THE PUSH

TOMMY
CALDWELL

THE PUSH

A CLIMBER'S JOURNEY OF ENDURANCE, RISK AND GOING BEYOND LIMITS

MICHAEL JOSEPH
an imprint of
PENGUIN BOOKS

MICHAEL JOSEPH

UK | USA | Canada | Ireland | Australia
India | New Zealand | South Africa

Michael Joseph is part of the Penguin Random House group of companies
whose addresses can be found at global.penguinrandomhouse.com.

First published in the United States of America by Viking, an imprint of Penguin Random House LLC 2017
First published in Great Britain by Michael Joseph 2017
001

Photograph credits
Insert page 1 (top left, right), 2 (top), 3: Terry Caldwell
1 (bottom), 2 (bottom), 4 (top right, bottom): Mike Caldwell
4 (top left): Estes Park Elementary School
5 (top, bottom): Jim Thornburg
6, 9 (top left): Topher Donahue
7, 8 (bottom), 9 (top right), 10 (top left, middle left, bottom), 11, 14 (top bottom),
16 (top, middle): Corey Rich Productions/Novus Select
8 (top): Associated Press
9 (bottom): © Nate Ptacek
10 (top right): Tommy Caldwell
12–13: Brett Lowell/Big Up Productions
15: Jimmy Chin
16 (bottom): Caldwell Family Collection

Printed in Great Britain by Clays Ltd, St Ives plc

A CIP catalogue record for this book is available from the British Library

HARDBACK ISBN: 978–0–718–18339–4
TRADE PAPERBACK ISBN: 978–0–718–18340–0

www.greenpenguin.co.uk

Penguin Random House is committed to a
sustainable future for our business, our readers
and our planet. This book is made from Forest
Stewardship Council® certified paper.

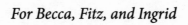

For Becca, Fitz, and Ingrid

THE PUSH

WIND

December 30, 2014. Day four, year seven, the Dawn Wall. Twelve hundred vertical feet climbed free, eighteen hundred to go.

We hear the wind racing from a half mile away, a roar in the darkness mixed with the pitch of a scream. The volume rises, drowning out all other sounds. We sit like gargoyles, legs stuffed in sleeping bags, backs against the wall. Kevin, my climbing partner, clutches the straps of our hanging tent and forces a smile. I can read his lips: "Hold on tight." A deafening *whap-a-pap-pap* resounds with the cadence of a machine gun. It's just fabric slapping the granite, but an involuntary shiver rattles inside me, shaking loose a decade-and-a-half-old memory born from the smell of exploding rock and visions of blood pooling onto the alpine tundra.

A sudden updraft swirls beneath the portaledge—our home, roughly the size of a sheet of plywood, with nylon strung between the aluminum frame and draped over its top. The floor begins to lift, and for a moment we hover in space, as if riding a magic carpet. I picture the three-eighths-inch stainless steel bolt from which we and all of our gear hang. Then the wind abruptly stops and the portaledge crashes down, straps snapping tight.

Each morning starts the same. I wake thinking about how to unlock the puzzle above. We brew coffee in our little perch and sit in awe as first light graces us—this part of the monolith of El Capitan, in Yosemite Valley, California, has long been known as the Dawn Wall. I brush my teeth, swish water in my mouth, and poke my head outside. I watch my toothpaste fall

1

as I count one, two, three . . . at around ten the white blob disappears into the forest below.

I pause and stare at my nine fingertips, cut, raw, but holding together. I often think of how this massive climb hinges on tiny details. Millimeters of skin contact and molecules of healing will make or break our ascent.

I gaze across the glacier-carved valley, and to the peaks unfolding on the horizon. I watch falcons tackle swallows in midair. Each day I feel the magnitude of my excitement in my restless legs. It's strange. In most ways I'm a pretty normal guy—self-conscious, shy at times, awkward. On the wall it's like I come alive; this place changes me. It always has. I take a deep breath and turn to the sheer face rising above.

Nobody had ever believed it possible to free climb the Dawn Wall, using only one's body (primarily fingers and toes) for upward progress, truly *climbing*, without relying on direct aid from the equipment to hoist oneself up. Legendary figures in the climbing world, some of whom I remember from my childhood, hanging out at our house with my dad, had long wondered if an ascent of El Capitan by any means was even possible. When the first ascent came, in 1958, it was a quantum leap. In subsequent years, countless climbers had made their way to the top following various routes. But freeing the Dawn Wall remained inconceivable. It existed as a kind of "here be dragons" on mental maps of the vertical landscape, virtually featureless and smooth.

Because of my father, I'd fallen for climbing long before I'd fallen for anything or anyone else. For me, free climbing the Dawn Wall is an act of purity. Getting to the top under my own power, unaided, is a way to express myself and my love of climbing and life in the grandest form and on the largest scale possible. If successful, and perhaps even if not, I'd validate not only my years of planning, but the entirety of my life.

When trying the hard pitches—which is pretty much all of them—I notice my mind an instant before my body. If doubt creeps in, even the tiniest bit, I hesitate. Just for a moment. Then my feet start to slip, my core starts to sag. I pull too hard with my hands, eroding precious layers of skin while trying to maintain my body position. To an observer, it happens in minute, imperceptible ways—until that micro shift pulls me from the wall and I soar through the air, racing toward the ground, sometimes falling as far as sixty feet but along a wall so steep that I hit nothing. The rope stretches, absorbing the impact and safely, softly, arresting my fall.

Sometimes, in those seconds after falling, a cascade of emotions flows through me. I drop my head to my chest in frustration and embarrassment. I question my strength, my balance, my willingness to endure. Other times, most times, I'm almost absurdly optimistic. In how many other areas in life do you get to test yourself over and over and over? How many other endeavors give you such immediate feedback? I analyze, regroup, and try again. *You've got this. You know you do.* Fears quiet, thoughts calm, mastery of the body and mind come into focus. Nothing else exists but that hold, that sequence of moves over stone, the information being sent from fingertips to brain. The vast world reduced to the size and span of my body as I force myself to override even the most rational doubts.

Rock climbing is a game of control.

When we aren't climbing, Kevin and I mostly talk about movement. The nuances of body position, the angle at which our toes contact a nearly invisible ripple of rock, how we place our fingers on a dime-thin edge in just the right way, in just the right sequence, with just the right combination of balance and body tension and footwork. At night I lie awake, visualizing the climbing, willing precision and perfection to wire itself into my body and brain. On the rock we rehearse the movement like gymnasts or ballet dancers, until we can flow from one position to the next. When things go well, we experience magic.

Sometimes, sitting on the portaledge between attempts, legs dangling over the edge, I think back seven years to the beginning of this journey-turned-obsession. To the countless days I've spent hauling heavy bags of gear and water up the wall, how I stuff my feet into shoes so tight that I sometimes lose toenails, and how I grab the same razor-sharp flakes over and over and over until my fingertips bleed and my muscles tremble.

In reality it's been far more than seven years.

One of my earliest childhood memories is of a raging blizzard, the wind roaring like it is now. My sister was six, I three, still in diapers, and we were nuzzled inside a single down sleeping bag beside our father, deep in a snow

3

cave, high in the mountains of Colorado. I shone my little silver flashlight on the ceiling of the cave and watched it turn blue. I listened to the muffled sounds of the wind and my dad's snoring just inches away. Every few hours he would wake, unzip his sleeping bag, put on his ski boots, and go outside to shovel the newly fallen snow so that we wouldn't get trapped. Then, as he lay back down, he would wrap us in his arms and squeeze us tight. We would snuggle close and fall back asleep, knowing that everything would be okay.

My first forays onto El Capitan were also with my dad, nineteen years ago, when I was still in high school. I found the exposure nauseating. I would glance down for a spot to place my foot and my focus would shift. Straight below, giant trees that looked like miniature broccoli sprouts would begin to spin, and my concentration would slip.

After all this time, I finally realize that these years of training, rehearsing, memorizing—they're as much, or maybe more, about building belief as they are about getting stronger.

The storm slows to a momentary lull, and I unzip the portaledge and peer outside, staring at the forest below, barely visible in the moonlight. El Cap meadow is, for once, void of human life. Roads in the park are closed due to the threat of falling trees. I turn my head and iridescent oceans of gold and white granite sparkle under a sea of stars. For the millionth time, a childlike wonder runs through me.

As I look into the night, again my thoughts drift. This time, my heart travels with them. A thousand feet below and less than three miles away, both close and terribly far, is the Upper Pines Campground. It's where we park our van when I'm climbing. I picture the drawn curtains and candlelight, and a recurring scene described by my wife, Becca. Inside, she tenderly strokes her thumb across the forehead of our one-and-a-half-year-old son, Fitz. Scattered around the bed of the van are books about animals. Tucked tightly in his chubby little hands, nestled under his neck, is a toy cement mixer. Becca sings good-night songs and Fitz's eyelids fade to slits.

Something triggers his little mind and he sits up, looks around, and asks,

"Where's Daddy?" Becca smiles. She brushes his head with her hand and says, strong but sweet, "He's climbing El Cap."

I've known this wall longer than I've known them.

Despite the discrepancy of time, my love for them far exceeds my love of the wall. It springs from something inside me that I seldom probe and infrequently check or test. I don't take them for granted; I just know in ways beyond words that the protection they provide me will hold.

Outside, again the wind howls like ghosts, reminding me that our luck can't last forever. We've got a perfect window, unheard-of winter conditions—dry, crisp, safe. Once the snow falls, it melts and then freezes to the rock, then melts again when the sun hits, sending terrifying sheets of ice roaring down—half joking, we call them widowmakers.

Another violent gust blasts us, shaking the portaledge and drowning out the tinny scratch of Bob Marley on our portable speakers.

"Even though New Year's Eve isn't until tomorrow, I say we party tonight," Kevin says.

He turns up the volume and we sing along, swilling whiskey and talking about good things, light things—life, relationships, and exploring places near and far—until our eyelids flutter and we fade. I feel my heart beating slowly, strongly, as if carried by gifts from the people I love.

The wind finally abates, rocking me like a lullaby. The forecast for tomorrow is clear and cool. I drift off to sleep, floating in the breeze midway between earth and the impossible.

PART
ONE

CHAPTER ONE

The steady and percussive clink, clink, clink *of metal hitting granite echoes off the towering rocks that border my parents' property. The shovel handle briefly blocks my vision before I bring the tool down again. Its impacts rattle my five-year-old bones. My efforts produce sparks, a handful of fractured rock, and a dulled shovel blade. I scoop the pebbles into a one-gallon bucket then continue to chip away. After an hour the bucket is full. I climb out of the shallow hole and empty the contents onto a growing pile. A slight, satisfied smile flashes across my face. I squint against the bright Colorado sunshine. I slip back into the earth before anyone detects my presence.*

I'm determined to make it to China. Sandy, my older sister, had planted the seed a few months earlier. Showing me a globe, she pointed out "here" for Colorado and "there" for China. I'd imagined the quickest route. What would the world look like if the sky was down and the ground was up?

The first few inches of digging went surprisingly fast. Then I hit bedrock. That's when the soft sibilance of a shovel easing its way through sand and silt turned to metal scraping stone.

I keep at it. I grow to crave the fleeting feeling of satisfaction from my efforts. Progress is slow, not quite a geological-age slow, but nearly. Every day, in some small way, I measure my progress and drink from that well of successes. When the garden spade breaks I rummage through the toolshed and find a trenching shovel. Later, I use a miner's pick that takes all my strength to lift over my head. When the winter winds rage and snow flurries float off the Continental Divide, I pull on a wool hat and keep going.

For more than two years I dig. The one constant is the sound of the shovel and the chalk scent of the earth. Somehow, someway, I am going to get there.

I barely drew my first breath. My mother, Terry, very nearly died while delivering me into this world. If it's true, as some say, that how you start is how you finish, then my exit is also going to be fraught with scratching and clawing and near misses. That's okay. Life is all about risk and reward. Better to have struggled, to have tried, than to not have seized an opportunity at all. Struggle is how I started and struggle is how I will probably finish.

Sometime after my sister Sandy was born in 1975, my mother had the first of three miscarriages. Her doctors told her and my dad, Mike, that there was little chance of having another child. I can't say that they kept digging but something like that. They assessed the risks and decided they could handle the consequences.

In mid-July of 1978, while carrying me into my third trimester, my mother began hemorrhaging. My dad rushed her to the hospital, where the doctors gave her a medication that could stop the bleeding but carried high risks of complications. Their intervention worked. The bleeding stopped. She returned home but was sick every day.

At thirty weeks she went into labor. The doctors fed an alcohol drip into her veins to stop the contractions; that measure nearly killed her. She rebounded after a few days and was released with instructions to rest as much as possible, and to stay calm—not easy given her past issues with fertility and childbirth and while looking after my three-year-old sister. On August 10, she went into labor again. She was delirious, her blood pressure dangerously high. The next morning they induced her.

At thirty-three weeks I made my entrance into the world, hovering around four and a half pounds, too early for fully developed lungs, but alive. Family lore has it that despite my size and fragility I came out screaming. My parents had no time to celebrate, however, because my mom was hemorrhaging badly. Emergency surgery. She has no memory of my birth. I had no sucking reflex and couldn't maintain body heat.

Many times, I'm told, the doctors feared I wouldn't survive. They kept me in the hospital for ten days before sending me home on the promise that my parents bring me in for daily checkups. There, in Loveland, Colorado, under my parents' nurturing, I thrived. After three months I had tripled my body weight.

As I look back, I wonder if something instinctual, born of my struggles on that hot August day in 1978, always made me try harder. As if from the start, something fierce beat inside my tiny heart. Not giving up seemed to come naturally to me. My parents hadn't, and their willingness to believe in my existence gave me life.

Leave it to my dad to put his stamp on those events. He referred to me frequently as their "Miracle Baby." I never asked why they never resorted to the kind of overprotective boy-in-a-bubble treatment you might expect given the tenuous circumstances of my birth.

All I can say is that I'm grateful that in many ways they just let me be. They didn't want my rough start to cast a shadow on my childhood. From my earliest days they allowed me the kind of independence that many of my peers didn't have—whether it was my period of digging, or the times in early elementary school when I went solo camping in the mountains several miles above our home. In solitude, I felt more deeply immersed in my surroundings. It felt natural. I don't remember how my parents reacted to my camping trips, but I went multiple times, with enough PB&J sandwiches to keep me going. It's easy to imagine my father's blessing (it was most likely his suggestion in the first place) and my mother's "oh, well" look of resignation.

My dad grew up in the Bay Area of California. His father worked as an engineer for the Army Corps of Engineers. They were solidly middle class and education was important to the family. Even more, it seems, Dad's parents wanted their kids to be strong and independent. My dad told me stories of the kayak he built for himself and the adventures he had with it. His parents encouraged his curiosity. I don't know how they felt about the gunpowder bombs he built and the homemade rocket he fired through a neighbor's garage door, but they did buy him a chemistry set. I guess they figured they'd guide his munitions work in a more productive direction.

On a Boy Scout trip to the Minarets in the Sierra Nevada Mountains, they camped near a group of climbers. The scoutmaster recognized that this was a rare species of creatures, which might be of interest to his thirteen- and fourteen-year-old boys. He invited the climbers over. Around a campfire, the climbers entertained the kids with their stories. My dad was intrigued, and upon returning home he bought a book called *The Freedom of the Hills*, a kind of Old Testament work from the early days of climbing. He started experimenting with aid climbing locally on Mount Tam with a bunch of his buddies. It took off from there. He hinted that he did some pretty crazy things, but seldom elaborated. All I knew was that whenever we were outdoors and active, I could see a look in his eye that was a mix of awe and audacity.

Then, for a while, after he married and moved to Colorado, climbing took a backseat to a different obsession. Before I was born, my dad converted our detached garage into a weight lifting gym and took up body-building. He soon started competing on the circuit. Mr. Colorado, 1976. Mr. Mid-America, 1980. He posed against the likes of Lou Ferrigno (the original Incredible Hulk from the TV show) and Arnold Schwarzenegger. He could do ten consecutive one-arm pull-ups, and he applied his training mentality to practically everything. He was a fitness freak with an outsized sense of adventure. As a two-year-old with buck teeth and freckles I would stand in the doorway and watch my dad bust out sets of curls with eighty-pound dumbbells, or hang upside-down, suspended by metal ankle cuffs with inverted hooks over a pull-up bar, letting out guttural growls with each inverted sit-up. Sweat dripped into the vertical fissure that ran from his chest to his navel. Short shorts and high tube socks with horizontal yellow lines encircled his bulging calves.

I was fascinated by it all. I was the proverbial ninety-eight-pound weakling, except that I wouldn't achieve that milestone weight until late in high school. Some of my earliest memories are of a variety of squat, bulging men—my dad's friends—wandering onto our property, walking that stiff monkeylike walk of the overmuscled, heading toward the weight stacks, the benches, and the racks. Grunts, shouts, and the metallic sounds of forty-five-pound plates banging together reverberated off the cement walls. Dumbbells and barbells dropped onto racks my father had fashioned from scrap metal and bonded into place with his buzz box welder.

Roars of human effort resounded over the strains of REO Speedwagon's "Take It On the Run" and Queen's "We Will Rock You."

Watching these older men press, squat, and deadlift weights, and then flex, their eyes fixed on whatever muscle or muscle group they hoped to develop, was like having the circus perpetually coming to town. I wanted to do whatever it was that my dad did; I learned to flex and pose before I learned to walk or talk. The laughs and applause I got and the high fives I gave fed my scrawny spirit.

Having a real life comic book character as a father probably warped my view of reality. A page in the family photo album shows a Polaroid of my dad in a red banana hammock, oiled muscles glistening, flashing a huge smile beneath his frizzy, dirty dishwater, beauty-salon-applied perm. He is flexing like a beast. Beside it is a shot of me, age two, knees wrapped just like my dad's, with a barbell on my back, doing squats.

What kid wouldn't want to emulate his dad, especially when he saw his father performing heroic deeds in real life? His encouragement—if you call it that—came early and in multiple forms. In my family, gifts were never simply doled out. They had strings attached. As far back as when I was three, when I received a Spider-Man kite for my birthday, it came with the requirement that its inaugural flight occur from the top of a rock spire. Since bodybuilding wasn't much of a family affair, rock climbing and skiing were regular weekend outings.

A short drive from our home in Loveland, above the east end of Estes Park, rises a series of gray granite domes dotting the skyline, ranging from small boulders to buttresses eight hundred feet high. We hiked uphill for a half hour to the base of a formation called Twin Owls, so named because it resembles a pair of three-hundred-foot granite owls nuzzled together. Dad strapped me into a homemade full body harness—seatbelt webbing wrapped around me in a series of loops and turns. I pulled on my climbing shoes, which my dad had made by ripping the soles off a pair of my little hiking boots and gluing on pieces of sticky climbing rubber. Our route was a dirty, bat-guano-infested chimney called the Bowels of the Owls.

At the start, a deep dark cave disappeared into the depths of the mountain. As if the climbing looming overhead wasn't exciting enough, my dad told me that mountain lions might live inside, and that I should carry a stick to poke them in the eye if one attacked. I can still hear his booming laugh echoing from the walls as he started up.

He went first, leading the way while dragging a rope behind him. After about one hundred feet he built an anchor and belayed my sister up. I went third, and since the climbing was above my ability level, my dad winched me up—my arms and legs flailed against the rock, scraping the skin off my knees, as my dad cheered me on. My mom went last, and then we repeated the process to the top.

On the summit we were surrounded by sky, with the town and the valley splayed out far below. We launched my kite, cheering in unison as it danced in the wind. It was my first roped climb, and, in my parents' eyes, that was the moment that I officially became a climber. I didn't see it that way. All I knew was that I'd done something that was fun and that pleased my parents. That was enough.

On another family outing, when I was maybe four, we took a climbing trip to the Vedauwoo Recreation Area in Wyoming. It's famous for its rocky bluffs, some of them adjacent to the campsites. We pulled in at night, our car's headlights slicing into a small bustling group of teenagers moving like wind-blown weeds. Once we got out of the car, we saw them pointing and heard their freaked-out voices. One of their buddies had climbed up a cliff, fallen, and landed on a ledge. He was dazed and bruised, perched some thirty feet from the top.

My dad went into action. Even though we had a bunch of climbing gear with us, he figured that time mattered. He began his free solo—trailing a rope but not bothering to place any protection. He Spider-Manned his way up the formation. I stood in the darkness with Sandy and my mom, craning my neck. I felt my mom's hand on my shoulder, grabbing tighter as my dad rose in the night sky. It seemed as if only seconds had passed before he was back on the ground with the kid. The trembling teen could barely stand, so my dad held him up. Multiple thank yous, and you're amazing, and that was so rad, wrapped us all in a kind of group hug. My dad waved it all off and pitched our tent. I went to sleep snuggled in a sleeping bag, encased in the belief that my dad could do no wrong, that he could keep everyone safe.

If my dad was a superhero, outsized in temperament and tenacity, my mom was the classic wallflower. She was petite, nearly frail, with the quiet and sweet demeanor of a saint. My mom looked like a librarian, with large, thick-lensed, gold-rimmed glasses that magnified her kind eyes. Nurturing came naturally to her. When she was only eight years old and living in Pasadena, California, her mother fell terribly ill and was bedridden for years. Since her father spent nearly all of his time working and believed in traditional sixties gender roles, my mom spent her childhood changing diapers and cooking meals for her dad and her three younger brothers. I don't think she ever learned how to play.

Maybe that's why she married my dad. Despite being a kind of mismatch, it was clear they loved each other deeply. When my mom was pacing the house stressing about something or other, my dad would walk in, take her in his arms, and start groping and kissing her until she laughed and my sister wailed in protest. It seemed as much about shocking us kids as it was about loving my mom. His mischievous smirk compensated for her furrowed brow. Her selflessness filled the holes left by his pride.

They met in college, at the University of California, Berkeley. When they entered in 1968, the place was a hotbed of antiwar and other antiauthoritarian protests. All peace and love. The flower power hippie stuff was part of their coming of age. It rooted in them a sense that you should do something meaningful with your life. It also fed my father's optimistic view of human nature. Everything was beautiful in its own way and nature could transform our lives and embolden our spirits. In an interesting bit of irony, despite their both being products of the psychedelic sixties, they never smoked dope. Not then or later. Heck, maybe it helped draw them together—they were probably the only ones left.

Much later in life, I learned that my mother had to nurture my dad early in their marriage. He was ambitious but scattered. He wanted to become a teacher, but he lacked the focus to do a proper job search. According to her, in those days he'd fallen under the spell of the climbing community—a counterculture bunch who rejected materialism and the conventional lives most people lived. Think hippies with a love of rock and testing their limits. They were, like a lot of wild children, into drugs. But my dad's experiences

15

as an athlete—he was first a gymnast—meant he wanted to keep the temple of his body pure.

My dad usually needed to believe that he made all the choices and decisions, but Mom sensed that if he was going to really make a go of teaching, she'd have to step in. Yet she had to be subtle. So she initiated his job search, nudging him along. A teaching offer in Loveland is how they landed in the Rocky Mountain State.

By the time I came along, it seems, all that planning and trying to control life had worn at my mom. Who can blame her? I shared living quarters for the first years of my life with a dozen wards of the state of Colorado. My mom ran a twenty-four-hour, in-house care center where kids of various ages were temporarily placed with us. I have this lasting impression of her racing around, corralling a dirt-smeared kid while dandling a baby in one hand and tossing a mini soccer ball into a bin with the other. In old photos she looks frazzled, wearing oversized sweatpants with worn-out cuffs that dragged on our green shag carpeting. Though I didn't know the term, many of the kids were likely to have been diagnosed as "behaviorally disordered." All I knew was that they were loud and frequently verging on seismic outbursts that shook my internal Richter scale.

Part of the reason I loved digging was probably that it got me out of our chaotic house. Maybe it's the same reason my dad spent so much time working out.

Over the years, reality would chip away at the heroic image I had of my father. When I see the old photos of him posing and ridiculously jacked, I realize it was before most people understood the detrimental side effects of steroids. Back then, bodybuilders got prescriptions from their family doctors. And I never recall witnessing my father act out in violence or anger. But when I scour my memory banks, I remember a fist-sized hole in a hallway wall. It was like viewing one of those "What's Wrong With This Picture?" puzzles from *Highlights* magazine. Maybe the shining image I held of my dad blinded me, because at the time I quickly dismissed this distortion, and a few others. They were so rare.

Looking back, however, I see glimpses of other moments that rattle my perfect perceptions of my childhood. When I was four and Sandy was six, my dad led the four of us on a cross-country skiing excursion. Though the sun was shining, the wind howled and whipped up snow devils that stung our cheeks and noses and watered our eyes. Being out when most remained inside made us special (as my dad reminded us, repeatedly, while exhorting us to press on and share his belief that this adventure was awesome). At one point I was lagging behind, and a ski skated out from beneath me. I slid down a small incline into a narrow ravine with a creek. A crust of ice had formed on each side of the stream. My skis spanned the edges of the crust, and suddenly I flipped upside down, dangling with my head inches above the frigid, rushing water.

I could smell the water and the dirt of the creek's embankment. Blood rushed to my head, and my vision pulsed with my heartbeat. I was simultaneously scared and ashamed. I wasn't sure if I should cry out for help. I wondered how long the ice above would hold me.

I have no idea how much time passed before my parents found me. They both wrapped me in their arms in turn. I watched as my father's pride in seeing me not cry turned into something ugly—anger at my mother. She was the one who should have been bringing up the rear. If she had been where she should have been, the whole thing could have been avoided. Why didn't she listen to him? Why couldn't she just do what she was told?

My mother remained silent. We all stood there shrouded in a fog of our own breathing. My dad loaded me on his back and double poled off, becoming a small dot in the flat light and then disappearing into the gloaming. My mother looked at Sandy, then looked longingly back at the trailhead, turned, and nodded in the direction my father and I had gone—away from warmth and rest and safety. They followed his wind-scarred tracks, my mother dutifully trailing behind, watching out for my sister.

In hindsight I know that deep down, my dad was probably terrified by what had happened. He couldn't unleash his anger at Sandy or me or himself, so he lashed out at my mom. Although he'd put us at some risk by simply being there, he'd also risked something else he deeply valued—the active lifestyle. If things went sideways, as I did in sliding down that hill and nearly drowning, then his whole plan for how he wanted to live his life could have been put in jeopardy. With stakes that high, he needed everyone to fall in line. We all had to pull our weight. I went along willingly, not feeling the weight as a burden, but as a blessing.

Mike Caldwell was a lot of things to a lot of people—teacher, coach, fanatic, and a kind of messiah of vigorous and adventurous pursuits. But how could I feel anything but gratitude for his providing me with a childhood in which I regularly felt like a pirate on the high seas or an explorer of great lands? I was lost in my own world with a perfect companion. I dreamed the sort of dreams that too often fade under the weight of adulthood. My dad's shoulders were wide enough to support both of us, and if he wanted others to fall under his magnetic spell it was because he wanted to help, not hurt.

For a long time, when I thought of those days I spent digging from 1982 to 1985, I wondered what they said about the man I would eventually become. Why wasn't I doing the things that my peers were into at that age? Why was I solo camping instead of begging to go to the playground? Why wasn't I plopped in front of a TV screen watching *Sesame Street* or *Scooby-Doo*? Why didn't I have crayons fisted in my hands instead of a shovel's handle? Sure, those experiences helped form me, but as Sandy pointed out to me later, why were we left alone so much? I didn't think of it that way, but she certainly did. And given how, as I got older, it seemed as if the four of us became two teams of two—Mike and Tommy and Terry and Sandy—what set us on somewhat divergent routes?

Like most of us, I am a combination of both my parents. More reserved than my father, I possess a quieter intensity and focus. I was small for my age and painfully shy, though not unhappy. We were churchgoers, and I would spend the hour-long Sunday school class silently facing the corner, speaking to no one. I dwelled in a world of my own, and developed an odd fascination with mundane tasks. In addition to my excavation efforts, I once spent ten hours straight, alone, fixated on the backyard orchard. I filled a miniature wagon with thousands of earthworms, piling them so high that they poured over the side rails. I also liked to take magazines and cut them up one page at a time into one-inch triangles. I would fill entire paper bags full of the confetti. Some probably considered me more than a bit odd.

A random incident in 1982 may have changed the course of my life, ensuring I didn't become a buffed-out meathead. My dad was spotting one of his gymnastics students on the high bar. The kid came off the apparatus, and in catching him, my dad tore a biceps tendon. The injury ended his bodybuilding career. That's when he shifted his focus back to his younger-years passion of rock climbing, in which, despite popular misconceptions, success isn't about big muscles. Finger strength and core tension, balance, mind control, and technique are far more important. True to form, he didn't dabble. And he was bringing his son along. Climbing and the outdoors became life and religion. We moved to the mountain town of Estes Park and bought a house that had thirty-foot cliffs on the property. My dad took a summer job as a guide with the Colorado Mountain School. He suddenly seemed intent on using mountaineering, rock climbing, and wilderness outings to purge me of my early childhood meekness.

While other kids spent their weekends playing games and going to birthday parties at Chuck E. Cheese's, being the son of Mike Caldwell meant that T-ball was for pansies, swimming was handy if you were caught in a flood, and adventure wasn't adventure without an unplanned night out. We didn't just hike and camp on family outings. We summited mountains and slept in snow caves.

In our household, obsessive tendencies were admired and nurtured. While most kids got money for chores, around the time I was four my dad implemented a physical fitness credit system: one hundred sit-ups, a lap around the block, or thirty push-ups would accrue credits. Aside from their intrinsic value, each credit was worth ten cents. After a while, I could buy a backpack, a BMX bike, climbing shoes. The credit system was interspersed with benchmark bonuses. The first time I did twenty consecutive pull-ups, I got a giant Danish waffle cone ice cream, with whipped cream and a cherry. The first time I ran three continuous miles, I got a ride on the back of my dad's motorcycle.

More than the money or prizes, I was driven by the desire to impress my dad. I always knew that my mom loved me unconditionally, but something about the way my dad would brag to his friends about my progress made me strive to win a larger portion of his approval. From those earliest days working out, I remember the burning sensation in my legs, and how I would cringe in pain and scratch at them until they turned red. Over time, as my body adjusted, the burning subsided. I didn't know anything about lactic acid or runner's high, but, before long, I knew that when I was working out I felt happy.

I am not sure I will ever fully understand my dad's intentions, whether they were a reflection of his ego, bravado, or need to stick out in the crowd, or if he was striving for something extra for me alone, something born of helping me compensate for my struggles at birth and my tiny size. By the time kindergarten rolled around, I had a physical tenacity that was rare for kids my age. Yet still I was small and, more so, endowed with my mom's sensitivity.

My mom seemed in favor of my engaging in more typical kid activities. The social nature of team sports seemed like a good approach to get me out of my shell. One afternoon, while we were out on the peewee baseball diamond for the very first time, the coach handed out balls and instructed us to play catch with one another. On the first toss from my teammate, I put my glove up and waved it in front of my face, looking as if I was on a parade float acknowledging the crowd. I could only vaguely make out the ball's location. My next memory is of lying on an exam room bed, staring into the bright light as a doctor's face loomed into view, a needle held between the glinting pincers of his forceps. A baseball has stitches, and the twelve bits of thread added to the skin on the orbital bones above my right eye, along with the associated swelling, were a nice approximation of the ball.

Of course, I couldn't just give up. I continued to play, though I was relegated to the purgatory of right field. There, I could stand and dig my rubber cleats into the earth, hoping that I could excavate a hole large enough to hide me and my embarrassment. The other kids were not overly cruel, but it was obvious by their frustrated outbursts that they pitied my lack of skill.

One benefit of the baseball beaning was that it revealed one of my deficiencies. I had very bad hand-eye coordination. Bad enough that I went to see another doctor. Now I had a pair of thick-lensed glasses that made my already protruding ears stick out even farther, adding to my daily humiliation of being ushered out of class to attend my remedial reading sessions.

I think my parents' efforts to help me overcome my rough beginnings were, at times, both a coordinated effort and each of them pulling me in opposing directions. I had to submit to the baseball experiment, just as I had to join my dad on outdoor adventures. I guess that wrestling, appropriately enough, put me on a sort of middle ground between the poles of my parents' influence.

Wrestling was a team sport. Each match contributed to an overall score. But it was also an individual endeavor.

When I entered the junior wrestling league at age five, I could run farther and do more pull-ups and push-ups than the other kids (and even the coaches). Toughness mattered more than technique at that age. In my first match of my first tournament, as I walked onto the mat, my miniature blue singlet flopped from my scrawny frame, and my headgear was too big. Then the whistle blew and I swooped in for a quick takedown, got the other kid in a half nelson, and pinned him within twenty seconds. The official slapped the mat, and my stunned opponent stood up and we shook hands. Then I saw tears running down his face. A lump formed in my stomach. I felt terrible. For the rest of the wrestling season, any time an opponent started crying (which was pretty much always in peewee wrestling) I let him win.

I imagine those losses frustrated my dad, but he knew what was going on. He had to be worried that if I was too soft of heart the world might be too hard on me. I'd also like to think my mother knew why I'd lose, and that my gesture gave her deep satisfaction.

My interests and my dealing with the competing influences of my parents took another form. During the summers off from his teaching job, my dad's work as a mountain guide frequently meant that he was away for days and sometimes weeks. As a result, Sandy and I were left alone with my mom much of the time. My mother liked to sew. I saw her doing it, so I had her teach me. Eventually, I became pretty good with a needle and thread. I'd make stuffed animals, teddy bears in particular. I'd spend hours cutting out the shapes and filling the carcasses with matting. My mom supervised my activity and praised me for my skills.

When my dad returned from his trips, I'd show him what I made. I could see from his feigned interest and thin smile, spread across his face like barbed wire, that he was disappointed in me. The glance that he gave my mom read like a sad tale of loss. She'd hold his stare for a few seconds, then look away, feigning interest in a magazine or searching for a thimble in her sewing basket. My stomach turned and my mouth dried. I ground my teeth and hunched my shoulders, making myself smaller as I packed my sewing things away. I felt my dad's glare cutting into me, rendering me into little triangles to be scattered and discarded.

I can see now that my father's "encouraging" me to become a climber was a gift. Even if it came at a cost to some of my other interests. While any parenting method can backfire, I see things like my dad's credit system and his dragging me around the mountains as pure genius. He successfully fostered in me a deep appreciation for the activities he loved most, and, in the process and decades before its time, he answered one of today's trendiest parenting questions: How do we build grit in our children? For my dad and me, it was a combination of bribery and exposure to minor traumatic experiences.

In the summers, our family piled into the car and drove to distant climbing areas. Sandy and I had become fascinated with one spot in particular, familiar from the classic Steven Spielberg film *Close Encounters of the Third Kind*. We hounded my parents incessantly about going there. Little did I know that it was one of the most iconic rock-climbing formations in the United States: Devils Tower.

Above the rolling prairies of northeastern Wyoming, the tower rises like a massive cylinder for twelve hundred feet. We set up camp and Mom pulled out a folding chair and reclined with her James Michener novel. My sister and I shouldered our packs and followed Dad up the trail, winding through ponderosa pines and over rattlesnake-infested boulders. At the bottom of the wall, Dad reviewed our techniques and systems. Although we were heading for the easiest route on the formation, a series of cracks and chimneys that my dad could have climbed without a rope, he made clear that this was serious. When he switched on his teaching voice, we knew it was time to pay attention.

"Remember, always double-check each other's knots, and stay clipped into two things. Don't just kick your feet into the cracks. Put them in sideways, then twist them so they don't get stuck. Put your hands in the crack and cup them like you are trying to hold a handful of peanuts. When it gets wide, look for V-shaped slots and try slotting your fists in. Make long reaches to save energy."

Early on I was learning that risk and recklessness are two entirely different things. We were never raised to be thrill seekers or adrenaline junkies. Climbing was about taking a stimulating and potentially dangerous environment and then using our heads, our attentiveness, and our skills to make it safe (with careful oversight from Dad).

The climb took us all day. We wiggled up cracks and chimneys, the grainy rock abrading our arms and backs. The pain and exertion were drowned out by the sensory experience of the Wyoming wind whistling past and the excitement of climbing with hundreds of feet of air directly below our feet. On the summit, Dad pulled sandwiches out of his pack, and we had a picnic.

When you are a six-year-old, not many experiences leave you with a lasting sense of accomplishment. After carefully rappelling down the route we had climbed, as we walked the trail back to the car I stood a little taller. I knew that the majority of people who came to the monument would never have the ability to ascend that rock. Our climbing hardware hung from slings over our shoulders and the ropes were strapped to our backs. Near the parking lot, a man stopped us and asked where we had climbed. "To the top," I confidently replied. He shot me a look that said, "Yeah, right, kid," and moved on.

Similarly, our first visit to Yosemite, when I was seven years old, left an enduring impression on me. We set out in our green cargo van and drove twenty hours through the sweltering Utah and Nevada deserts to the fabled, glacier-carved valley. The walls towered skyward. It was so much bigger than anything I had seen, so much bigger than even my imagination.

I learned to love everything about Yosemite, from the smoky campgrounds with hordes of kids riding around on bicycles, to the mosquito-infested meadows, to the towering redwood and cedar trees so old and so huge that it seemed as if dinosaurs should be walking among them. Sandy and I spent most of our days floating down the Merced River on our raft, listening to the roaring waterfalls that threw mist a half mile. Then we would watch my dad climb the walls, and afterward stand by his side as he'd tell stories among his friends. The ragtag climbers were my heroes. Their passion and determination were so obvious that even a child could connect with it. By that time my dad, with his bulging biceps and bandana wrapped around his head, was exactly what I wanted to be when I grew up.

One summer, Dad introduced me to one of the most exposed climbing games around. Our family loaded packs full of rope and hiked for hours to the top of upper Yosemite Falls. It's North America's tallest waterfall, and the water free-falls from the valley rim down toward the valley floor. To the side of the falls, splitting off a vertical rock wall and separated from the rim by a deep notch, rises a granite tower called Lost Arrow Spire. It's a three-hundred-foot-tall finger of rock with daunting exposure—because it starts near the top of an already sheer wall, its freestanding apex is nearly 3,000 feet above the valley floor. It was one of the last prominent landmarks to be reached in Yosemite, a vertigo-inducing hanging island surrounded by space and air.

My dad's best friend and main climbing partner, Randy Farris, accompanied us, serving as a safety double-check for me. We tied our ropes together and descended to the notch where the base of the spire splits from the main wall. We then spent several hours climbing the spire to its top.

My sister and mom, now finished with their portering duties, lounged on the rim, relaxing in the Sierra sun and wind and watching us climb.

While we were on the Lost Arrow Spire a helicopter passed below us. We could look straight down to the tops of the rotors. I thought about how rare it must be to see a helicopter from this angle. Once we reached the top of the spire we gathered up the rope that had been trailing behind us, its far end still securely affixed to the rim at our starting point. We pulled it tight, creating a horizontal highline between the top of the spire and our starting point. Dad and his friend finished their rope-rigging wizardry and double-checked our systems, triple-checked me after I secured myself.

I peered across that gap. Nothing but our lines and the ground below us. *How cool*, I thought. I knew my dad wouldn't put me in a spot where I could be hurt. I stepped off the rock into open air. A few minutes later, I'd completed a spectacular Tyrolean traverse (picture a crude kind of zip line) and made it back to where we had started. The excitement of it tickled my belly, like cresting a hill at high speed.

I looked across to where my dad was positioned. He smiled and gave me a thumbs-up. I felt some of that satisfaction and success that I'd experienced while digging. This time, though, I didn't feel the need to shrink from sight. I nodded back to my dad and returned his gesture.

I felt that I belonged, that I fit in.

CHAPTER TWO

A disheveled old man with a gray beard and a bulbous belly stands on the shag carpeting of our living room. Behind him a dark oak bookshelf, overflowing with my dad's dog-eared climbing books, frames him as if he's enshrined on the wall. He stands beside a bedsheet nearly as rumpled as he is. On it, a projected photo of El Capitan glows dimly, cutting through and rising above a cloudbank of ground fog. I'm five years old and wearing my Superman pajamas. I've worn them all summer long. The knees are threadbare. Around the room men in grubby clothes hoist beers and chatter and laugh so loud, it all becomes white noise; they're adult versions of the kids my mom usually watches over. Only she's not in sight. She must be in the kitchen getting them drinks or preparing more snacks.

My dad moves around, grinning broadly. He wraps his arm around the shoulder of one man, grabs another by his biceps. One of them says something and Dad throws his head back in a loud laugh. The other guy doubles over, resting his hands on his knees as he slowly shakes his head.

I weave through the forest of legs. Though I'm trying to be careful—I'm so grateful that I can be hanging out near them—I bump into someone. I look up. He looks down. I smile. His face shows confusion and surprise. I hurry off, and suddenly I'm flying. Someone else has hoisted me by my armpits and I'm squirming and laughing. I land and scoot off again. Then a laughing bearded man snags me and says, "You going to say uncle?"

The disheveled guy at the front of the room hoists a glass to his lips. He straightens it and sets down the now empty container. The smell of beer and body odor swirls in the space around me.

"Let's get this shit show—uh, slide show—started, shall we, gentlemen?" he shouts. It takes a minute, and a few of my dad's whoots, before the show within the show can begin.

Along with my parents, there were a number of other influences in my early life. My dad's climbing buddies had gathered that night in 1983 to hear, at my father's invitation, one of the legends of climbing deliver a presentation on his extraordinary exploits.

I remember being fascinated by Warren Harding's eyes. Bloodshot, wild, the kind of eyes that held secrets, that had lived through perilous adventures and remained stuck wide open with surprise and delight. Between his eyes, a beet-red nose traversed his wrinkled face. Harding had started the evening relatively sober and with his standard storytelling fare. He told scandalous tales of womanizing, drinking, and recruiting young climbers who didn't know any better and dragging them up El Capitan for weeks on end. "Rock climbing is a fine kind of madness," he always claimed. Despite his gruff mannerisms, he had an undeniably genuine nature. He was a hero to us all. His stories had me wide-eyed and grinning. I remember looking around the room and seeing my dad beaming and nodding his head.

Later, when I became fully engaged with the sport of rock climbing, I read and heard more about the bearded fat man's history. In 1958, Harding became the first person to climb El Capitan. His belief and his will—his indomitable spirit—got him there as much as his strength, and his ascent elevated rock climbing to another dimension. Back then, El Cap was considered impossible. It was too sheer, too smooth, too big. Another pioneer of Harding's era, his chief rival, Royal Robbins, said, "In the early days you noticed El Cap, but we didn't pay much attention to it, because it was kind of 'out of the question.' We didn't even consider climbing it—it was too much of an imaginative leap."

To Harding—and probably only Harding—El Cap wasn't out of the question. He spent two full seasons sieging the wall, fixing ropes from the ground to his team's ever-inching-upward high point, shuttling equipment up the ropes and pounding in pitons made from various shapes and sizes of scavenged scrap metal to allow progress. In some of the wider cracks,

Harding famously used cut-off sections of stove legs. In stretches devoid of cracks, he hand-drilled bolts and masonry rivets into the rock. He burned through multiple climbing partners. But he never gave up. The final push cemented Harding's status, as he drilled a virtual ladder of twenty-eight consecutive bolts up blank granite, hammering through the night for seventeen hours straight.

Given the magnitude of the endeavor in that era, he was mostly aid climbing. Aid climbing, occasionally called "artificial" climbing, means you achieve upward progress by pulling on your equipment. When free climbing, however, upward progress comes exclusively from engaging your body (typically hands and feet) with the rock. Free climbing simply means free from aid. Much to the frustration of those who climb, nonclimbers routinely mistake free climbing for free soloing (free soloing is climbing without a rope). When free climbing, you climb under your own power, with the rope and equipment present only to protect against a fall.

At the time, getting up El Cap by *any* means was, for most, pure fantasy. Harding's route, aptly named the Nose, ascended the defining feature in the center of the 3,000-foot rock face. Today it is probably the most famous rock climb in the world.

Harding went on to make thirty first ascents in Yosemite, pioneering big-wall techniques that are still used today. His self-deprecating motto was *Semper Farcisimus!*, and his traveling presentation, which he gave at our house, was titled *Downward Bound: The Rise and Fall of a Rock-Climbing Legend.*

I was probably too young to realize that I was a child of rock-climbing privilege. When I read more about Harding and others, I got it. Yosemite was the equivalent of Yankee Stadium or Fenway Park. And I didn't just get to spectate, I was actually out on the field. Or at least in the clubhouse. Having Warren Harding in my living room was as if Babe Ruth had come over for dinner—a past-his-prime and hard-drinking legend, but a legend nonetheless.

Though the Warren I met was a shadow of his former self, I could imagine what he'd been like in the 1950s and early 1960s, when he ventured up Yosemite's walls for the first time. He still retained much of his mischievous energy. He was a legendary joker, a guy who took climbing—but not himself—seriously. When asked why he climbed, he'd say something like, "Because we're insane, that can be the only reason." When asked how he made a particularly tough ascent, he'd say, "I started at the bottom and went to the top." My dad loved that kind of attitude and made sure I understood that staying humble was the best way to the top.

Harding's era in Yosemite was characterized by exploration, freedom, and fierce competition. Climbers made their own rules and chased the first ascents of massive, untouched walls. But different factions had distinct ideas of how the ascents should be carried out.

The front-runners were Harding and his tribe, and another group of climbers whom he derisively called the "Valley Christians" for their righteous adherence to a self-imposed code of climbing ethics. This group had its own leader, the great Royal Robbins. Robbins's style emphasized minimal damage to the rock and reducing reliance on siege tactics, such as fixing ropes. He placed a greater emphasis not on *if* you can make it to the top, but on *how*.

Harding, on the other hand, was a rebel to his core, even within the counterculture of climbing itself. He seemed to thrive on the idea of telling people to buzz off as he did things his own way. He once said: "Oh, God, I was always a total mess. I hate climbers like Royal Robbins who are so superior. He doesn't mean to be, he just is. He's methodic, scientific, capable, and so competent it makes me envious."

The rivalry between these two legends forms some of climbing's richest history, and it came to a head in the race to climb the southeast face of El Capitan, to the right of Harding's 1958 Nose route. It was the biggest, steepest, most unclimbable-looking wall in all of Yosemite. If this route could be climbed, regardless of tactics, it would prove that ascending any wall was in fact possible.

In 1970 Harding and his partner Dean Caldwell (no relation) started climbing with twelve days' worth of food and water. Midway up, weather rolled in and they hunkered down in their hammocks. They kept going, intermittently climbing through storms. They stretched their rations to two weeks, then three. Other climbers couldn't believe that they could survive so many days on the wall and tried to rescue them—but, in true Harding spirit, they refused assistance. They continued, almost entirely aid climbing;

to even consider free climbing on such an unfathomably sheer and smooth wall was out of the question.

At one point Caldwell scribbled a message, stuffed it inside a tin can, and dropped it from the wall. It read: "We must be the most miserable, wet, cold, stinking wretches imaginable. But we're alive, really alive, like people seldom are."

Their saga had grown into such a spectacle that word spread, and scores of onlookers had gathered in the meadow below and congregated atop El Capitan (you can walk up the backside). After twenty-seven continuous days on the wall, they pulled over the top, where they were greeted by throngs of TV cameras and reporters in what had become the biggest media feeding frenzy in rock-climbing history. Even the irreverent Harding was worn so thin from their ordeal that he hid behind boulders, bawling, before he could face the crowd.

Harding's famous aid climb became known as the Wall of the Early Morning Light. Over the years that section of El Capitan, where the sun's first rays bathe the most daunting portion of the world's most iconic big wall in brilliant orange alpenglow, became known by a similar name: the Dawn Wall.

I didn't realize it at the time, but during that presentation back in 1983, Harding had ignited a spark in me. As I learned more about him in the following years, that spark fanned itself into a tiny flame. I wanted to emulate guys like my dad, Harding, and my dad's group of climbing friends, be up there on those big walls, doing things that nobody had ever done.

Warren Harding wasn't a member of my dad's group of climbing buddies. He'd accepted the invitation to speak at our house because my dad was part of the local guiding company, the Colorado Mountain School (CMS). At the time of the slide show, my mom had just stopped running the day care center, and started working in their office. The owner and operator of the school, Mike Donahue, was one of my dad's great friends.

Mike Donahue was a remarkable man. He shared with my father a love of the mountains and the outdoors. While my dad spread word of the wonders and benefits of climbing with messianic fervor, Mike went about the same mission with a more laid-back approach. If my dad was a warrior then Mike was a poet-philosopher. Their differences can probably be best summarized by this: When assessing the clients they led up mountains, if the group had a get-to-the-top-or-bust vibe, then my dad would lead the group. If they seemed more into the experiential nature of the endeavor and the peak was a bonus, then Mike led them. Mike took a slow and meditative, stop-and-smell-roses kind of approach. It never seemed to bother him that he hadn't climbed the area's most iconic wall, the east face of Longs Peak—even though many considered it a "must-do," in terms of status in the climbing community. As Mike put it, "A great adventure without success is far superior to a climb where everything goes as planned."

Mike was the master of the unplanned bivouac. On several occasions my dad and other guides went out to rescue Mike and his clients, thinking they were in trouble. Most times, Mike's mellow manner had simply lengthened the trip beyond the originally scheduled time—sometimes by days, not hours. That's not to say that Mike was a slacker. In his estimation, he climbed Longs Peak—a nearby 14,259-foot summit—more than 250 times.

He was almost stereotypically the grizzled mountain man—full-bearded, lean, and topped with a mass of knotted hair. But so gentle. Even as a kid I connected with his big heart and big laugh. I imagined that birds might have nested in his beard and hair; they were already tangled with bits of twigs. I can still picture the many photos of Mike taken during cold weather outings—his face a blob of frozen snot and exhaled water vapor that looked like soft serve ice cream clinging to his grinning face.

Our family spent a great deal of time with the Donahues. They lived in the neighboring community of Allenspark, and their lifestyle significantly influenced me. My dad couldn't have been earning much from his work at CMS—it wasn't a not-for-profit organization, but nearly so. It wasn't the kind of mega-outfitter they competed against. The Donahues did the work for love and not money.

As a kid I loved visiting the Donahue home. Mike, his wife, Peggy, and their three kids lived amid a thick forest of lodgepole pine trees, in what had once been a dirt-floor cabin. By the time I came along, they'd installed a rough-sawn pine floor. Their outhouse was surrounded by long rows of

31

stacked wood. The fireplace provided the only heat and light in the house. They had no running water, so they kept big barrels and plastic jugs in the corner of the kitchen. The adults would sit outside around a fire pit, drinking alcohol and swapping stories while the fire crackled and sparked. Their youngest son, Tobias, was about my age and we became best friends. Together we ranged out among the trees until the adults' blaze was a pinprick of light.

With an ax in hand, we'd supplement the deadfall we'd gathered and build teepees and lean-tos. Sometimes we'd ride out from our fort to conduct raids on enemy Indian camps, avenging ourselves on tribes that had attacked us. Other times, we'd sit in the teepee and imagine that we were back from the hunt and preparing hides for the coming winter. With pinecones as our weapons—some of them as big as apples and even grapefruits—we'd wage war on each other's encampments.

Tobias and I would start a fire and do our best to keep it going for days on end. We'd alternate watches, one boy sleeping, the other tending the fire. I can still feel the sting of smoke in my eyes, the dried nasal passages from those hours hunkered down by our creation, the pine sap tackiness and stains on my hands and my clothes.

I was at home in the woods, and seeing how the Donahues lived was inspiring. In Tobias, I found someone with similar interests and a vivid inner life of imagined adventures. Together we ran in the deep of the night until our sweat-covered arms cooled and our exposed skin pebbled before retreating to our (or our parents') circles of light.

"Hey, Tommy. C'mon, bud. Time to get up."

Bleary-eyed, I can barely make out my father's face in the darkness. He gives my legs a shake and a quick pat.

An instant after his blurred body recedes, my feet are on the cold floor. It's two fifteen in the morning. I can feel my pulse quickening. I stand in front of the toilet nearly hopping from foot to foot, wishing I could get all of my pee out of me quicker. Done and shaken, I trot back to my room.

My bag, packed the night before, sits on my desk. I've laid out all my clothes and quickly tug them on. I scramble down the stairs and out into the driveway. The door of my dad's rusty old Nissan Sentra barks its displeasure and resists my tug. Once in the car, the aroma cloud from his massive mug of black coffee signals the start of another adventure. My insides bubble, a mix of anticipation, sleeplessness, and fear that I might not be up to my dad's challenge and trust.

At the trailhead, under shimmering stars, the cold penetrates my fleece and jolts me into alertness. Within minutes, hiking the steep trail with a rope coiled over my shoulder, my chill turns to sweat.

"Do you think any other kids my age have climbed the Diamond?" I ask, as my feet scurry over roots and rocks.

"Definitely not. You will be the youngest for sure." Dad steps aside and lets me lead.

After an hour in the forest we cross into the barren alpine tundra. A cold wind blows. We skip across boulders as little alpine mice, called picas, dart through the beams of our headlamps. Thirty miles to our east, scattered lights dot the sprawling Front Range.

All those people are comfortable in their beds; they will be for hours.

My legs quiver and my lungs burn. We have found a higher plane of existence. My dad's preaching has converted me to his way of seeing our world. I feel a hint of pity for those who don't get to experience the crisp air and excitement of mountain climbing. Are they ever really awake?

The ice-cold water of Chasm Lake stings my teeth. Our brief stop for a refill over, we continue through talus fields to the foot of the wall. I still feel the buzz of exertion from more than three hours of hard hiking as I uncoil our climbing rope. My dad ties into one end, and then watches me properly tie into the other. He grabs a blade of rock for chopping steps up the frozen snowfield that splays from the bottom of the wall like a skirt. The Diamond towers above.

In August of 1990, when I was twelve, my dad had decided I was ready for Colorado's premier alpine wall, almost 2,000 vertical feet of granite. Named the Diamond because of its shape on the east face of Longs Peak, it's the highest elevation big wall in the Lower 48. Beginning at over 12,000 feet in elevation, the wall is visible from the flats of the Front Range.

Thousand-foot streaks of water ooze like black fangs down the tan-colored shield of stone. When one stands at the base, it looks as if the wall is canted at an angle, as if it might topple over on you. How we would get to the top seemed beyond comprehension. Except I was with my dad, and I knew that he believed in us.

Given my age, my dad had targeted the easiest route on the Diamond, but the Diamond by any route is a lifetime climbing achievement for many. I'd already climbed the mountain itself when I turned eight—it was all I wanted for my birthday—but we had ascended a relatively mellow route on the north face. Essentially we had hiked it, with only a couple hundred feet of roped climbing. Now, finally, I was ready for the real deal. I knew that fewer than 50 percent of the climbers who started up the Diamond ever reached the top. There were many factors involved—the elements, the level of experience of the climbers, and so forth—but I didn't know of anyone my age who had even attempted the climb. That excited me even more. It wasn't about the thrill or the facing of danger, it was about pushing my limits and seeing if my hard work had paid off.

The Diamond was my first real test.

Although I was shy and socially awkward, and I would have never admitted this to anyone, I viewed myself as a little warrior. I'd spent hours and hours working out. I took great pride in being able to outwork and outlast older kids, and even adults, when at the gym or when climbing at the crags with my dad. I beat almost everyone at wrestling—except for the criers whom I let win. Still, if anyone saw me walking down the hallway at school, if anyone truly saw me at all, they would have no idea of my capabilities. I never did anything to show anyone up, and I never made any kind of gesture—never a fist pump, a chest thump, or the other kinds of "Hey, look at me" things that athletes do.

Still, I reveled in opportunities to show everybody that I was more than that kid with the big glasses and the special education schedule. Like in seventh grade, when my PE teacher created the Hundred-Miler Club, a contest to encourage physical activity. We were to track what we did—hiking, running, biking, push-ups, sit-ups, and so on—on a score sheet. Different activities had different point values, and the goal was to reach a hundred. I was so excited that the first afternoon following the announcement of the challenge, I ran home from the bus stop and dutifully recorded my mileage.

The top three kids would earn special recognition at the end of the school year assembly. I was easily doing one hundred points of activity a week. Hell, every weekend my dad and I went on twenty-mile hikes. I worked out maniacally, as usual, and recorded it all. At the year-end assembly I sat quietly, eagerly, in the stands of the gym, knowing that I had outdone everybody. The regular kids were called up first, receiving certificates. Then another few who did pretty well. The PE teacher and principal were saving the best for last—the top three.

From behind my huge glasses I grinned in anticipation. *Third: Bryan Mecray with 200 miles.* Even my big ears glowed. They let the teachers participate, so, *Second: Mrs. Wolf with 327 miles.* My self-consciousness evaporated. And the *Winner: Tae Ludlam with 548 miles!* Everybody cheered.

I was crushed. They didn't believe me. My score of over 800 miles was so far beyond everyone that they simply didn't believe that the little nobody, the kid who kept to himself all the time, had done what I'd recorded. But I stuffed away the welling tears and turned them into motivation. Dad always taught me that it's not what happens to you, it's how you deal with it.

By the time I stood below the Diamond, I was ready. All of the training, and even the rejection, had developed mental discipline, and I'd been climbing nearly since the time I could walk. My dad never talked about failing or quitting. He never talked about fear either. He talked about preparations and precautions. He talked about controlling as many elements of a climb or other adventure as you could.

I paid out rope as my dad carefully made his way up the frozen snowfield and onto the rock. He would lead every pitch, or rope length, climbing up and placing removable protection at intervals of his own choosing, based on his judgment—what is known as trad, or traditional, climbing (in contrast to sport climbing, where you clip permanently affixed bolts for protection). His pieces of gear, if placed well, would protect him. If he fell, of course he would fall twice the distance above his last piece of protection.

Intellectually I understood what it meant to be afraid, but I never felt fear when I was with him. I wasn't worried about the massive weight differential between us, and how it could affect my ability to safely belay him. He weighed about 170, about twice as much as I did. That meant that if he fell, I'd be violently yanked skyward against the anchor, while simultaneously trying to cinch down the belay device to hold the massive impact. Realistically, I'd probably have lost control, which could have been disastrous for my dad. I shudder to think of his being injured, it being my fault, and our being stranded up there. None of this occurred to me at the time, of course. Dad was confident enough in his abilities that he was going to essentially free solo the Diamond.

After making short work of the snowfield and a six-hundred-foot steep and loose chimney, we reached "Broadway," a huge ledge at the base of the real climbing.

I belayed as my dad moved like King Kong scaling a skyscraper, confident, efficient, graceful, and methodical. He'd carefully place his fingers on the rock's natural edges and in the cracks, testing each hold before pulling hard. He'd climb 150 feet or so, then look for a good stance with solid protection and build an anchor. When he called to me that I was "on belay," I could remove my anchor and begin climbing. I'd scan the rock for possibilities, and in an instant analyze which holds I could reach and, instinctively, position my body to allow upward progress. My oversized yellow helmet tilted awkwardly to one side. My undersized legs wobbled as I stepped high onto an edge. I zoomed-in my focus, studying the shapes of the holds and alternately grasping and relaxing, trying to conserve energy, sucking in the thin air, and resting on every good foothold. The cold rock numbed my fingers. At every stance I'd stop and balance, releasing my fingers' grip on the hard surface. I curled my reddened hands into fists and blew my breath into them.

"You can warm your hands on your stomach!" Dad yelled down to me.

As I climbed I'd remove each piece of gear from the crack and clip it to a sling around my shoulder. When I reached my dad's anchor he'd grab the gear, rerack it on his gear sling, and within minutes set off on the next pitch. By the time we reached the third pitch above Broadway, the sun was warming the wall. Little patches of ice that had formed the previous night began to drip.

Chunks of ice fell from a chimney far above. They floated past, peaceful and silent. The truth was, they could be deadly. One, nearly the size of a watermelon, crashed on a nearby ledge. I shut my eyes as I was sprayed with shrapnel. I felt as if I was on the edge of a gun battle. I'd eventually learn about 9.8 meters per second squared, gravitational acceleration, but back then my frame of reference was being pelted by one of Tobias's pinecones. I adjusted the strap on my helmet and took a deep breath. I eyed the wall above me and then took in the larger scene.

Boulders cascaded down a gully far below and to our left as they melted from the glacier. The mountain seemed to be coming alive. I looked at Dad, hoping he couldn't read the twinge of fear in me. I felt so small. His eyes narrowed and his lips grew taut. The tendons in his thick arms stood out like rivers on a relief map below his pushed-up sleeves. From the deep furrows that creased his forehead, I could tell that he was deep in thought, deciding something.

"Okay, as I climb this next section it is your job to watch for ice and warn me when you see it coming." A smile stretched across his face and immediately I felt at ease. He trusted me. Suddenly I wasn't as cold as I had been. I was taking care of him as much as he was responsible for me.

The earth disappeared below, the shimmering waters of Chasm Lake far away and the mundane life in the cities and towns even farther. Around 11:00 a.m. storm clouds roiled overhead. The electrostatically charged atmosphere prickled the skin on my arms. The air popped and rumbled. We hurried.

Soon we topped-out the wall at nearly 14,000 feet, completing the Diamond. We raced upward, tagged the summit, and then boogied down an adjacent, lower-angled face. As we rappelled the skies opened, pelting us with hail. My dad shifted into fast-forward. "Keep going down that ramp while I coil the rope! I'll catch up in a minute," he shouted to me over the sound of rumbling thunder. The air smelled different, some electric scent overpowering the smell of the rain and the rock. In the distance lightning fractured the bowl of the sky.

We moved in perfect synch, and soon we were skipping down the trail, passing groups of dripping-wet hikers. As we neared the trailhead, the dull pain of exhaustion pulsed through my legs. My chapped lips bled. We eased ourselves into our car seats, soaked and tired. I sat completely still for the first time in thirteen hours. It was my biggest day yet in the mountains. On the silent drive home Dad reached over and, grinning a huge grin, squeezed my shoulder.

I closed my eyes and sank back in the seat, tired but happy. I'd proven to myself that I had what it took to tackle a monumental challenge.

A month later, I am still tired but no longer happy. I sit in math class as the sun dazzles the foliage of a withering aspen tree. My eyes, now more fit, follow a few leaves as they drift from the tree and fall to earth. The teacher is going on about something. Like the sound of water running in a distant stream, the words "integer," "whole number," and "imaginary number" tumble by me. I can't imagine that anyone really cares about any of this. I can't understand why no one seems to care that my dad has taught me that riffles form mean-ders in rivers, that the Big Thompson River that flows through our town flooded in 1976, tossing cars and houses and lives aside as it rampaged down the canyon. Erosion grinds away at rock and leaves behind fissures and foot-holds and ledges.

Reflexively I flinch when I hear my name. I look to the front of the room and realize that my teacher, Mrs. Tierney, has asked me a question. I sud-denly feel as if I have to pee. I look down at my desk and scan the surface's grain, hoping I can spread those lines and climb inside the wood. When I don't respond, she adds another question, "Were you paying attention, Tommy?"

My classmates' laughter bounces off of me like the hailstorm on Longs Peak.

Somewhere in the world lightning strikes the ground one hundred times a second. The United States receives twenty million hits a year. Every year an average of eleven people die of lightning strikes in Colorado. Those are some of the numbers I know. Just like I know that I can do thirty repetitions on the pull-up bar and hang in the front lever position for twenty-five seconds. Those are the numbers that really matter.

I say nothing, hunker down, and wait it out.

THE PUSH

As I grew, my parents recognized my early academic struggles, so for the latter part of middle school they decided that I should transfer to Bill Reed Middle School, where my dad taught. He was impressed by his fellow teachers and thought that with his involvement they would be able to help me. On my first day I walked through the doors scared, still small and shy. My dad walked in ahead of me, cutting a swath through the kids in the hallway. They shouted, "Hey, Mr. C!" and he ran a gauntlet of high fives until he was out of sight. I went to my locker and struggled with the combination. I imagined myself tearing the door off its hinges; instead, I finally got it open. I looked at its bare walls and mentally arranged all the photos and stickers I'd affix to its surface—a stash of them from Neptune Mountaineering in Boulder. I just hoped that the other kids wouldn't notice my battles with remembering my combination. I'd struggled with that at my other school, going through periods of days when the numbers eluded me. I'd walk into class without the right textbooks and notebooks and folders. How could I explain? Why couldn't I remember my class schedule? What could I do but duck my head and scuttle off, hearing the laughter and dork-calls in my wake?

I was okay with my dad being a rock star in school. He helped me earn some street cred. As my confidence grew, I became more engaged and focused. I stopped forgetting things like my locker combination. Before, I felt as if my teachers had written me off. At my dad's school I was getting a new start. For most of his career he'd taught PE and health, which he did wearing brightly colored spandex and tight neon tank tops. But for some reason, in the years I attended his school he taught English and social studies, which he still did in spandex and a tank top. His English class was a high-energy affair of verbal quizzes in which he hurled candy across the room as rewards for correctly answered questions. As with my earlier credit system, he charted progress and had the kids competing against each other.

He built a climbing wall in the gymnasium and started an after-school program, which quickly became the school's most popular activity. For even more fun, he rigged a rope swing from the hanging balcony of the gym. He also held lead-fall practice, in which kids climbed to the I-beams in the ceiling, protected by a rope, then scurried farther out along the beams and leaped off, to be caught by the students who were holding the other end of the rope and learning to belay.

Climbing became a cool thing at the school. Because I knew more about climbing than the other students, for the first time in my life kids started looking up to me, even asking me to teach them. With this kind of attention my grades improved and I started to love school.

Climbing became another form of my education. In the summer of 1993, I got to join my dad on a CMS assignment to guide in Bolivia. I'd traveled around the western United States a bit, of course, going to Yosemite and Wyoming. But getting a passport photo and traveling to another continent with my dad was different; if someone had told me that I had to fly on the wing, I'd have said set me up with oxygen bottles. I counted down the days to departure, pored over maps of the country, and lingered over photos of the Central and Eastern Andes in my dad's climbing magazines and books. To condition my legs, I rode my bike to school a few times, a sixty-mile round trip.

We flew to La Paz, the country's capital, which sits in a high bowl nearly 11,500 feet above sea level. I was lightheaded from the thin air, along with my excitement. We took a taxi to our hotel, and everything was a blur of bright primary colors and the rust and ochre tones of the earthen homes. The streets were frantic with cars, buses, motorcycles, scooters, and pedestrians. Though I'd sought quiet and solitude when I was younger, then, just shy of my fifteenth birthday, I loved the commotion. I couldn't help but laugh when I saw a mother, father, kid, and a pair of chickens clinging to a soot-spewing moped as they wove through traffic, as if stitching a seam. I cracked the window and inhaled the smell of exhaust and a low-level tinge of cabbage gone bad.

Magnifying the sensory overload was my inability to understand a word—it was the first time I'd been surrounded by a language other than English. I could make out a few words on street signs and billboards, the omnipresent Coke and Fanta soda emblems.

My dad had to prove to the clients that his scrawny kid could carry his weight, so he treated me like an adult from the start. Shortly after arriving, Dad handed me a stack of twenty-dollar bills and told me to go to the man on the street corner—that guy with the calculator—and exchange our money. Then get water that wouldn't upset our gringo bellies.

"Make sure the caps are still factory sealed, that way you know they didn't just refill the bottles with unclean water. Then buy beer from the kid with the blue cart."

I nodded and made my way out of the hotel. Momentarily blinded by the bright sun, I stood for a few seconds taking in the scene. Businessmen in Western-style suits quick-stepped along the sidewalks, dodging street vendors in traditional Bolivian dress. I wondered why so many of the women wore hats that resembled the ones I'd seen in photos of outlaws in the old American West. The hats perched at funny angles atop their heads, and they wore colorful embroidered shirts with puffy sleeves, and wide skirts that triangled down from their waists in a cascade of brilliant blue fabric. Above the street noise, I heard the sound of music. On the sidewalk, just down from the hotel, a group of men blew into various wooden instruments. Pan flutes looked like angle-cut test tubes set in a rack. A tambourine rattled and a drum beat time to my rapidly thumping heart. A man plucked at wires attached to a stick and a bucket. I squinted down the street in the direction my father had told me to go. As I took the first few steps my head felt light, like a balloon on a string.

When I found the moneychanger, I didn't know what to say. He reached out his hand. He then scrabbled his dirt-darkened fingers at the calculator and showed me the screen. I nodded, gave him money, and he handed me a stack of bolivianos. I held the currency in my palm, surprised at how many more bills I'd received than I'd given. I nodded my thanks and walked away, casting sideways glances, wondering if someone was following me.

The beer vendor was just a few years older than me. I pointed and held up fingers to let him know how many I needed. He smiled and pulled the beer from its place. He gestured to me for payment. I pulled the wad of bills from my pocket and began thumbing through them. A few seconds later his hand covered mine. He took the bills, counted out a few and handed back the rest. Transaction completed, faith in humanity still intact, I walked away marveling at how cool it was that I could legally buy beer in a foreign country.

At the hotel my dad thanked me, and I glowed at his "Atta boy, Tommy!" Over the course of the next few days he encouraged me to take in as much of the city as I could before we headed to the mountains.

One morning I wandered the narrow, hilly streets, casting glances overhead to the spiderweb of power lines. At one corner, I noticed a row of market stalls. A group of older women clad in uncustomary black clothes and hats sat on chairs or squatted on the curb. I'd later learn that this was a famous part of La Paz's markets—El Mercado de las Brujas—or the Witches' Market. At first my eyes were drawn to a shelf of stone carvings. As I moved along I was struck, nearly in the face, by something dangling from the stall's hanging roofs. I stepped back in shock—it was a dried llama fetus. Nearby were dried frogs, condor figurines, and bottles with liquids and powders, all for sale. Through a bit of gesture, give and take a few words, I learned that the witches were good witches. Most of what they sold was intended to deliver good fortune. I bought one small bottle from one of the most witchy-looking of the *brujas*. She gestured to her heart and her head and gave me a thumbs up, letting me know that my selection was proper. She smiled a toothless smile.

I decided to bring the potion home for my mom or Sandy. Thinking of my sister made me a little sad. At first, she'd been a big part of our family's climbing outings and other activities. Lately, she'd not been much of a part of them at all. She had other friends and other interests. I sensed that as the miracle baby and the little guy who idolized my dad and followed him everywhere, I was getting more than my fair share of my dad's attention. But I thought that she would have loved the trip to Bolivia. I knew that the potion was just a silly little trinket, but I wanted her to know that I was thinking of her.

After our organizational days in La Paz, we crammed into old jeeps and drove to a village below a 21,125-foot peak called Illimani. When we arrived, some fifty children ran to our vehicles, climbing onto the hoods and roofs before we even stopped. They crowded around us, playing with and pushing one another and calling for candy in their native language, Aymara. They lived in mud huts with tin roofs, had dirt-caked faces, and wore tattered clothes. Entire families, from the newborn baby to the great-grandpa with cavernous lines across his face, all lived in the same small shack. Yet the joy and laughter surrounding us made my school playground seem like a morgue.

My dad hired five strong young men as our porters, to help carry our gear to base camp over the next two days. We divided everything into sixty-pound piles, which they wrapped in large canvas blankets and hoisted onto their shoulders as if they were as light as my school backpack.

The men spoke amiably with one another, smiling and laughing along the trail. The clients complained of blisters from their shiny new boots. They slowly trudged up the valley with pain etched on their faces, labored exhalations and muttered curses falling from their gaping mouths. The barefoot porters stepped lightly and nimbly, hopping over rocks and roots that tripped up the clients. The first time we stopped to rest and the porters sat down, I saw that the bottoms of their feet were yellow and black, thickly callused and tough as a Vibram sole. When they drew ahead I followed, trying to keep up through a terraced valley as alpaca wandered past. For half a day we walked up the gently inclined valley, alongside fields of potato sprouts and the occasional patch of grass. As we gained elevation, the green yielded to gray rock and silt, contrasting brilliantly with the snow-covered mountains ahead.

At one point we took a break on a small rock outcropping, overlooking the valley below, and I pulled a nutrition bar from my pack. The porter next to me unwrapped a packet of cooked potatoes and carrots, still steaming hot. With a nod he handed me some, and then I offered him my snack, but he declined. A cold gale blew from the glacier above, and I dug out my jacket. As it flapped in the wind, I accidentally put it on inside out. The porters noticed with good-natured laughs.

The next day, in blustery conditions at 16,000 feet, I took three breaths for every step. It felt like the air had slowed my internal engine to low gear, and trying harder only made it worse. I spent most of the day hiking alone, with the porters ahead and my dad behind, looking after the clients. Copying the porters, I chewed on coca leaves to fend off altitude sickness. No more powerful a stimulant than caffeine, it eased my headache. Still, at fourteen, I thought it was so cool to be imbibing the plant from which cocaine was derived.

Despite the hypoxia, I took joy in the rhythm of movement. Something had always appealed to me about laboring away alone, as long as I was outside.

We camped that first night on a flat perch on a glacier. A maze of crevasses surrounded us on three sides. While two of the clients were pitching their tent, a sudden gust of wind ripped it from their hands. Without even thinking, I sprinted across the glacier, jumping onto the tent and stopping it just before it would have disappeared into a crevasse. That night I was the hero in camp and I beamed with pride.

In the following days we climbed Illimani, and then another mountain called Huayna Potosí. I don't recall much about the actual climbing, it was mainly easy snow and ice, and more like a fairly strenuous hike. Although I liked the work, if this was mountaineering then it wasn't for me. Rock climbing, the sort of thing we did on the Diamond, lit my fire.

In a very real way, I'd gone to school that summer in Bolivia; I learned what really mattered to me. To this day, what I remember most is the deep impression the porters made on my fourteen-year-old self. They seemed content, despite their lack of material wealth. I was from a different world, couldn't even speak the same language, yet I felt a bond with them unlike any I had with kids my age back home. I had been feeling the early pressures of our society telling me to go to college, get a good job, and make money. Deep down it felt like a false lure, one without meaning. The thought of conforming, of settling for less than the adventurous life I craved, scared me more than any mountain.

Thanks to my dad, Mike Donahue, and those porters, I was starting to unlock essential feelings about myself and how I viewed the world and my place in it. I started thinking that climbing could be my path to what I considered a greater truth—that simplicity, solitude, and natural beauty were the real gems in life.

CHAPTER THREE

I stand and stare skyward. *Refrigerator-sized blocks arc overhead like a sixty-foot crashing wave, splotched and mottled in various shades of brown, black, and white, all part of a continuous shield of stone. I study the features and try to identify weaknesses. I shut my eyes, visualizing what lies ahead. Each climb at Rifle is like a thirty-minute high-exertion chess match. Cerebral athleticism. I know that once I start it will be a strategic battle to balance the physical, mental, and emotional, when my heart pumps harder and harder, the lactic acid sears my forearms, and I fight for calm. Precision, composure, power, and control. I play out each move in my mind, telling myself that I am good enough, that I can do this.*

My drumming heartbeat tells me it is time to go.

I open my eyes, nod my head. Okay. I'm ready. I inhale deeply. I reach up and grab the first hold. I'm on the wall and climbing. A zoomed-out image flashes before me, of my body moving through the sequences like a gymnast in the Olympics. Only for an instant. I exhale and narrow my focus to the intricacies with which my fingers grasp the rock. Before I know it, I'm more than a dozen feet off the ground. I can feel my muscles beginning to work, the lactic acid starting to burn.

Breathe, relax, exhale . . . hold on just hard enough, just loose enough, shake out, milk this rest, get it back, breeeeathe.

Okay, whew, now hanging here is costing too much, gotta move again before my fingers fail.

Go, go, go.

Clip the bolt.

Breathe, breathe, breathe.

Get it back. Look ahead.

Crux sequence. Relax. Don't talk yourself out of this.

You know what to do.

Step left foot high. Feel that tiny nubbin.

Pull your hips in; pull hard with the right. Not too hard.

Easy, easy.

Stay calm.

Focus. Focus.

One more sequence and you send this.

I clip the anchors and slouch, hanging in my harness, my chest heaving and my heart pounding. I rest my palms on my thighs, feel the sweat stinging my eyes and blurring my vision.

This is utterly ridiculous. And absolutely beautiful.

Upon returning home from Bolivia, we had just enough time for my dad to fill in my mom on a few of the highlights. My dad let her know that I had acquitted myself well as a young guide. She asked me how I liked it and I said, "Fine."

"Fine," my dad said, twisting his face into a portrait of disbelief, "It was better than *fine*! The little dude was on his game. Showed the clients what a real man looks like. I had him guiding them, I swear to God. And the porters? They totally tried to drop him, but he kept pace. They saw his hustle and embraced him like he was one of their own."

I walked to my room and lay down on my bed. I wondered briefly where Sandy was. I heard some commotion coming from the kitchen but I shut my eyes and drifted off to sleep. That night in the darkened house, I went to Sandy's room to give her the little bottle I'd brought back for her. She wasn't there, so I left it on her dresser amidst a tangled coil of bracelets and necklaces.

A week later, Dad and I were on the road to Arizona. He'd read about the Mount Lemmon area in either *Climbing* or *Rock and Ice* magazine. He subscribed to both, and we tore into them as soon as they hit the mailbox. Mount Lemmon was a hotbed for a new type of climbing that had yet to gain mainstream acceptance in the United States. My dad was intrigued and I trailed in his considerable wake, eager to see what all the excitement was about.

Times were changing. The climbers of Harding's era and the one that followed lived fast and free. Climbing ropeless (free soloing) was common, as were hardcore drugs. Yosemite climbs were given names like Mescalito, Tangerine Trip, and Magic Mushroom. Many of those climbers became so absorbed in ascent, and in maximizing their experiences at any cost, that they made little of their lives afterward; maybe they overdosed on the gems of life.

By the early eighties, high-end Yosemite big wall climbing had become a turnoff for my dad. The prevailing style eschewed any breach in "ethics" such as rehearsing pitches on the wall in order to free climb them. To some it might seem absurd, but that was how it was back then. Imagine a gymnast who faces communal scorn for bastardizing the purity of his sport by practicing his routine in advance. As a result of that hard-line thinking, free climbing hit a natural ceiling and progress on big walls shifted to dangerous aid climbing. The gear placements were so precarious that the slightest shock loading could rip the pieces from the rock and trigger a wave of successive failures below. In the worst-case scenario, this could blow out the belay, sending both climbers plummeting to their deaths. Since placing bolts for protection was frowned upon, machismo prevailed.

For my dad, that was enough. He saw high-end big wall climbing becoming a game for off-kilter adrenaline-junkie types who cared little for self-preservation. Ultimately, such a direction for climbing would prove to be a dead end.

During this time, however, the Europeans had completely rethought rock climbing. Europe was home to the Alps, the birthplace of alpinism. Climbing mountains was a celebrated act, bordering on sacred to some. But many climbers were becoming more interested in the challenge and enjoyment of climbing difficult rock, without the risk inherent in alpinism, mountaineering, and even traditional rock climbing. The French spearheaded the use of portable, motorized drills and started bolting otherwise unprotectable rock faces with small but solid, permanent anchor points every few meters. They used incredibly strong, lightweight nylon ropes that stretched to absorb impact from falls. Between the bolts and the high-tech ropes, falling was no longer a life-risking terror, but an expected part of trying hard. With a reliable safety system in place, climbers could focus on the athleticism of free climbing the most difficult features of sheer cliffs, and the internal voyage of exploring their personal limits.

This new form of climbing—today the most popular type of climbing in the world—became known as sport climbing.

In the eighties, as sport climbing made its way to the United States, it was met with heavy resistance. Despite climbing's de facto mantra of freedom, the staunch traditionalists—most American climbers back then—saw sport climbing as an affront to their sacred pursuit. They touted an overt, defiant anthem: Sport Climbing Is Neither. Sport climbers would seek out smooth, crackless faces and establish routes with bolts (which are usually permanent fixtures), and then the traditional climbers would come along and remove them—what was known as chopping them. Fistfights broke out between members of the two factions. The ugliest, most contentious era of American climbing had settled down some by the time I came along, but only slightly.

My dad always looked forward, never backward. As a result, at Mount Lemmon my dad and I clipped bolts, rehearsed the hard moves, and safely fell off routes. We dipped our hands into bags of gymnastic chalk to dry the sweat from our fingers. Hard sport climbing felt like a constant battle between self-doubt, precision, and effort, waged over stretches of difficult rock usually only sixty to eighty feet tall.

While in Arizona, we ran into other like-minded climbers. One of them was a former gymnast who came from a traditional climbing background. She then embraced sport and competition climbing (a new form of structured events held on overhanging plywood walls with artificial, bolted-on holds) before moving to Europe to compete on the international circuit. She was so good, she won the World Cup and multiple major titles. At Mount Lemmon she was climbing circles around everyone else; she had previously climbed the unfathomably difficult grade of 5.14—the first woman to do so. Later this lean, strong woman, standing only five-foot-one, would use her vast array of skills to become the first person to free climb the Nose, on El Capitan, shattering preconceived notions and making what many still consider the greatest rock climb in history. Afterward, she also dropped one of climbing's all-time greatest lines, a pointed quip directed at the machismo of the day: "It goes, boys." It wasn't only Lynn Hill's phenomenal skill, but her vision of climbing that helped change the game.

I knew none of this at the time. I just watched as she floated up the rock, climbing a steep wall that looked as smooth as a plane of glass. At one point she splayed her legs out into a full split, toes pressing against opposing dime-width edges. Then, holding that position, she stopped to chalk her hands and started chatting with her belayer. I looked over at my dad and our jaws dropped. We were witnessing a new paradigm in climbing. My dad, never shy, seized an opportunity to speak with Lynn. I stood there not saying a thing, just marveling at what that woman could do. Like her, I was light and flexible and strong for my size. I liked the feeling of being on rock and solving the puzzle of what sequence of moves to make, even on routes that were only a single pitch. The creativity of it appealed to me.

Although we had little time to develop a full sense of sport climbing, what we'd learned and what we'd done had a strong allure. We returned to Colorado with our appetites whetted. But we had more work to do in that summer of '93.

We were only in Estes long enough to have my mom do a few loads of laundry. Dad helped me pack, and our summer of alpine guiding took me to a new destination—France. In exchange for a salary, my dad had made arrangements for me to join the trip. Once again, I was on an airliner bound for a foreign land.

Given that the French had invented sport climbing and were the acknowledged world leaders in it, Dad wanted to get us on the famed cliffs of Southern France for two weeks before the clients arrived. We purchased a guidebook to the premier sport climbing areas, and from Paris we hopped a train. Most of our climbing had been on granite, where the walls rarely exceed vertical. In France, most of the sport climbing is on smaller limestone cliffs, where the cleanest rock tends to be on the undersides of depressions, creating severely overhanging routes.

The climbing was far more gymnastic—success seemed to depend on contortionist-like body movements for maximum efficiency, where strength-to-weight ratio was crucial and big muscles seemed to only add unnecessary ballast. I'd always thought the ideal climber was built like a lumberjack or fireman. But the Europeans were light and skinny like me. They seemed like modern dancers in a vertical and overhanging arena.

I remember watching a particularly strong Frenchman at a crag in an area called Cluses. He was petite, lean, and absurdly honed. As he climbed his shoulder muscles rippled with every movement. In his tiny climbing shoes and spandex he cruised up a wildly overhanging route. When my dad tried the same climb, his fingers immediately opened under his body weight. He grunted and moaned. Compared to the French climber, my dad looked like a Sumo wrestler. He couldn't do the climb no matter how much he tried. It was the first time I had seen my dad physically outdone by another human being.

At the time, I didn't fully appreciate or understand what I was seeing, or even how lucky I was to be in South America and then Europe that summer. My parents didn't believe in spoiling their kids with material goods, but lavishing them with the opportunity to fully experience life was part of their parenting.

In the South of France we climbed voraciously. We tried to imitate what we saw, from studying the holds from the ground to moving swiftly through the hardest sections so we could rest on the larger holds. The climbing had a different flow and pace. Traditional climbing was usually more methodical, due to typically longer routes and the crucial safety considerations of placing one's own protection—perhaps akin to running a marathon through a potentially perilous obstacle course. Sport climbing was a bit like boxing or wrestling, with their spurts of intense action followed by brief clinches along the ropes or pauses on the mat. Regardless, they're still both climbing and they share a complex strategic component.

As the two weeks went on, our fingers hardened and we started getting the hang of limestone. Gradually we made our way up steeper and more difficult routes. Despite our progress, at every cliff we found climbers who were much better than my dad. Instead of frustration, my dad admired what he saw and expressed his appreciation in his usual optimistic way.

When it came time for Dad's work, we took a train to Chamonix. The jagged skyline of peaks shot sharply above the town in an unfathomable scale, spires of ice and granite rising 10,000 feet above the cobbled sidewalks. The Mont Blanc massif is one of the most storied in the history of alpinism, and climbing pulses through the culture of Chamonix. The mountains look at once hostile and sublime. Climbers occupied a place in French sporting culture similar to that of a major ball sport star in the United States. An unfortunate side effect of the adulation and popularity of climbing is that, as my dad told me when we first arrived, more than a hundred people die each year in the mountains around Chamonix. As soon as we arrived, my dad pointed out the route we would follow to the top of Mont Blanc. Several thousand feet of steep, forested hillside would lead us to a barren rock balcony, which we would traverse onto the slopes of a disintegrating glacier. We'd then weave around crevasses big enough to swallow twenty-story buildings, ascending onto the upper slopes of the mountain, skirting a several-thousand-foot face of blue ice and eventually topping out on a distant, domed summit. To me, at fourteen, it seemed an inviting yet nerve-jangling universe far, far away. I spent the better part of an afternoon studying the route from the balcony of our hostel, my neck craned back and my heart beating at double speed.

On an acclimatization day we took a gondola called the Téléphérique de l'Aiguille du Midi, which whisked us nearly two vertical miles in less than thirty minutes. We watched the landscape shift from streets and shops to grass and forests, then to the terminal ends of glaciers, with their icefalls and crevasses, and then to an inhospitable realm of rock, snow and ice. We hopped out of the lift and went sport climbing on spires high above the icy glaciers. The environment was dazzling, but somehow it didn't feel real. Somehow, I wasn't as engaged. Not arriving at the destination under my own power, while making access easier, seemed to diminish the size and beauty of the mountains and rock formations. I still held on to that dig, dig, and dig some more mentality. I felt as if I had watched the day on television, without fully participating myself.

The next morning we met Dad's clients, took the lift midway up, and started toward the summit. We walked across the first glacier following a route marked by painted rocks. An ice trench, formed by hundreds of cramponed feet, weaved between the boulders. We watched a man try to leap across a crevasse and disappear into the glacier. Within minutes a helicopter arrived, dropped a rope into the crevasse, and the man, relatively unharmed, clipped in and dangled on a brief but thrilling ride back to Chamonix. We spent the night in the very crowded Grands Mulets hut, spectacularly located on a rocky outcrop surrounded by tumbling glaciers, where I watched someone pass out at an elevation not much higher than our house in Colorado. A soiled hole in a plywood platform above a thousand-foot drop served as a toilet, with paper and excrement littering the mountain. The route was so crowded that on our summit day we simply stood in line and hiked uphill, alongside clients with little experience and what appeared to be an interest only in reaching the top, being dragged by their bored-stiff guides.

After climbing Mont Blanc we traveled to Zermatt, Switzerland, and had a similar experience climbing the Matterhorn.

It's hard to complain about such iconic locations, and from afar these mountains were the most beautiful I had seen. But the whole experience felt so urban, the paths to the summits so well marked, that the unknowns were virtually eliminated. By the end of the summer I found myself reminiscing about the remote and undeveloped Andes, as well as the simple focus of complex movement on overhanging stone. Regardless, one thing I knew for certain: I was now officially a climber.

In the spring of '94 my dad began looking at steep, blank sections of rock around Estes Park with a new eye—and a drill. As was typical of him, he took to sport climbing and its methods with full-on fervor. He wasn't bolting existing routes or rock that was protectable by traditional means, but that didn't matter. While it wasn't like those Wild West frontier days when guys beat up on each other, we'd arrive at routes he had bolted and find the bolts removed. The message was clear and a line was drawn. Some people did not like the idea of sport climbers "polluting" their favorite crags with bolts. No one ever confronted my dad directly, and that's probably a good thing. He was beyond his steroid days, but he was still a massive physical presence who held his beliefs firmly and would have stood up to anyone who challenged him.

My dad refused to see climbing as a zero-sum game. In his mind, there was room enough for everyone, every style, and every type of climbing. This open-minded approach cost him friends. It seems weird now—why couldn't people from a mountain background also embrace the gymnastic style and techniques of sport climbing? After all, in addition to having more fun, those who could combine new-school skills with a big-route mind-set might just change the game entirely. His sense of inclusiveness was deeply influential as I grew older and met more and more climbers. I'd see people doing things differently from me, and instead of dismissing them and their efforts out of hand, I'd try to learn, try to add to my own bag of tricks. In some ways, I took that "let's-all-do-our-own-thing" approach off the rock and into the rest of my life. At school I recognized and rejected the cliques and pressures to conform to others' values and expectations. I thought the social hierarchy—jocks, hicks, cool kids, bullies—was all petty and lame.

Despite fears surrounding this Euro-style "invasion," in small pockets of the United States sport climbing was taking hold. One manifestation, indoor climbing facilities, started popping up in major cities. We'd sometimes drive to Denver, a three-hour round trip, to train at Paradise Rock Gym. One afternoon, my dad was attempting a route on a twenty-degree overhanging wall when he encountered a big cross move that he couldn't do. He tried it a few times, hanging on the rope between attempts, and ultimately couldn't figure it out. I suggested that I might try. Dad flashed one of those "yeah, right, good luck" eye-rolling looks, but put me on belay. When I got to the move I pulled through with little trouble. This was the first time I'd demonstrated greater mastery than my dad. No shaft of sunlight came down to illuminate me and no torch appeared for my dad to hand off. I felt no rush of adrenaline, superiority, or anything like it. In fact, if I hadn't suggested that he try a different approach and use a higher right foothold and

twist his hips a little farther to the right, the moment might have gone unnoticed. Usually my dad's expression was easy to read. After I'd offered my
advice, reading his face was like looking at an array of thumbnail photos, all
waiting to be clicked. He was confused. He was disappointed. He was
pissed. He was proud. He was determined to get back on the route.

He was also determined that we take on some of the best (toughest) sport
climbing routes in the United States. For the first time I can remember,
come summer of '95 our road trip wasn't centered on Yosemite's towering
walls or faraway mountains. We went to Wyoming, California, Utah. Before
our experimenting with sport climbing, our life on rocks and mountains
had been more about gaining experience than progressing the physical
challenge. At least at the levels we were pursuing, success in mountain
climbing was virtually assured, and my dad wasn't interested in upping the
risk. On sport climbs the emphasis became improvement—how fluidly
could I move from one position to the next? How quickly could I get from
point A to point B? How could I most efficiently string together a sequence?

The focus required to climb at my limit seemed to heighten my senses.
The contrasts in the rock would jump out at me. I would notice things like
the sweet smell of juniper in the wind. I was more aware of the rhythm of
my breath and the preciseness of my body movements. We would climb
every day, testing ourselves and expanding our library of movement skills
on different types of rock, before spending our nights driving to the next
climbing area. Each time I felt stronger, lighter, and more skillful than the
last. I began to crave the sense of progress I was making.

To wrap up our trip, we rolled into Salt Lake City to spend a week in a
small canyon called American Fork. We'd climbed so much that summer
that my caloric intake couldn't keep up. My fingers got strong and little
muscles bulged from my back and veins protruded from my forearms. After
climbing but before heading home, we swung by the Snowbird Competition.

The first major U.S. climbing competition had been held on the side of
a lodge at the resort in Snowbird, Utah, in 1988. Artificial holds had been
bolted to the wall and a ten-foot swooping overhang had been built near
the top of the twelve-story hotel. The event was televised and we recorded

it; then we rewatched it so many times on our VHS tape deck that eventually the images flickered and faded. In each ensuing year the comp had attracted the best sport climbers from the United States, so we were eager to check it out in person.

We learned that the event included a citizen's competition the day before the pros—anybody could sign up. I'd been climbing well, but I didn't like the idea of competition. I'd experienced failure too often when directly competing with others in organized sports. But my dad urged me to give it a shot, and to please him as much as anything, I entered. Mentally I tried to force myself to simply treat it like another day of climbing.

The afternoon of the citizen's comp, I pinned a number onto my baggy tank top, and with my eyes to the ground walked out to the first route. Mountain bikers raged down a ski slope in the distance while nearly empty bleachers surrounded me, with a handful of amused spectators. Beck's "I'm a Loser Baby" blasted out of speakers the size of televisions, probably in an attempt to spruce up an event that's about as boring as watching paint dry. The twelve-story wall with artificial holds rose overhead. I tied in to the rope, pulled on, and practically sprinted to the top.

Hmmm, I thought, *that's weird. I wonder why they made it so easy.* The next three routes were mildly harder, the route setters making each round more challenging by bolting on smaller holds spaced farther apart. I felt a twinge of excitement to be on the same wall that the best sport climbers in the country would be on the following day—even though the routes they set for the citizen's comp were way easier.

After my final climb, my dad threw his arms around me and gave me a bone-crushing squeeze. "That was incredible, Tommy, you made it look so easy."

"It *was* easy," I said with a shrug. "The route setters botched it."

"No—you're the only one to finish all the routes." In climbing competitions participants aren't allowed to watch the other climbers, so I assumed everyone was making it to the top. I was way wrong.

Suddenly I felt my body tingle. "Does that mean I have to climb tomorrow?"

"Heck yes it does," my dad said. "And you're going to kick butt."

I stood there feeling as if someone had come along and scooped out my insides. The next day I would compete against rock stars like George Squibb and Christian Griffith. These were men, grown men, guys I'd read about in the magazines. These guys were pioneers in sport climbing in the United States, Griffith especially. He was the like the guy who'd brought fire down from the mountaintop for the rest of the primitives. One of the first to adopt the French style of sport climbing in the United States, and he advanced the sport.

Either ignoring how overwhelmed I was feeling or doing his best to give me the kind of talking to I needed, my dad said, "You can do this, Tommy. It's just climbing. Go out there and have fun."

Come morning I stood in a room with my climbing heroes, too intimidated to talk. Wide-eyed, I watched as they sanded their fingertips and stretched their legs. Some sat in the corners with their eyes closed, breathing deeply. Everyone kept to themselves. Griffith, one of the favorites, was doing standing high jumps. He was on the cover of the current issue of *Rock and Ice*. I figured that if he was jumping up and down, maybe I should, too. So I snuck into a hidden corner and imitated everything I saw.

From outside, I could hear that the crowd's throbbing intensity matched that of the silent isolation room. Though I hadn't yet seen the bleachers, I knew that the number of spectators had grown beyond the measly few who had sat through the citizen's comp. I licked my dry lips and scanned the ceiling of the room. A water leak had left a rust-brown stain.

We were each to compete in two rounds, both with a twenty-minute time limit. Since I had never timed a climb before, I decided I should try to climb each route as fast as possible. When I walked out I inhaled full, deep breaths. The music blared and the spectators softly buzzed. I was a nobody, an opening act before the headliner came out and got the crowd on its feet.

I looked at the overhang nearly one hundred feet above me. Just another kind of ceiling. Just another water stain up there.

I started up.

Everything felt foreign to me. Hollow plywood walls that thumped when my feet touched them. Formed cement holds. Spectators. But I had low expectations, so I wasn't overly nervous—still, I didn't want to make a fool of myself. As I climbed the first route and then the second, though the holds seemed small and far apart, I had this out-of-body sensation that I was floating; I felt weightless and flexible. Not once did I second-guess a move or think that I might fall. In fact, I thought about nothing but what was before me. On my second route, as I pulled the last few moves to the top, the spectators all stood up, cheering, stomping their feet. I could only think of how weird and surreal the whole thing was, and how they must have been cheering only because I was a kid.

When I returned to the ground and saw my dad, he was trembling. He looked like a caught fish—his mouth moved as he tried unsuccessfully to force a few words. His eyes grew wide and glassy. Deep crevasses creased his forehead and circled his eyes. He shrugged, palms up, and then hugged me.

To others the results were obvious, but an hour or so later, when they announced me as the winner, I felt as numb as I had the day before. A couple of event organizers hustled me over to an area near the grandstands. A raised platform held a dais. I looked at a couple of other climbers standing near me. They were men. I could see the beginnings of beards etched on the crags of their faces. I felt featureless, a blank inside and out.

I heard my name and was suddenly gripped by a sixteen-year-old's self-consciousness. I felt small, insubstantial. I hugged my arms around myself, uncertain what to do with my hands. I walked onstage not knowing what to say, what to think of the fact that some of these climbing legends were cheering for me, and that I had just outclimbed them. The emcee handed me a trophy and shook my hand. He lowered the microphone to my level. It was as if he'd put a lit torch in front of my face; the heat and the brightness repelled me. I stepped away. He reached for my hand to raise it in victory, but I was already gone. I wanted out of there.

I walked into the waiting arms of my dad. Tears ran down his cheeks. He gripped me so tight, I felt as if my body was being rearranged. I wondered for a minute what the big deal was, why he was crying.

Days later, when we got home and watched the video my dad had shot, I got a glimpse of it through his eyes. It was as if some seismic event had taken place. The footage of me on the wall was so shaky as to be nearly impossible to make out, a product of my dad's overwhelming pride and joy. My parents had realized for the first time that something remarkable was going on. That climbing might one day be more than just a hobby for their son.

His pleasure in my success continued in those days after our return home. When we went to the climbing gym for the first time, one of the regulars said to me, "Hey, Tommy. How's it going? What you been up to?"

I didn't hesitate, "Nothing much."

As I walked over to begin the first route, I heard my dad's raucous laugh, "Nothing much? Nothing much? Tell him, Tommy. Tell him what you've been up to."

I was used to my dad telling the guys about our exploits at the sport crags and some of the routes we'd sent. This was different.

"My kid went out to Snowbird and it was like he had those routes wired. He sent everything. Didn't even look like he was breaking a sweat. Right, Tommy?"

I pretended that I didn't hear him. A month later, when my name appeared in the Hot Flashes section of *Climbing*, I felt a sense of satisfaction again. I had known for a while that I was a climber, but now others would, too.

My parents bought a camper van and we started hitting the road on weekends. A four-hour drive took us to the closest limestone canyon we knew of: Rifle Mountain Park. A sublime creek meanders through its floor, green trees and shrubs line its banks, and walls up to three hundred feet of blue and tan limestone soar skyward. Wildly overhanging caves punctuate the undulating walls, like clerestory windows high up in a cathedral. As if a piece of Europe had been dropped into western Colorado, it offered some of the best sport climbing in the United States. Mom would come, sometimes belaying but mostly reading novels in the van. Sandy usually chose to stay home with her friends.

Rifle's complex, highly featured routes demanded a gymnastic climbing style, making them among the hardest climbs in the country at the time. In the United States, difficulty for rock climbs is expressed on a scale called the Yosemite Decimal System. Climbers arrive at a consensus in assigning this grade. They take into account both the hardest moves and how continuous a given pitch is. The first number, a five, denotes class five climbing, which means most everyone would want a rope, and without one a fall would be fatal. Then there's a decimal point and a second number, which indicates the technical difficulty. It's an open-ended scale, growing over time as standards evolve. These days, 5.9 and below is usually considered moderate to fairly easy. Starting at 5.10, difficulty gets subdivided into letters *a* through *d*. Thus, a 5.10d is slightly easier than a 5.11a, and considerably easier than 5.11c. At the time of our weekend pilgrimages, the hardest climbs in the world were rated 5.14c. Rifle had a handful of 5.14 climbs, and back then anything in that range was rare.

In my dad's mind, climbing—like anything—was all about preparation and hard work. If you put in your time in the gym and on climbing walls, you put yourself in the best position to succeed. To be your best and to win competitions and acclaim, you had to outwork everyone else. In that regard, I was ideally suited to the task. My whole life I'd been able to dig deep mentally and physically, work past a point of exhaustion, and revel in the moments of exquisite torture when mind ruled body and pain surrendered to persistence. I willingly sacrificed what many kids put atop of their list of priorities—a social life. I didn't care.

More than anything I wanted to be good, really good, exceptionally good at climbing. At that point in my life, the only other realm where I'd enjoyed significant success was in shop class. My school held competitions in bottle-rocket building and CO_2 cartridge model car races, which I won. I loved solving three-dimensional puzzles and was, I later learned, what was termed a kinetic learner. If I could put my hands on things and physically manipulate them, I was completely engaged. Just like solving the puzzle of the rock while lead climbing, which was only enhanced by the psychological intensity of razor's-edge performance, at least when trying climbs at our limit. The abstract didn't do the same for me. I had an active and vivid imaginative life as a younger kid, but those stuffed animals and geometric shapes I cut out and pasted together were the first signs that I had a compulsion to build things.

Building relationships was tougher for me. Some of the kids at school fell under my dad's spell and took up climbing. I could talk with them about that. Even better was when I could show them my expertise in the subject. But those relationships were almost entirely superficial and more about the activity than anything else. I always felt that I got along better with the adults at the climbing gym. As much as I kept to myself, I'd at least engage in conversations with these men.

If winning the Snowbird competition hadn't fully alerted me to the fact that I'd arrived as a climber, then having Christian Griffith walk up to me at a gym in Boulder and ask me to climb with him at nearby Flagstaff Mountain certainly did. I'd defeated him at Snowbird, but I was pretty sure that he had no idea who I was at that point. He was a legend. He was thirteen years older than me.

In my mind, I was still that scrawny little dude. It was totally cool to me that the chariot he was going to take me to Flagstaff in was a Volkswagen GTI. I got in, noted the checkerboard upholstery of the bucket seats and the tiny aftermarket steering wheel he'd installed. Even before I could buckle my seatbelt, I was thrust against the checkerboards, and the acrid smell of burning rubber filled my nostrils. Our route took us up a serpentine mountain canyon road. Above the noise of the engine I heard the sounds of violins, cellos, and pianos blasting from the car speakers. He zipped in and out of lanes, passing other drivers, ignoring the solid line as if it didn't apply to him.

As we neared the Crown Rock Trailhead, I had a realization. This guy was trying to freak me out—and he was succeeding. Barely slowing as we entered the parking area, he grabbed the emergency brake and gave it a violent yank. The rear end of the car slewed around to the right and we did a perfect 180-degree turn. Well, not so perfect. The car bisected two parking spaces. I sat frozen in my seat. Christian switched off the car and grinned at me for a few seconds. Without a word he got out and grabbed his gear, leaving me and the unlocked, open-windowed, bumper-stickered, ticking car behind. I gathered myself and my things and hustled after him.

I remember that ride but the climb has receded in memory. Christian and I would take other trips together, and he was one of my first sponsors. He had a clothing line called Verve, and he hooked me up with a few items. I asked my parents to keep it quiet, though. In the end, it didn't matter that they'd agreed to my request. Somehow a few guys in the climbing community learned of the more or less informal sponsorship. In their minds, I'd sold out by accepting free stuff. I'd violated the purity and the sanctity of the endeavor, so they chose to not speak to me anymore. I understood their point, but I'd been working part time as a busboy at a local restaurant and hated the work and hated being confined in tight spaces. If I could start saving money on gear, maybe I could eventually leave my job and not suffer too much financial damage—my dad's pay-as-you-work-out system was no longer in effect. Besides, this was Christian effing Griffith offering me some swag. Who was I to say no?

I was thrilled to climb with guys like Christian, but they were all much older than me, and I was so square that we didn't hang as friends. When the climbing was done, we went our separate ways. At school, I wasn't ever going to sit at the cool kids' lunch table. I was fine with that. I'd gained, and enjoyed, a reputation for not giving a shit about school. By virtue of not fitting in, by default I gained acceptance with a small group of like-minded kids who needed to fit in somewhere. But I had climbing. I had somewhere else to go, some other activity to occupy my free time. As a result, I was a kind of absentee member of the antisocial club.

I self-identified as a climber. But as time went on, I began to wonder if that was going to be enough. And just what exactly did that mean? What kind of climber was I going to be? What was truly going to make me happiest?

As much as I would have preferred to ignore those questions and just keep climbing, I was in the grip of transformational forces in my body and my brain. I was a climber, but I was also a teenager.

CHAPTER FOUR

Five, four, three . . .

"Fuuuuck!" I shout, shattering the tranquility of the canyon. My words bounce off the rock walls and strike me in the face. I'm dangling in my harness fifty feet off the deck.

"Just lower me," I shout at my dad, who's on the ground, belaying. He pays out rope and his face comes into better focus. His lips are drawn tightly against his teeth, not because of the effort of lowering me, but because of his sadness.

"Why do I suck so bad?" I yell as I untie. My vision has narrowed into a tunnel of anger. I claw at the laces of my climbing shoes. The lactic acid time bomb has fried my fingers into useless stumps. Unable to undo the knot, I tear at the heel of my shoe and pry it off. I do the same with the other, chucking the offending footwear into a nearby bush.

A few climbers stride past me; they drop their eyes as they approach, either afraid of what I might do or because they are embarrassed for me.

I drop onto my butt and sit in the dirt, squeezing my knees to my chest and sagging my head into my arms. I can't believe that I'd pumped out so quickly. What the hell is wrong with me?

I turn my head and spit. A thin rope of saliva clings to my lip and slowly lowers to the ground. I can't even spit right. Why am I even out here?

I pop up and do the walk of shame to our van. I don't look up; I watch my bare feet kick up whirling dervishes of dust. I imagine that everyone who recognizes me wonders if what they've read in the climbing mags is true.

I clamber into the van and slide the door shut, slamming it into place. I lie *down and press the flat of my hands into my eyes and watch the closed lid light show do its shimmer dance, turning from blue to red.*

Where is my dad? Doesn't he know that I just want to get the hell out of here? I should just fire up the van and leave him behind if he doesn't get it. I can drive. I just can't climb for shit anymore.

I'd adopted my dad's "work hard" mantra and become maniacal in my pursuit of fitness and skill. In the summer of '96, I trained for five days a week, for five to ten hours a day. I drew a curtain on the rest of my existence. It was just me, the walls, and my will. Every day I exerted a dogged effort until my body simply failed. I never quit. I drove my body until it was unable to respond to commands from my brain.

The idea that I could be the best at something was the most tempting elixir in the world. Those childhood times of feeling invisible, pitied, or ignored drove me to desire climbing success more than anything else. My teenage body was in the perfect state to absorb the massive training stimulus. My hands strengthened, my forearms grew, my back expanded, and my mind toughened.

I'd become one of the most successful sport climbers in the country. I was climbing routes that other top climbers couldn't, and getting written up in the mags. People recognized me, gathered at the bottoms of climbs to watch. One person had even asked for my autograph.

As my climbing ability grew, so did my confidence and my willingness to put myself out there—in climbing and the rest of life. For years, I had felt like a light rubber band, elastic and powerful, immune to gravity. My progress had flowed like the waters of Yosemite Falls, unimpeded and plentiful. I was taking greater control of my climbs and of myself. Instead of turning away from other climbers at the gym and downplaying my accomplishments, I adopted a matter-of-fact tone. This is what I did. Nothing more and nothing less. If they offered praise, I took it with a simple thanks.

My dad and I watched an annually released video called *Masters of Stone*. We would sit and stare, enthralled at footage of the hottest walls and crags. My dad took notes and, eventually, we'd visit those spots. When we went to Shelf Road in southern Colorado, a limestone cliff reminiscent of some of the toughest sport climbing zones in Europe, I climbed the appropriately named Chomping at the Bit and earned more press. Before long, that would transition to my appearing on the cover of *Climbing* magazine.

But my body was changing.

I plateaued, stopped winning the comps, things didn't progress as fast as my dad and I would have liked. When *Climbing* magazine arrived, I would watch my dad flip through the pages and then casually toss it aside, trying to hide his disappointment (but not succeeding). I felt like shit. I felt like I'd let my dad down. My dad couldn't always attend the competitions, since he was teaching. I'd return to my hotel room and hesitantly dial the phone. I remember how knotted up I felt inside, how those butterflies had turned into buzzards and picked at my guts and my nerves.

We'd cut to the chase, "Sixth."

"Sixth. As in, not even top five?"

"Yeah."

"What went wrong?"

"I got a little nervous. I had trouble with a—"

"It's all in your head, Tommy. That's where your trouble is. It isn't on the wall."

I'd sit on the bed listening, trying to inventory all of the things swirling inside my head.

In time, I came to hate the competitions, especially the local ones, because my dad was there. Somehow the distance of a phone line diminished his disappointment; in person, it struck me full force. Yet, I took it for how it was intended—as a means to inspire me to work harder. Cheerleading had gotten us only so far. My dad sensed that my work ethic was my greatest strength. Praise wasn't going to keep fueling me and my desire. We were at a crux sequence and he was checking out all the options for solving it.

But the truth was that the main cause of my struggles was me. Not just my mind but also my body. In going from my mid to late teens, my muscles grew and my body weight increased. My finger strength had no chance of keeping up. Nor, apparently, did my technique.

On hard sport routes I would battle my way up a climb, and at the crux sequence I'd feel like an observer, hopelessly watching as my fingers oozed open and my body disconnected from the wall. I would let out an angry yell, my teenage voice faltering into an atonal shrill as I dangled on the end of the rope, panting and defeated.

I knew how I felt about climbing and success, but I'm not sure I understood what it meant for my dad. For me, being the best wasn't about outperforming others. My dad was always on my side, but part of me still heard his voice in the back of my mind telling me that my troubles were due to something not being right in my head. That meant that I was my own worst enemy, an opponent I knew well but still couldn't defeat. Was that true? And was there something about the competitive environment that didn't suit my temperament?

Later that summer, we took our annual summer road trip. This time, we would have a companion along. While watching the *Masters of Stone* video, we saw a kid even younger than me who could be considered a true master. His name was Chris Sharma.

From the beginning I was somewhat jealous of Chris. He seemed preternaturally gifted, charismatic, and graceful. In comparison I was more of a plodder, the hard-working sort with a lunch pail mentality.

I had just turned seventeen when we met; he was fifteen, and a competition prodigy. He was from Northern California—Santa Cruz—and there wasn't much outdoor climbing where he lived. Since he didn't have a driver's license, he'd climbed mostly indoors. So we decided to take a road trip together.

Like me, Chris was small for his age, but he was a lot more scrappy. When we first met, he told me that he was struggling with his climbing due to an injured hand. Some bully at school had been picking on him and Chris had punched the kid in the back of the head and fractured a bone. He wasn't just feisty, he projected a laid-back California surfer dude vibe that hid an active mind and an aggressive curiosity. Not to mention a ferocious ability.

We met in Logan Canyon, which cut through the Bear River Mountains, an offshoot of the Wasatch Range in northern Utah. We had selected a route called Super Tweak, rated 5.14b—it was one of the hardest routes in the whole state. Given Chris's minimal outdoor experience, attempting Super Tweak was like throwing Chris into the deep end to see if he could swim. On our first day I ripped a big flapper on one hand. I taped up the torn end of my finger, but blood oozed out, making the sharp holds feel as if I was grabbing slippery razor blades. I made multiple tries, failing, trading attempts with Chris. Near the end of day Chris sent it. *I'll be damned if I'm not gonna send now*, I thought. I tried for two more days. Well, guess I was damned.

I nursed my finger and my frustration all the way up to Lander, Wyoming. Chris seemed oblivious to it all, zoning out and listening to Bob Marley on his Walkman, while my dad and I alternated stints behind the wheel of the van. We pulled into an area known as Wild Iris to try a route called Throwing the Houlihan.

"What's a Houlihan?" Chris asked, smirking, as he set out.

"No idea," I said, watching with a twinge of envy as my dad belayed him.

A few hours later I was tempted to throw a tantrum and not a Houlihan. Chris had sent it but I'd once again had trouble with the crux and come down pissed and doubting myself. Was it in my head?

Chris was sending routes, but was he also sending messages to me, ones that I was translating into distress calls. I wasn't angry with him—only with myself. The seeds of doubt had sprouted again. I don't know if my dad saw it happening, but we swung back south and got me on familiar turf at Rifle. Chris and I were both able to send all of the toughest routes, but even I could see the writing on the walls.

Chris was simply a better climber. He moved with a fluidity and grace that I admired. It was as if he was climbing unburdened. Meanwhile, I was laboring up the climbs, weighted down by expectations both self-imposed and from outside, by doubts, and by the lingering sense that what had once been fun was now more like a job than an adventure. Even back at Rifle, where I climbed well, I still was feeling the lingering effects of a kind of mild hangover. Even my senses felt dulled. Colors seemed more muted and the air smelled slightly stale. The sound of the creek was like a distraction.

Our road show continued for a little bit after that. Chris was oblivious to what was going on inside me. We got along well, and we've remained good friends to this day. In time, the flappers I'd sustained to my ego were going to heal. I'd have to toughen them up the only way I knew how: with more hard work, rather than tender loving care. But the harder I beat my head against the walls of sport climbing, the less it seemed to help. Something was missing.

After the summer of Sharma in '96, I entered a period where I mourned for those days when the world was filled with wonder and color. Those days of embracing nature, of running from lightning, of seeing my dad's eyes sparkle with love, not sadness, at my behavior. *This was stupid, it's just rock climbing. It's supposed to be fun.*

Then one beautiful autumn day in Rifle Canyon in 1997, after one of my wobblers I stared at the carpeting on the floor of the van. The sounds of Rifle Creek bubbled in the background, and an idea occurred to me. Maybe I needed to bring a bigger version of adventure back into my life.

I looked over at my dad. He was looking across the canyon to the climb I had been failing on. I could tell he was formulating some kind of pep talk. I knew I needed some spark, some new challenge, something to get me out of this rut.

"Dad, do you think I could free climb El Capitan?"

To a nonclimber the question probably sounds like a shot out of nowhere. But any rock climber with a pulse is inspired by El Cap. To free it would be like flying to the moon.

A long pause ensued. "That's an interesting idea," he said before a slow exhalation.

He sat for a moment, chewing on his lower lip. His eyes slowly shifted from side to side. I could see him weighing the different scenarios. His climbs of El Capitan had been some of his biggest adventures. In 1968 he made the nineteenth ascent of the Nose. It took three and a half days, a fast time for the era. They wrapped seatbelt webbing around their waists because harnesses had yet to be invented, and used old Goldline ropes, scores of homemade pitons, and heavy steel carabiners. Soon after, he climbed two more routes on El Cap. Later, he had to be rescued off another route in a terrible storm.

In his Yosemite days Dad had endured many unplanned bivouacs, shivering through the night, along with dozens of unforgettable sunrises. For climbers these moments of suffering and beauty can take on the quality of transcendence.

But years earlier, my dad's two best friends had been swept away by an avalanche while ice climbing in Rocky Mountain National Park. He had spent a stormy night and day searching hopelessly for them. He returned home and collapsed into a pile on the floor, too tired to pull off his mountaineering boots. Tears streaked his wind-burned face. He was the kind of dad who cried because he was happy, or because he was proud. I had never seen him cry because he was sad.

"Ice and alpine climbing have too many objective hazards," he would later tell me, reflecting upon the uncontrollable risks of climbing everchanging mediums. I took his words as gospel. If we stick to rock climbing, we are responsible. When my dad brought me up the Diamond, or the Lost Arrow Spire, or even icy mountains like Mont Blanc and the Matterhorn, he didn't even consider it dangerous. He knew the environment well, and I was under his care.

I don't think he worried so much about El Capitan as about what it might lead to. Sport climbing is safe. It's controlled. It's great. But how far do you take it? He saw my drive and toughness, and he feared that my ambitions would push me closer to the alpine realm and lead me to distant and dangerous summits. Too many climbers he'd known had died this way.

He'd surely also noticed that I'd begun taking other risks. I don't know if it was because of my frustration with feeling as if I'd stopped improving and stopped enjoying the pleasures of sport climbing, but I'd started earning other "performance awards." A couple of speeding tickets, bordering on the reckless driving spectrum, had me on the verge of losing my license. I liked the sensation of moving fast a little too much. I was doing some of the usual things that high school kids did. I drank a bit and smoked some pot, but I wasn't like the bingers and the pukers and the partiers whose exploits I heard about when I half dozed in study hall or at a cafeteria table.

Maybe deep down I was looking for an anchor, some kind of protection. "Dad," I asked again, "Would you show me how to climb El Cap?"

Every time you drive into Yosemite Valley, the sight of El Capitan, shooting skyward for 3,000 vertical feet above the lush green meadow, inspires absolute awe. When you're trying to climb it for the first time, that awe can feel more like terror. In terms of absolute move-by-move effort, the route we chose—the Salathé Wall, named after a Yosemite pioneer—should have been relatively simple to free climb. It was a full grade easier than what I had done on sport routes. But that didn't account for the exhausting continuousness, or the intimidation factor. I would glance down at the tiny treetops and the specks that passed for cars and feel as if my brain was on fire. Even when I could make myself focus on the moves, I wasn't climbing daintily with my fingertips and clipping bolts anymore. I seemed to be either skating on slippery slabs, calf muscles pleading for me to stop, or shoving my body into cracks and thrashing around, an unpleasant combination of claustrophobia and vertigo tightening my guts and my throat. Then there was the mental game beyond just the moves. In traditional ("trad") climbing, you place your own removable gear in the rock for protection as you go. Your life depends on properly calculating the need for, and availability of, that protection versus the physical and psychological costs of placing it.

I knew there would be added difficulties on a big wall. "I'll be able to figure it out," I'd told my dad. He had taught me the basic systems used in wall climbing, but I had drastically underestimated the realities. We had packed enough food, water, and equipment for six days. A thousand feet of rock climbing a day seemed reasonable. At that pace: three days. But this would be my first wall, and a few sections might take me several tries. So we'd better double that. You need three liters of water per person per day. That's seventy-two pounds of water alone. Add in our camping gear and food, and our haul bag weighed close to 150 pounds. I would climb a pitch and set up a pulley system to raise the haul bag. Then I would pull as hard as I could, my feet high, pressing straight out against the wall. The bag would inch upward despite the mechanical advantage of the pulley. Hauling one pitch was the equivalent of thirty minutes straight of barbell squats.

Day one turned into seventeen hours of nonstop labor. Most of the effort came from getting our damned equipment up the wall, and I had to climb with an unaccustomed and weighty collection of gear hanging from me as well. Plus, it was scary. There always seemed to be a loose block or sharp flake that, if not properly accounted for, could damage the rope. I couldn't shake the gory, irrational visions of ropes breaking, gear pulling, and my body bouncing down the wall until it exploded on the boulders far below.

Slowly, things got better. I got used to the relentless exposure and the constant labor of the climbing. We spent our second night on a beautiful detached pillar called El Cap Spire, a perfectly flat ledge about halfway up the wall. Sitting in our sleeping bags, looking out across the glacier-carved valley as the last fluttering rays cast soft beams of violet and orange, the ledge felt like a lavish spa. An inexplicable sense of contentment swept over me. We had pushed through one of the most demanding and hair-raising days I had known. That night I slept like the dead.

The next day it was back to the gallows. Strain, labor, fear. It didn't take long until everything hurt, including my brain. I completely abandoned the idea of free climbing the wall. I judiciously yarded on gear. All I wanted was to reach the top and return to the serenity of the sport crags. My dad seemed over it, too. During the day clouds rolled in, providing much needed relief from the sun, but the threat of rain added a sense of urgency. We did whatever we could to climb faster. I was hurting, but was also surprised at my ability to keep up with the constant workload.

On our fifth day, we finally pulled our tired, aching bodies over the top. Rain droplets splattered onto the rock. I wasn't old enough to drink, but staggered like a drunkard from exhaustion. Deep soreness, a combination of fatigue and pain, throbbed through my bones. My eyesight was blurred. I wobbled down the backside in silence, barely speaking to my dad, vowing to myself never to return. I wasn't tough enough to cut it on the big walls.

On our drive home, I wondered where my life was headed. I was nineteen, had recently graduated from high school, and had little interest in university. Back in Colorado I took the first step to enroll at the local community college, but the moment I set foot on the campus, it was as if I was zipped up in bivvy sack of anxiety and frustration. What about all those dreams I'd had of travel and not conforming to the usual expectations?

One evening around the dinner table I stared down at my hands, fumbling with how to begin.

My mom slid her hand across the table and took mine in hers, "You know you don't have to go to college right now, right?"

I looked up at her. I hated the idea of worrying her, and in that moment I saw that she looked hopeful.

"Listen," my dad began, "school will always be there for you when you really want it."

I almost laughed. It was as if he'd read the mental script I'd prepared earlier that day.

"If you want," my mom said, her eyes shining and her mouth twitching into a poorly hidden smirk, "you can ditch your dad and me for a year and hit the road."

"You'd be on your own," my dad said. His expression turned serious. "But there've got to be a few things we make clear."

The few things were truly a small number. This was to be a reality check for me. I could raid the pantry to start out and whenever I came back through Estes. Other than that, no financial support. Though he didn't say this, I sensed that my dad wanted me to experience the dirtbag life. I also think he thought that I might enjoy it. As usual, he was right. Funny thing was, I'd been wondering for a while if getting some space from him would help me find the direction I needed. My mom and he had been thinking along the same lines.

Within a day or two I replaced the passenger seat in my car with a piece of plywood for a bed and hit the road. Where to?

When in doubt, go with what you know.

I traveled from one sport climbing area to the next, checking off a few routes I hadn't sent on previous trips. I continued attending competitions, usually placing in the top three, but almost never winning. After entry fees, the prize money typically left me with about a hundred bucks a month, enough to keep climbing and going to comps. I showered maybe twice a month at YMCAs, and spent my rest days at public libraries and dollar movie theaters. I shopped at dented can and expired food stores, and even did a bit of Dumpster diving. I always slept in my car. Seeing how little money I could spend became a fun game. I cherished the freedom associated with a lack of material need. In between trips I'd go home, empty my parents' pantry, and head back on the road.

One of those trips took Chris and me to Smith Rock State Park, in central Oregon's high desert. We'd kept in touch and he'd dropped out of high school to compete and climb full time. He was doing well, and we both reveled in the vagabond lifestyle we'd chosen.

Like every climber, we'd heard of the route Just Do It. At the time, it had the highest grade of any climb in America at 5.14c. It had been bolted by an American named Alan Watts. But before he could send, in 1992 a Frenchman named Jean-Baptiste Tribout came to Smith and essentially stole it. Every sport has it rules—both written and unwritten. Instead of using only the holds that naturally existed on the face, he defaced the route with a chisel, artificially creating better holds in the spots where he needed them. What Tribout did was raise a middle finger to everyone who had tried that route, especially Watts. He named the route Just Do It, to signal his distaste for the ethics of those who believed that a climb should be done using only existing, naturally formed features on the rock surface.

For more than five years America's best sport climbers tried to repeat the climb. It had become a symbol of French climbing domination on American soil. Chris and I decided it was time that an American just did it. After only a handful of tries, Chris sent. It took me seven tries over three days, but I hung in there and was actually surprised by how easy it was (compared to how I'd built it up in my head, anyway). With Just Do It on our résumés, Chris and I had a solid claim to being among the best rock climbers in the United States. We were ready to take on that world, the sport climbing world, and that meant going to France.

For a month Chris and I hitchhiked around Southern France living off only what could fit in our backpacks. Chris had told me that his hippie father had spent several years living in India, his only worldly possessions being a walking stick and a pair of reading glasses. We liked the idea but needed to climb. So we added a small bag of climbing and camping equipment to enable our pilgrimage. We slept in farmers' fields and the occasional public campground. During that month, Chris beat everyone at the world championships comp, and climbed some of the hardest routes in Europe. His success silenced the many critics of his unconventional style—Chris used momentum as he climbed, much like a monkey swinging between branches, and the old-schoolers chastised him for poor footwork and lousy body control. But Chris knew what he was doing, and from that point forward every young climber entering the sport tried to imitate his dynamic style.

Given all his success, Chris was still that little fifteen-year-old I'd met—humble, good-natured, and physically from a different planet. I felt privileged to witness the magic. I, too, tried to mimic Chris—or at least, to climb with the same kind of confidence and poise—but only got partway there. While he pushed and inspired me to become better, in the realm of sport and competition climbing I would always look like a beginner in comparison.

Something bigger kept nagging at me. Life after El Capitan felt dull. I kept thinking back to a moment on the Salathé Wall. It was the evening of our third day, and I'd climbed out a large roof and onto the headwall, an overhanging shield of rock that is a definite contender for the most exposed spot on the planet. The massive trees in the forest below looked tiny. A perfect crack split the otherwise smooth barrier. In terror I had yarded my way upward in aid slings, thankful for the security of being firmly attached to the wall for my every move.

Over time, my memory of that moment of fear and failure had faded. I had visions of developing enough control, enough calm, to sink my fingers into that perfect crack, climbing free, surrounded by nothing but wind and sky, the world dropping away in the distance. If only I could get there. My mind kept spinning with ideas, logistical improvements I could apply if I were to go back.

I started to analyze where things had gone wrong. The sun had been a major factor, causing dehydration, swollen feet, and less-than-optimal climbing conditions. We could have avoided this by starting our days in the dark and climbing through the cool early morning hours, finishing when the sun hit. I broke the route into sections. The first 1,000 feet were comparatively easy. We could climb that in a day. The next 1,200 feet were harder, but if I conditioned myself well enough I might also be able to climb that section in a day. My dad had taught me outdated, old-school tactics rather than the new strategies free climbers were using for El Cap routes. By hiking around to the top, rappelling in and prestashing food, water, and sleeping gear along the route, I could avoid the heavy hauling. And if I rehearsed the hardest sections, I could figure out what gear I needed and what I could leave behind. I could more closely replicate what I had been doing on sport climbs over the years. On big routes, strategy is as important as ability.

After we returned from France, I trained with newfound zest. While my previous training had mostly consisted of climbing, I started lifting weights and running. I needed more all-around fitness, and I definitely needed more toughness.

I'd been saving money from some small-time sponsorship contracts and my comp winnings (almost always second place, behind Chris—I placed second in the Phoenix Bouldering Contest seven years in a row). I bought a beater 1980 GMC Savanna conversion van to replace my car, moved in, and headed west.

Yosemite Valley without my dad was a wholly different place. I tried, awkwardly, to fit in with the eccentric tribe that composed the valley's climbing core. People like Cedar Wright and Timmy O'Neill, guys with no money and worn-out clothing, but with a fire in their eyes and a badass, go-for-broke climbing style. This crew had not only climbing prowess, but a quick wit and a demonstrable countercultural belief that an impoverished lifestyle was an ethical choice rather than a desperate reality.

Their de facto spiritual leader was a bold, athletic climber named Dean Potter. He stood six-foot-five and looked like a pterodactyl. Ripped, intense, and with a looming presence, he ran around the valley shirtless in his cutoff khakis and bare feet, alternately making short work of the biggest rock faces—often climbing solo—and departing into his own trippy versions of serene vision quests.

One day he was kind enough to take me on a bouldering tour. We wandered the valley in search of the biggest boulders we thought we could climb without breaking our legs. Showing off a bit, I climbed so far up one boulder that I would be lucky to break only my legs if I fell. At thirty feet, the rock turned sloping and mossy. I couldn't go up, and I couldn't reverse the moves. I started to quiver. In a moment of quick thinking, Dean climbed into an adjacent tree, hung from a branch with one hand, and used his enormous wingspan to reach toward me with his other. "If you feel yourself start to go, just grab my hand!" I refused to give up, barely managing to pull myself over the top by delicately tugging on clumps of moss.

Dean seemed impressed—perhaps he would be my portal into the tribe. The following morning I saw him in the climber's camp, and sheepishly walked up to him.

"Hey, Dean," I said, trying to sound casual. He'd just scooped an apple core off the ground. "So what are you doing today?"

"Climbing the Nose with Timmy," he said, taking a bite.

"B-but, it's like eleven a.m."

"Yeah, man, it only takes like five hours."

It had taken me five *days* to climb the Salathé Wall. Sure, I was trying to free climb it, but even considering their "anything goes" speed tactics, which mixed high-end free skills with yarding on gear at breakneck pace, my mind nearly short-circuited trying to fathom climbing the Nose in an afternoon. The diehard valley crew was shattering the standards of the day, and I wanted nothing more than to fit in. But I wasn't eccentric enough, and I hadn't proven my worth.

To save money on camping fees, I'd entered into an arrangement with one of the park's rangers. He had formerly worked at Rocky Mountain National Park and knew my dad. With that connection, I had what I thought was a pretty good gig. When he was out of the house, I could go in, shower, and hang out. When he was home, I was back in the van or elsewhere. At this time, climbers and rangers were involved in a kind of bear and garbage can game. Turns out that my ranger "landlord" was notorious among the climbers as a hardass bent on busting climbers for smoking pot and illegally camping. When word got out that I was living at his place, the climbers shunned me. It was just guilt by association, but at the time nobody told me why, and I was too reserved to ask.

I spent a month hooking up with random valley vagabonds and doing smaller climbs. As a shy, skinny kid, convincing people to follow you up big walls isn't so easy. I spent most of my time by myself, and alone is how I fell deeply in love with Yosemite. Hiking around to the top of El Cap I would stop and listen. I'd pause to smell the manzanita and run my hands over the rock, studying the texture of the granite. The rhythm of moving through the mountains has a way of wearing away the rough edges of the ego. I felt myself becoming part of the landscape. I listened not only to the sounds of roaring waterfalls and wind, but to an inner voice preaching serenity and simplicity. When storms rolled in I went on long hikes, rediscovering a giddy fascination with the trees and sky and, most important, the rocks.

Eventually I recruited a local high school student named Mike Cassidy to climb El Capitan with me. Mike was sixteen years old, the stepson of a ranger, and had boy-band good looks. "I'll teach you how to climb big walls," I told him, trying to sound convincing.

We spent a week day-tripping onto the Salathé Wall, stashing bivouac gear on ledges and rehearsing the hardest sections. In the process, as I feigned expertise—Mike none the wiser—I gained a greater understanding of big wall climbing systems. I memorized the free moves the way I used to do on a sport climb. I wrote down all of the gear placements, in order, so I could carry only what was necessary on each pitch. Over the previous month I had felt my body strengthen. I'd gradually become familiar with the slippery stone, and how it could be climbed. Even more important, something in my mind started to shift. What was once vertigo-inducing exposure no longer bothered me. I reasoned that I fell all the time on sport climbs, and being thousands of feet off the ground on something so sheer would actually be safer.

My second attempt to climb the Salathé was poles apart from the first. Climbing in the shade, unburdened by haul bags, I felt as though I was levitating. I karate chopped my way up cracks that had taken me hours. My hand- and finger-jamming technique—that same method of carefully stuffing your hands into the cracks that my dad had taught my sister and me on

Devils Tower all those years ago—was now dialed in. It felt like one of those dreams where you are breathing underwater or flying. Mike followed along on jumars—mechanical ascenders that clamp onto the rope and slide upward, allowing a person to rapidly follow a route without having to actually free climb it. At the end of each pitch we high-fived. It was as if I had somehow unlocked the secret to free climbing El Capitan.

Three days after starting, we pulled over the top. It was only the fifth free ascent of El Capitan. Despite the initial learning curve, it had felt almost easy. I had a hunch that in this realm I could become the best in the world. I was twenty years old, and suddenly I knew the direction I wanted my life to take and how to get there.

CHAPTER FIVE

The candlelight dances in her eyes. I hear the faint buzz of mosquitoes as they try to penetrate the wall of citronella scent. I look up and see the white wall of El Capitan twenty feet away, glimmering under the moon, shooting out of the forest and into the night sky. Candles sit on small boulders around our little campsite in the woods. A flickering flame holds my gaze. Our backs are propped against a boulder, feet tucked in sleeping bags. I let my leg rest against hers. She slips one hand onto my knee. A moment later she waves the other in front of my face, "Hello?"

"Yeah. I'm here. Just thinking." I reach out to put my hand on top of hers but it's already gone. An instant later she lies down, propping her head on a small pile of clothing, looking upward. She smiles, her white teeth nearly glowing in the candlelight, and I feel a tickle in my belly, that lovely, unsettling, cresting-a-hill-too-fast sensation that I think might be love.

I hope that she wants me here as more than a climbing partner. She's giving me not-so-subtle hints. The shrine of candles, arranging our sleeping bags side by side in a clearing just big enough for the two of us. Even the way she had smiled, her head down, not able to look me in the eye when she asked if I wanted to climb together.

"You want to do Lurking Fear with me?"

"Love to," I had said, not hesitating for a single instant.

I had been treating her like every other climbing partner, not because I wanted to, but because that's all I know. Now I think she is giving me an invitation. But I don't know for sure. I hesitate, my mind spinning.

What if I'm reading the signs wrong? Are the candles just to keep the

78

mosquitoes away? Could it be that she arranged our sleeping bags beside each other because there was no other flat place in the forest? I can't shake a friend's words from my mind: "You will never meet a girl, all you love is rocks." In this moment I would give up rocks in a heartbeat to be with this girl. I should just lean over and kiss her.

The night goes on. We lie on our backs, eyes wide open. I can feel the heat from her body, smell the scented shampoo in her hair. I know she isn't sleeping. My courage builds. I decide I am going to turn toward her. Her sleeping bag rustles. She slips out, walks over, and blows out the candles.

"Fire danger's pretty high right now. Good night, Tommy."

I curse myself. Dammit.

Why can't I be brave, like I am while climbing?

My sudden attraction to Beth Rodden had been a surprise. The girls who had caught my attention had been more of the crunchy type, Birkenstocks, ratty hair, girls who could swear and laugh and drink and drove rusted-out Subarus.

She was one of those girl-next-door suburban types. She smelled nice and had smooth blond hair. Small, thin, she couldn't have weighed ninety pounds soaking wet.

It definitely wasn't a case of love at first sight. I'd bumped into her in Europe when Chris and I were hitchhiking around. She was there for a climbing competition, traveling with her parents, and I remember thinking how different our lives were. In many ways I looked down on her perfectly groomed existence. She'd learned to climb in the gym and did the comp circuit. She barely climbed outside and rarely talked to others, but over the years our paths had crossed again a few times. I learned that she was a straight-A student and lived in pancake-flat Davis, California.

Then one day in March of 2000, two years after we first met, I saw her at a climbing gym in Boulder. I'd been asked to give a slide show. As I stood in front of a not-so-full room of about fifteen people, flipping through slides, she walked in with a friend. They sat in the back, looking at me, then whispering and giggling like schoolgirls. Afterward, Beth confidently walked up to me.

"Hey, Tommy, ya know I just climbed El Cap."

"Really?" My eyebrows shot straight up. "How did you like it?" I asked.

"I was scared shitless," she said with a smile. Wow, the girl from suburbia has a potty mouth. "Want to see some pictures?" she asked. I looked at her smooth oval face, her cheeks that shined along with dancing eyes as she smiled. She was damned cute. And she was hitting on me.

She launched into her tale of post–high school freedom. How she had bailed on college and hit the road. Despite almost zero outdoor climbing experience, she went to Smith Rocks, Oregon, where she spent a month working on a sport climb called To Bolt Or Not To Be, which a decade earlier had been considered the hardest in the country. She managed to make the first female ascent of the route, becoming the youngest woman to climb 5.14.

On a nearby route at the same time was none other than Lynn Hill. When Beth lowered to the ground after her successful ascent, Lynn walked over and invited her on an expedition to Madagascar. The trip was sponsored by The North Face (Hill's sponsor at the time), and they established a difficult 1,200-foot big wall climb. Beth showed me photos of soaring faces and rock arches that looked like images from another planet.

We found excuses to hang out over the next few days, and I learned more about her life and her adventures. I secretly fell fast and hard. By the end of the week I was canceling all other plans, "coincidentally" aligning my travel schedule with hers.

I was giddy with excitement. I'd come to believe that my friend's line about never being able to meet a girl might be right. True, I did love rocks. But my being single was more because I was deathly afraid of women. I still saw myself as a clumsy kid with big ears. I'd had a few girlfriends, but I'd always fallen too fast and probably too hard. The only strategizing I'd known was with routes and moves and sequences, so each of my brief romances flamed out because I was sucking the air out of the room.

At this point, at the age of twenty-one, when I wasn't living in the van, I lived with my parents. I had no money and was dreadfully awkward in every aspect of life but one. And that one thing was what mattered most to me.

Still, I dreamed.

Beth and I traveled with a group of friends to the crack-climbing mecca of Indian Creek, Utah, where towers and walls rise from the high desert like natural fortresses, painting the landscape in vibrant shades of deep orange and red that contrast with the endless cobalt sky. We stayed up late talking by the campfire, staring at the stars after everyone else had gone to their tents. Before I knew it I'd lost my appetite, couldn't hold a thought for more than ten seconds, and no longer seemed to need sleep.

I wasn't sure what love was supposed to feel like, much less first real love, but this felt as if I'd been swept up by a tornado. Little halos formed around Beth's head and I started to see every quirk, from her bowed legs to her nerdy sayings, as incomprehensibly endearing. But I was not sure whether she was attracted to me.

A few weeks later, we reunited in Yosemite. When she suggested we try to free a route on El Capitan called Lurking Fear, I was overjoyed. The route had never been freed; we could be the first.

On the route, the sun burned hot and the rock felt sharp. Our fingers bled and some of my toenails fell off from my tight shoes, the baking rock, and the minuscule holds that required intensely technical footwork. Under normal circumstances I would never have considered the conditions workable. But Beth never complained, so neither did I. She climbed with impeccable balance and a feel for movement that allowed her to use holds so small that they could hardly be seen. She seemed unaffected by the exposure. I found her strengths both baffling and exceedingly attractive.

I could never bring myself to make a move. So our first night in a portaledge together she took it upon herself to shift the relationship past the point of just friends. Usually in a portaledge, you sleep head to toe, with a divider creating a little cocoon for each person. On that first night on the wall, Beth took down the divider, put our sleeping bags in the same direction, and cuddled up close. To me it seemed like a fairy-tale start to a relationship, two lovebirds sleeping together on a small ledge above the clouds, on America's premier big wall. On Lurking Fear, Beth became only the second woman to free climb El Capitan.

After that neither of us wanted the magic to end, but Beth was leaving soon on another North Face expedition, to an alpine granite paradise in

Kyrgyzstan. Lynn Hill and another team of North Face athletes had journeyed to the same area a few years earlier and returned with stories of soaring walls, spectacular mountains, and kind, simple-living villagers who farmed in the valley below. We couldn't bear the thought of being apart, so I accompanied her to The North Face headquarters in San Leandro, California, to see if we could get me hired on to the trip as rope rigger for the photography. We spent two weeks planning and packing. I didn't much fit in. I followed Beth around like a lost puppy dog, while the trip leader, a young climber of sharp wit and intellect named Jason, had a field day with me. Beth saw my growing angst as I was being bullied. I took it, thinking it best not to be confrontational. Beth saw it as my not standing up for myself—not the most attractive quality for someone in a budding relationship.

One night, lying together in my van, she told me it was over. I didn't want her to see me tearing up, didn't want to support her notion that I was somehow weak. I slipped out of the van to go for a run. Ninety minutes later, I slid the door open as quietly as I could. Beth and I barely made eye contact, but whereas before her expression was hard, I saw that she had softened. She knew she'd hurt me, and she knew, at least in the sense of having someone to help her on those big walls in Kyrgyzstan, she needed me. By the next afternoon, we were back on.

Soon after, we learned that our ploy to get me hired as a rigger had worked. Together we were off to Kyrgyzstan.

I used to fantasize about what Yosemite would be like without the cars and people. Now I had the answer: like the rock-climbers' paradise of Kyrgyzstan's Karavshin region, specifically its adjacent Ak Su and Kara Su valleys. In fact the area, nestled deep in the Pamir-Alai Mountains and long popular with European and Russian climbers, has been called the Yosemite of Central Asia. It was wild and remote, with no infrastructure and no chance for rescue. We were four climbers on the adventure of a lifetime.

We'd arrived in the belly of a beast, flying from Bishkek in a monstrous Russian military helicopter chartered through our Kyrgyz travel logistics company. On the way, we'd pressed our faces against the tiny round windows, watching as the dry desert yielded to pale green hillsides and alpine meadows, and then to rocky cliffs rising in every direction. Around corners and up valleys, we'd caught glimpses of the mountains we had come to climb. We hopped out and the helicopter flew away, its earthquake-like vibrations and diesel fumes vanishing along with our sleep deprivation, replaced by pure wonder and isolation.

We dragged our duffel bags to a flat patch of grass in the heart of the dead-end Kara Su Valley. Craggy hillsides rose and fell into braided glacial rivers. Massive blades of granite shot skyward. Behind the walls sat blue and white glaciers, crawling slowly toward the basins below. Wildflowers bloomed in the meadows.

Beth and I climbed to the top of a boulder where we could peek over the stunted trees and gaze up the valley. A towering granite monolith named Mount Asan-Usan framed the left side of our view, and on the right was a golden shield called the Yellow Wall, a 2,000-foot rock formation that resembled a massive snowplow blade. Up-valley, miles of rock culminated with the icy Piramidalny Peak, rising to over 18,000 feet.

Warmth grew in my chest and extended to my fingertips. The overwhelming awe left me feeling as if we were under the influence of some bigger, unexplainable power, as if a valley so perfect must have been designed by the divine. I wrapped my arms around Beth in a huge bear hug and lifted her off the ground as we both giggled.

We began unpacking the rainbow of duffels splayed out beneath a patch of juniper trees, establishing our base camp. Beth and I pitched a shared tent, while our two climbing partners set up theirs.

The photographer The North Face had hired to document the trip, John Dickey, ambled around, a relaxed smile visible behind the camera. Technically he was my boss. I'd been hired to rig ropes for him. At twenty-five Dickey was the oldest member of our expedition. Six feet tall, dark and handsome, he gave off a well-adjusted but shaggy cool vibe. In comparison, the rest of us were kids.

For Dickey, raised religious in Texas, recreation had meant Bible trivia competitions, at least until he rebelled and headed west. He landed in the Mission District of San Francisco, got into climbing and gravitated toward

Yosemite and the High Sierra, where he'd made some quality ascents. Along the way he'd graduated from San Francisco State with a degree in recreation and leisure studies, making him the educational dean of our trip. Beth, in second place, had done a semester of college.

"Hey, Beth, do you know where my CDs are? We need to crank some fuckin' Metallica." The other member of our expedition, our team leader, Jason "Singer" Smith, was fiddling with a small set of speakers and a portable CD player. His nickname came from his penchant for repairing his own ragged clothes. Singer grew up small like me, sitting on the bench alongside the fat kid during games before finding his way exploring and climbing in the mountains near Salt Lake City. Twenty-two years old, about five-foot-six and a buck thirty, he was three inches and twenty pounds lighter than me.

After high school Singer headed for Yosemite, where we had first met. I recall thinking him interesting, contortionist or sword swallower interesting, obviously on a mission to be noticed. He'd hold court shirtless and barefoot, wearing patched-up cutoffs, and embark on thirty-minute monologues about topics like the proper technique for brushing your teeth. All his rants were choreographed like a stand-up comedy routine, his dirty blond mop bouncing with his animated delivery. His always-spinning mind made him seem untouchable, as if he was too smart for his own good, either a loose cannon or a genius. Maybe a bit of both.

Singer's notoriety was well earned. He'd made a handful of impressive ascents on El Cap and a free-solo (no rope) climb of a hard Yosemite route called the Rostrum. His crowning achievement was a fifty-day expedition to Baffin Island, where he'd made the first solo ascent of a 4,000-foot big wall on Mount Thor. He used a rope, self-belaying the difficult route, and it was certifiably out there in a remote region above the Arctic Circle. He didn't speak to another human for three weeks. During the climb he came across the equipment from the last person who'd tried to solo Mount Thor, a Japanese climber who'd died in the attempt.

Singer's mind-blowing—and surely mind-altering—solo on Baffin had put him on the climbing world's radar. The North Face took him on as a sponsored athlete. Singer lived in his van, and he and Beth had become friends. So that's where our trip began, with Singer as the trip leader, Dickey as photographer, and me as tag-along-boyfriend, there to put the rope up for Dickey. But really, I was there because of Beth.

As we were settling in, a local yak herder walked into our camp. His clothes were stained brown, the skin on his face weathered, and his cheeks were covered with a dark patina speckled with pink spots. Smiling and dipping his head in a quick bow, he approached. He grabbed a twig and started to draw lines in the dirt. Through various charades we learned his name and that he and his family lived in a stone hut a short distance away. They were the sole residents of the upper valley, but a larger seminomadic community existed farther down at the convergence of the Kara Su and Ak Su rivers. Though these valleys are popular climbing destinations as far as remote Kyrgyzstan goes, Westerners were enough of a novelty that during our first few days at least a dozen local shepherds came to visit.

We must have looked like aliens who'd landed in a spaceship. I couldn't help feeling like an intruder, trespassing on their simple lives with our CD players, fancy tents, and mountains of climbing gear.

The yak herder returned the next day with his family, and gifts of fresh bread and yak milk. His wife was dressed in traditional Kyrgyz clothing, with a pink scarf wrapped around her head, a long red skirt, and an ornately embroidered blouse. The kids wore jeans and Western logoed T-shirts, but tattered to the point where any mom back home would have pitched them in the trash. We spent hours sipping tea, communicating through gestures, and mutually enjoying one another's company.

The stress of the world back home began to fade and I felt as contented as I had on my trip to Bolivia when I was fourteen. At night, the chill of the air would drive us into our tents and sleeping bags where we would drink tea and play cards. In the mornings, as the sun dried the dew from the grass I would wander from camp, lie on my back on a flat boulder, close my eyes, and listen as the buzz in my body calmed.

Back home, the State Department had issued an advisory against travel in Kyrgyzstan, but that seemed so improbable that we felt right for having ignored it. It called conditions in the region "fluid and potentially dangerous." Like everywhere, right? Everywhere but here, it seemed. We reasoned that camping and climbing in a dead-end valley in the mountains posed no greater risk than the actual climbing. Dozens of climbers visit the Karavshin annually; the Russian Mountaineering Federation had held an international big wall climbing competition in the Ak Su the previous year. Still, a couple of friends who were planning to come canceled their plans. Their call, but we thought they were overreacting to the omnipresent be-scared-of-everything warnings. We were so sure of our safety that, since our plane arrived late and we needed to climb, we didn't bother to check in at the U.S. Embassy in Bishkek.

After our arrival, we realized that one of our duffel bags hadn't shown up— it must have gone missing during an airline transfer. Singer and Dickey set off on a multiday quest to find a phone to call our travel arranger in Bishkek. They navigated between shepherd huts, tiny villages, and military outposts where nobody had telephones and hardly anybody spoke English—not that any of us spoke any of the primary languages of Kyrgyz, Russian, or Uzbek.

While those two were familiarizing themselves with the surrounding areas the hard way—they were gone for four days, with no luck in tracking down our bag—Beth and I went on hikes. Our excuse was reconnaissance for climbing objectives. But for me it was about being alone with her. We wandered the banks of turbulent rivers and through steep pastures with grazing yaks, their white and brown dreadlocked fur hanging to their knees like skirts. We walked up massive talus slopes into side valleys with glacier-formed cirques composed of nothing but rock and water. We dipped bottles in streams so clear the water could be seen only by the way the light refracted off its surface. At times I would hang back just so I could watch Beth as she hopped across boulders and scrambled up shelves of rock. She'd turn around and I'd light up at the sight of her high, round cheeks and silky blond hair. I noticed how each day her face became a little more tanned, her legs smeared with a little more dirt. I could no longer imagine a life without her.

"I have a surprise for you," Beth said, turning toward me. She smiled and touched my thigh.

Dickey and Singer had returned from their bag-chasing foray, and we all went climbing. Instead of heading up on the biggest walls first, we'd chosen a warm-up: that 2,000-foot blade of rock called the Yellow Wall. We were halfway up, sitting in pairs in our two portaledges, feet dangling over the edge. The day's last light flickered along the jagged horizon and we listened to the distant, pleasant purr of rivers far below.

Beth pulled out a packet of instant chocolate pudding, plopped a candle in it, and lit a flame. It was our first night on the wall, and my twenty-second birthday. For a moment the universe was reduced to the flame and the space it illuminated. I blew out the candle and our worlds broadened to the sky around us, billions of vibrant stars, unpolluted by all we had left behind. Even at night I felt small, utterly insignificant, and completely content. The most spectacular peaks on earth surrounded us here, at the confluence of the Himalaya and the Hindu Kush, Tien Shan, and Karakorum mountains. The stars twinkled and we talked and laughed and I fell asleep with a smile on my face.

We slept soundly, unaware of the torture and murder that were happening in the neighboring valleys. Just days earlier, heavily armed militants from the Islamic Movement of Uzbekistan (IMU) had slipped across 15,000-foot mountain passes on the Kyrgyzstan-Tajikistan border. This southwestern tip of Kyrgyzstan, where we were climbing, overlaps with Tajikistan and Uzbekistan like interlocking fingers, and includes ethnic enclaves from each country. The Taliban-affiliated IMU had declared jihad against the Uzbek and Kyrgyz governments, the former for its well-documented human rights abuses, including ruthless repression of Muslims, and the latter for allegedly aiding the Uzbek regime. The IMU was intent on creating an Islamic caliphate in the region.

The rebels had moved undetected across the border and split into groups. Earlier that day, August 11, 2000, while we climbed, less than ten miles away one group of the militants had ambushed a Kyrgyz army outpost called Mazar. It's one of the places Dickey and Singer had been during their search for a phone. The militants slaughtered ten soldiers, some of whom they tortured first. They also captured a Kyrgyz soldier who had been patrolling the valleys and who, therefore, knew our whereabouts. Along the way the militants had already learned—probably from frightened locals—of foreign climbers in the Ak Su and Kara Su valleys. The same day another group of militants entered the Ak Su and captured several German and Ukrainian climbers, holding them in the valley. Meanwhile, the murderous group moved from Mazar toward the Kara Su, where they knew there were four foreign climbers—us.

The piercing echo jolted my eyes open. The noise was too distinct to be anything but a gunshot. I'd been in a deep sleep, the bliss of the previous week still coloring my every perception. Why would anyone be firing a weapon? *Maybe someone's trying to tell us something? Did our bag arrive?*

A second shot sounded. A bullet ricocheted off a small rock roof just above, knocking gravel onto our portaledge. Beth instinctively sat bolt upright and pulled herself close to the rock wall. Her chest heaved in and out in short, labored breaths.

"What the hell was that?" Singer barked.

"We are being shot at," she said. Her eyes darted from place to place.

Fear rattled through me, unlike anything I had experienced, different from rock fall, exposure, or lightning. We sat for a moment, unsure what to do, before easing our heads over the edge. Far below, on the scree slope at the base of the wall, stood three figures.

Dickey peered through his telephoto lens.

"They've got guns. They're signaling us to come down," he said, his voice matter of fact.

We talked it over—*What should we do?* They had already demonstrated the accuracy of their aim. We had little choice.

Dickey was the first to show courage.

"I'm the oldest," he said, continuing calmly, "and I look at least ten years older than all of you. I'll just go down and offer them a cigarette."

He grabbed one of our two-way radios, tied all of our ropes end to end, and descended 1,000 feet to the base of the wall to discover our fate.

"Uh, yeah, so these guys just want to have some breakfast with us over at our camp. You guys need to come down, please," Dickey radioed to Singer. Something about how he pieced together his words seemed odd. I figured he knew that Beth and I were listening, and he didn't want to scare us.

At age three after my first technical roped climb with my dad, Mike. This was the moment my parents said I became a climber.

My dad, a competitive bodybuilder: Mr. Mid-America, 1980.

By age three I imitated everything my dad did, including weight lifting.

My mom, Terry, me, my sister, Sandy, and my dad
on a hike in Rocky Mountain National Park.

One of my earliest 14,000-foot summits, Mt. Sherman, at age four.

Right: At age six on Devils Tower,
the formation that was featured in
Close Encounters of the Third Kind.

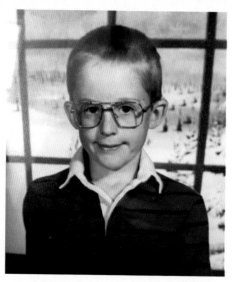

My third-grade schoolmates would never have guessed that I would become a professional athlete.

At twelve years old, I became the youngest person to climb the Diamond on Longs Peak in Rocky Mountain National Park.

My first climbing competition in Snowbird, Utah; to everyone's surprise I (center figure) won.

Chris Sharma (fifteen) and me
(seventeen) on the first of our
many sport climbing trips
around the world.

My days sport climbing taught me
how to move on the rock as well
as strengthened my fingers.

On my first attempt to free climb the Salathé Wall in 1998.

My second free route on El Capitan,
Lurking Fear, was climbed with Beth Rodden.

In 2000, Beth Rodden, John Dickey, Jason "Singer" Smith, and I, on a climbing expedition in Kyrgyzstan, were taken hostage for six days.

After cutting off my left index finger with a table saw, my doctor told me I should reconsider my profession as a climber.

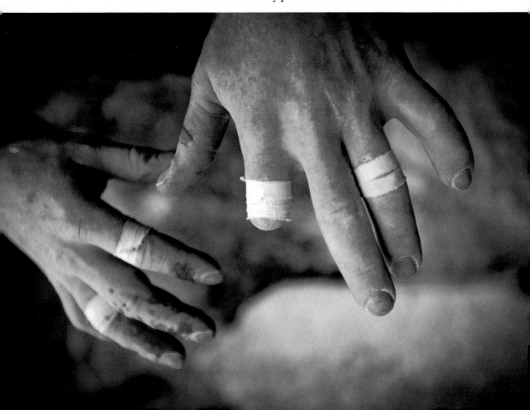

One by one we rappelled to the ground. Singer went next, then me. Beth would descend last.

A man named Abdul, clearly the group's leader, greeted us. He was heavily bearded and stocky, but with a thin waist, and the pockets of his camo army fatigues bulged with ammunition. He carried a Kalashnikov rifle loosely in front of him.

Except for being armed, the other rebels looked like high school kids who'd cut class to hang at the video arcade. One of them, long and lanky, with a slouched posture, wore a Patagonia Gore-Tex jacket, surely taken from some Western climbers or trekkers, with a military-style camouflage vest over top.

When they saw that the last person down the rope was a woman, their eyes widened. Petite and twenty, though she looked much younger, Beth could have passed as a child.

To my surprise, the rebels shook our hands pleasantly and escorted us back to our base camp without force. I immediately noticed our slashed-open tents. They didn't even bother to unzip the doors. Gear and food was scattered all around. Another man—the fourth rebel—was hunched over, vomiting. He'd apparently had a bad reaction to our food.

Through hand gestures, grunts, and whistles, they told us to fill small backpacks with food and warm clothes. But first, our passports.

That's a good sign, I thought. *At least they want us alive.* As we handed over our passports, the reality of our situation began to sink in.

Dickey said it out loud: "We're hostages."

We sat in the grass while they finished looting our scattered gear. Nearby was another man I had somehow failed to notice earlier. He was familiar—a Kyrgyz soldier named Turat. We had met him a few days earlier when he had wandered through our camp on a standard military patrol. At the time, like the other people we'd met in the Karavshin, he was pleasant and relaxed. Now he was different. He was still clean-cut, of medium-stocky build, but now his beige army fatigues were stained with blood. As I watched him, my pulse thumped at my temples. He looked haggard and resigned, yet his eyes darted around in panic. When they paused, they held a look of sadness mixed with determination.

When our captors were distracted, Turat turned to me. He pointed to the blood on his pants, held up three fingers and then ran his fingers across his throat. Horror flooded through me: *After they kill us three, the IMU would keep Beth.*

"*Nyet, nyet!*" Turat said. He must have read my petrified expression. Through sign language and very broken English we finally understood what he meant. The IMU had killed his three friends. And he was next. They had kept him alive only to guide them to us.

Turat then picked up a tent pole from the scattered equipment and made a stabbing motion. I blinked slowly, trying to absorb what he was telling us. It was unmistakable, but I didn't want to accept it. He wanted us to attack heavily armed men with tent poles. Setting a mousetrap in our home had been the extent of my willingness to kill, and even that made me queasy. I shook my head adamantly, and, whispering harshly, said, "No, no."

Over our stunted murmurs, a hum in the distance grew nearer. We stood in the grass and looked to the sky. Abdul sprang to his feet. He stood there for a second like a hunting dog on point, then he started shouting. For the first time since we'd been on the ground, they pointed their guns at us, indicating "Stand up." They hurried us into some bushes and forced us to hide amid the leaves and thorns. Hiding didn't last long. Shouts and whistles and chaos followed. Up again. We ran as two Kyrgyz military helicopters circled overhead. For miles we scurried along the banks of the Kara Su River, past its convergence with the Ak Su, panting from exertion and terror, alternately hiding in bushes and trees and then running again.

During one of our brief breaks, trying to comfort Beth, Singer said, "You have to think of this as a video game." His words also struck a chord with me—we had to disassociate ourselves from reality, try to pretend this wasn't real.

The helicopters continued hovering overhead, and the rebels forced us to flee onto a rocky hillside. Shots rang out. The four of us huddled in a deep impression in the rock. I didn't know who was shooting at whom, and if the military knew there were innocent hostages being held. They must have, or they'd have indiscriminately unloaded on us. Unless it was Turat, not us, holding them back.

Before we knew it, a full-fledged firefight had erupted. By now a small number of Kyrgyz troops had arrived and gave pursuit. I heard a deep *thunk*, followed by a high-pitched whistle. A moment later an explosion spewed rock and dirt. The rebels blasted machine guns and fought fiercely, holding their ground.

Beth and I cowered with Turat beneath a nearby tree. Bullets ripped through the brittle branches, showering down wood and kicking up plumes of dust. I shivered with fright and wrapped myself around Beth as she wept. Turat sat beside us, forearms propped on his knees. He was strangely calm, accepting, as if he had made peace with the world. The smell of junipers swirled amid the metallic odor of machine-gun fire. Then Turat did something I will never forget. He took a piece of candy from his pocket and pushed it into Beth's palm. He looked her in the eyes, and in broken English and gestures he said, "Please don't cry. I am about to die and I don't cry."

A loud whistle, distinct from the hailstorm of bullets in what had become a war zone, sounded from a huge boulder just uphill. Abdul, the rebel leader, stepped out and motioned with his arm. Another rebel, beside us, paused from his shooting and directed his weapon at Turat. Turat marched toward Abdul, his face a blank mask. Abdul led him behind the boulder.

We heard two loud pops. Beth's whimpers turned to sobs.

Abdul signaled to us next. I felt sick to my stomach. Bullets snapped all around us, and we had no choice but to follow. We huddled beside Turat's body as it grew cold and stiff. A pool of blood had spilled from his head, and as the hours passed the maroon color lost its sheen, leaving only a dark stain on the sandy soil. He lay with his limbs twisted, his fingers curled. I tried not to look, but found my eyes drawn to him. Turat's was the first dead body I'd seen. I tried to will some strength into my legs to keep me from wobbling.

I turned to Beth, expecting to see my own terror reflected in her expression. As if Turat's strength had infused Beth the moment she saw him dead, she spoke to me calmly, enunciating every word. "Keep your eyes locked on mine. Do not look away no matter what."

Rock dust rained onto us as bullets continued to ricochet off the boulders. The noise rang in my ears, magnifying in intensity. I shut my eyes against the discomfort. When I opened them again, the evening alpenglow shone on the horizon. How could something so lovely occur simultaneously with such horror? Suddenly another whistle. Collectively, we flinched as an object sailed overhead. Abdul snatched an apple from the sky and stuffed it into his mouth. The rebel who had tossed it turned and resumed fire. Abdul made some adjustment to his weapon. He let the apple fall from his mouth into his hand. He stood and munched away, as casually as if he was at home watching television. He finished the fruit, dropped the core, and wiped his hands on his pant leg. He calmly repositioned the tripod of his AK-74 among the rocks, and resumed shooting.

The fire intensified, both sides trying harder to kill in the day's last light. What seemed like hours passed in minutes as the sun dropped, and Abdul and the other three rebels laid down their guns and rolled out mats. Another rocket-propelled grenade exploded nearby on the hillside. The four of them turned toward Mecca, knelt, and began to pray.

Once the sky turned black, the shooting stopped. Along with our captors we fled, leaving Turat's body to rest in peace. Later that night, two of the rebels left, searching for a goat to slaughter for food. They never returned; we would eventually learn that they were picked off by Kyrgyz forces. Only Abdul and Sharipov, whom we would eventually know as Su, remained. Su was twenty years old, the same age as Beth. A prominent mole protruded from his upper lip. Short sprouts of hair shot from beneath his wool cap, and thin stubble tried to take hold on his chin. At times he looked frightened, had that perilously wide-eyed look of someone lost and dazed. He took orders without protest and I worried that he might have an itchy trigger finger.

We were hostages, but in a way so were our captors, hunted by the Kyrgyz military. We bolted through the night; I shadowed Beth. The frantic pace and terror had overwhelmed us, leaving me at once numb, shocked, and pulsing through a surreal existence. At sunrise, we hid. To keep us weak, Abdul split us into two groups. He took Beth and Dickey, and sent Singer and me with Su. When we knew what was happening, Beth and I turned to each other.

"We're going to be okay," she said. "Just do what they ask."

"I will."

"Promise me? Nothing stupid, okay?"

"I'll see you soon."

I feared I would never see Beth again. I had vowed to stay with her, to protect her, and in that I had found purpose, a shred of hope. But our fate no longer belonged to us.

For the next fourteen hours, while the sun shined outside, Singer, Su, and I sat stuffed in a damp hole, pulling reeds and branches over our heads for cover, thirty feet from the mist of a fast-moving river. The tiny space soon filled with the sour smell of wet foliage and our collective breath, a sharp contrast to the high alpine air. Our clothes soaked up the moisture, adding to the teeth-chattering chill. Our suffering warped time. Almost a day had passed since our last sip of water or bite of food. My tongue scraped the roof of my mouth. Complacency washed through me in waves. Yet it all seemed minor compared to my worry for Beth.

I questioned myself and God. I needed something to hang on to, some glimmer of hope. I mouthed or said silent prayers. I needed to believe that we were being watched after, that this was our destiny. I thought of my mother. She had always believed that she possessed a psychic sense for the suffering of people she loved. I sat in that hole and wondered if she knew I was in trouble.

Singer and I sat side by side, knees tucked against our chins. Minutes felt like hours, hours like days of bone-rattling cold. I mostly stared blankly at the dirt. But at one point, when Su had drifted off to sleep, I noticed Singer eyeing Su's gun. I wondered what he was plotting.

When the sun set again and we finally emerged from our hiding place, we milled around as stiff as old men. But when I saw Beth, I straightened and felt revitalized. She was alive, standing in front of me. She even managed a smile. We stood on the bank of a river, the water roaring so loudly that we couldn't hear each other unless we shouted. So we simply hugged. Then we looked each other in the eyes until we knew we were okay. I wanted to hold her forever.

Soon after, under cover of darkness we ate our daily meal—one Power-Bar split among the six of us. Before fleeing camp on the first day, we had grabbed a small bag with a half-dozen bars. It was our only food. Away from the river and able to speak, I learned how much worse the day had been for Beth and Dickey. Abdul had forced them under a boulder on the bank of the river. During the midday swell the water had come into their cave, soaking them both. The riverbanks had eroded the earth beneath the boulder, and they worried that the boulder would collapse on top of them.

Beth would later tell me that Dickey was like a father figure throughout those awful days, holding her shivering body tight for warmth. At times she wept, and questioned what we had done to deserve this. While Abdul and Su interacted nominally and sternly with us guys, they didn't know what to make of Beth, acting visibly awkward, almost afraid at times. At one point Dickey, thinking fast, communicated through sign language that Beth and I were husband and wife. Maybe that would touch some part of their humanity that seemed to have been buried.

We continued moving, Abdul in the lead. We crossed various small rivers, as we did each night, which provided our only opportunities to drink. Silty, gritty liquid that left sand grinding in our teeth, but each sip gave us a tiny burst of energy.

Later that second night we stood on the bank of a swift river, looking for passage. Abdul and Su tried to push a mangled log across to create a bridge. But as they grappled with the awkward and heavy log, they barely got their feet wet. It was obvious: They were deathly afraid of water. Suddenly, without warning, Singer plowed waist-deep into the raging torrent, fighting to keep his footing. At one point the river nearly swept him away, but then he gained control, struggled back, grabbed the log, and pulled it across. Abdul trembled as he crawled along the log, and at a particularly vulnerable spot Singer, standing in the river, reached out to offer assistance. Abdul, to free his hands, gave Singer his gun. Singer continued guiding him, then handed the gun back and yelled to us to cross. One by one we reached the other side. Afterward, Singer pulled himself from the current and sat on the riverbank, panting and soaking wet.

"What was that?" I scowled. I looked at him with confusion and even disgust.

But then Abdul raised his gun above his head and triumphantly shouted to Singer, "*Soldat!*"

Suddenly it dawned on me. In the midst of a nightmare, while the rest of us were overwhelmed by the terror around us, Singer was scheming our escape. He was building their trust.

While each of us had privately contemplated what action, if any, we should take, Singer forced strategy to the forefront of our minds. From then on, in semiprivate moments, in measured tones to avoid detection, we talked. And we were divided. Beth insisted emphatically, unequivocally, that we do nothing risky—our captors were clearly capable of killing, and nobody knew what they had planned. Why risk our lives when we could withstand this treatment? Our captors wouldn't last forever, not with the military in pursuit.

Singer and Dickey insisted on devising an escape plan immediately. We were four, they were two. We could catch them at a vulnerable time and overpower them, take their guns. We had to act.

I recognized their point, but I was torn. Since Beth was my primary concern, I sided with her. Yet I remained mostly quiet—even in such a desperate situation, I didn't want to create friction.

As the next couple of days and nights wore on, when the eastern sky grew bright we would hide from our pursuers, our potential saviors—the Kyrgyz military—and then, under cover of darkness, move toward an increasingly bleak future.

Day after day, we grew ever more depleted, our already lean reserves of fat gone. Our bodies metabolized our own muscles for energy. Worse than hunger and fear, sleep deprivation tormented our minds. During our nightly reunions, when the four of us huddled together, Dickey and Singer plotted and planned. Beth and I tried to ignore their senseless babble.

The Kyrgyz army continued its relentless pursuit. At times we could see them from our daytime hideouts, hear their helicopters. The skirmishes generally lessened, but sporadically flared up with gunfire exchanges. Like constant reminders, we could hear the sounds of distant rounds—mostly clashes between the army and other, nearby IMU militants. The nights wore on. Sometimes I stopped caring. The army had effectively herded us off. We were moving in a big circle to the north of the Ak Su and Kara Su valleys. Down in those valleys were rickety stick bridges and a handful of now abandoned shepherds' huts.

While we were hiding, Singer droned on, continually plotting—or maybe it was fantasizing—our escape. Inside some hellish hole or beneath thick bushes, he spoke in a low voice and an even tone to avoid detection.

"When Su is sleeping I will grab a rock and bash in his skull, then I'll grab his gun—the safety is just behind the trigger on the right side. We can shoot Abdul before he even knows what is happening." He schemed incessantly, insufferably, playing out vivid, gory details of murder. "I'll bite his throat and rip out his jugular, while you grab the gun."

I could hear him talking to Dickey during safe moments when we came together. Beth remained resolute: Better to spend months in captivity than resort to the evil that personified the IMU. But Singer wouldn't stop. "We'll just kill them. We'll take a rock and smash their skulls and take their guns. They trust us now, we can do it." I wanted him to shut up. I willed him to shut up. He kept going. I stared at him like an alien, with cold eyes. We couldn't kill. Killing is wrong. Killing is what separates us from them.

But we were wasting away, losing energy. Losing our will. Beth's angelic face was hollowed and drawn. She'd lost fifteen pounds. As our bodies grew weaker, I slowly came to wonder if Singer was right. If we were to live, we might have to kill.

Maybe Singer was just waiting for the perfect time. At the river, Su still had a gun. Both Abdul and Su had always been with us. Overpower one and risk a shootout with the other, with weapons we don't know how to use?

In one way, though, we had the upper hand. We were in a foreign land, but as the military forced us to evade onto ever-steepening ground, we had to guide our captors up the rocky terrain. At times we even put our hands on their backs and spotted them along the way.

It's only now that I can clearly see Singer's strategic brilliance, even if it tears at me. These weren't nice men. They weren't holding us until some fairy-tale moment, when they would set us free. What were we waiting for? Were the Navy SEALs going to charge in and rescue four climbers in the middle of the mountains of Kyrgyzstan?

We would have been hostages until the ends of our lives.

But when we were guiding Abdul and Su up mountainsides, I would hear Singer scheming, would hear him talking with Dickey about throwing them off. *When? Now! Do it!*

For all of my uncertainty, I had confidence in one element: my ability to endure. I seemed to be holding up better than the others. And I didn't fear death. It's how I have always been. I fear losing the people I love, but death itself, my own death, leaves a blank spot in my mind.

I finally came to accept that the violence I so detested was our only way out. And I came to another realization: Nobody else was going to actually do it.

Starvation is a funny thing. You feel it first in your stomach, a nauseating pain low in your gut. Your breathing becomes labored and your body slows. Your face turns solemn. Any movement seems like too much bother. Your mind goes next. Indifference takes over, emotions dull. But after several days, the pain in my stomach went away. I still don't know how it happened or where it came from, but as everyone else grew weaker, I felt stronger.

I noticed my night vision improving. Lines became crisp. By the time the sun had set on the sixth day, I was aware of every sound, every movement. I felt a lightness, a vitality, as though I could race straight uphill without my heart rate rising. The others stumbled every few feet. Delusional or not, I saw myself again as a warrior.

With my confidence came acceptance. Singer was smarter, but I was stronger. Singer could be the commander, I was the soldier. Clarity overtook me. My love for Beth transcended my need for her. I willed my heart to harden.

On our sixth night, our captors hatched a plan. They, too, were starving and cold, so Abdul would return to our base camp to scavenge any remaining food and warmer clothes. The rest of us would ascend a 2000-foot mountainside, a mixture of talus fields and nearly vertical cliff bands. To us, at least in our normal states, it was easy terrain. Abdul, after gathering more rations, would come up another side, a less treacherous way, and meet us on top. For the first time, we were alone with Su.

The moon plays tricks in the darkness, casting shadows that dance across the cliffs. A jumbled mess of stone disappears below. Blackness. Far in the distance, stars illuminate the jagged spires and snow-covered mountains.

Su's feet skid and he lets out a pained grunt. I watch as Singer guides him, pointing out footholds and handholds solid enough to grab. The plan had been for Beth and me to stay above, out of the fall line.

We climb higher. Su wobbles again and I hear the clatter of rocks tumbling down the nearly sheer dropoff.

Now.

Now.

Silently I'm urging them to do it. Willing them to do it.

Dickey and Singer resume their guiding. More spots pass where Su is exposed and insecure. I try not to think about what it is that I'm wishing they would do.

As the top nears Su gains confidence and scrambles ahead of them, using his hands to keep his balance as he clambers over loose rock. At a more difficult section just fifty feet from the top, but twenty feet to our right, he slows. Singer and Dickey are still below. I glance down. Our eyes meet. They nod.

I look at Beth. "I'm going to have to do this," I whisper. "It has to be me."

She trembles. Shadows cross her face. Her lips open slightly, but no sounds escape. For a moment we stare at one another. She dips her head.

I know.

The strength has been growing into a monster inside me, emerging from nowhere, from everywhere, unlike anything I've known. I accelerate across a series of footholds with the swiftness of a mountain goat, staying silent though the shadows. Fifteen, ten, five feet away and still Su doesn't see me coming. The barrel of his rifle glistens under the stars. I see the outline of the grotesque mole on his upper lip. My foot dislodges a loose chunk of rock.

He turns sharply toward me. Our eyes lock. I lunge for the strap of the gun slung over his shoulder. I pull as hard as I can and push his shoulder. His body arches backward through the blackness, outlined by the moon. He cries out in surprise and fear. His body lands on a ledge with a sickening thud, and then bounces toward oblivion.

For a moment I hear and feel nothing. Then vertigo strikes me. I think the sun is rising. Glimmers of light blur into long, indistinct streaks, somehow real and surreal at the same time. Suddenly, as if a stone has crashed down on my head, every muscle in my body contracts and I squeeze my eyes shut as hard as I can. I scramble and sprint the remaining distance to the top of the mountain where I stand alone, panting. I drop to the ground and tuck myself into as tight a ball as possible. I rock back and forth, sobbing. Everything I've held inside floods out of me.

I had just killed a man. Not an evil villain, but a man not so different from myself. Scared, juvenile. A man who probably had a family at home, waiting for his return. I shouted at God to wake me from this nightmare. It was too horrible to be real. I shook uncontrollably and wondered if I was going mad.

I heard a voice and felt a hand on my back. Singer. I reflexively flinched away. "You did what had to be done."

I buried my head further between my knees, twisted my face into a hateful knot. I needed to place blame. I had chosen to kill. Singer's incessant babbling had infected me like a virus. This was supposed to be his job. How could he have put me in this situation? He was Satan and I was the doer of his deeds. I had become the evil that surrounded us for the past six days. I clenched every muscle I had, hoping to squeeze the last bit of life from my body.

But then I felt warmth. Beth knelt behind me, tucking my back between her knees and wrapping her arms around my shoulders. "You saved our lives," she said.

"How could you love me now? I'm a terrible person!" I wailed.

"You are my hero."

I lifted my head and looked at the other three, huddled around me. I saw their sense of urgency. This was where we were expecting to meet Abdul, and I had just killed Su. I took a breath.

Get hold of yourself, I thought. *This is not over.*

Ahead and to the east the angle softened to more of a steep hillside. We ran farther along the ridge crest until what looked like a decent break, where we dropped to our right, tumbling and falling down loose dirt and boulders in half-run, half-panic, weaving around the occasional cliff and leaping off the smaller ones, guided by fear, luck, and moonlight.

Dickey and Singer knew the valley below—it's where they'd gone when trying to track down our missing bag. There were shepherd huts and an army outpost, if we could only get there. If they didn't think we were the enemy and shoot us. If it hadn't been overtaken. Hiding in the shadows, in the boulders and in the trees lining the valley would be men with guns, either Kyrgyz soldiers or the rebels who had killed them. They would surely kill us, too.

At the valley floor we kept moving, running along cattle trails and ignoring the terror of imaginary figures cast by the shadows flickering through the trees. Our breath burned in our lungs, the frigid air seared our noses. For three, maybe four hours after pushing Su, we ran like skeletons in the night fueled by adrenaline and fear. Just before sunrise we paused. Ahead we could see a small hut with ibex skulls hanging on posts. Dickey and Singer remembered the place. Not far beyond was the army outpost.

Frost coated the bushes and I stared at my breath, rising in shimmering white puffs. Again we picked up the pace, and soon we saw figures moving in the shadows off to the sides, so we ran faster. *Bap-bap-bap!* Bullets flew, my heart pounded in my ears, the gunfire increased and we kept running toward an enclosed area, like a courtyard, inside the army outpost. We didn't know if they were Kyrgyz soldiers thinking we were rebels, or the soldiers were dead and the rebels were shooting. With no time to think and nothing to do either way we dove into the dirt as men swarmed over us, shouting and pointing rifles at our heads. Over and over we screamed, *"Americanski! Americanski! Americanski!"*

PART
TWO

CHAPTER SIX

Snow falls and settles on my eyelashes, distorting my vision for a moment before melting. A front has moved in and turned day into night. Outlines and indentations created by snowshoers pack the trail, enhancing the tenuous footing. Spring snow's heavy moisture, the heat of the sun, and the cold nights make everything slick and hard. Still, slip sliding as I am, I'm happy to be out and running. Sweat beads down my back and I feel a shiver.

Another mile or so and I come around a bend into bright sunlight. Wisps of clouds dance across the sky, as if they're polishing the peaks to my north and west. The sun reflects off the snow, as if I'm running on a field of sequined white carpet. The only disruption is the squeak of my shoes.

The trail rises steadily, no more than a few degrees of incline, but at more than 9,000 feet elevation, the going gets harder. I settle into a shorter stride, increase my cadence, bow forward slightly at the waist. Once I reach the crest it's all downhill to home.

Hours later, I sit on the couch. Pictures Beth has framed of the two of us hang on the walls. I have been trying to get up the nerve to propose to her. But as always with this sort of thing, I am having trouble committing. She had made an offhanded joke about this being our Date Night. I knew it wasn't genuine. In reality, she feels nervous, edgy; I feel the same. Wondering what they're going to say, wondering what it's going to feel like to have to relive some of what we'd experienced twenty months earlier in August of 2000. So much has happened since then, the Twin Towers, wars, the list goes on.

NBC's Dateline begins. The teaser at the beginning of the show has me shifting in embarrassment. We all look so young, and there I am looking *overwhelmed. I turn toward Beth and she's either completely riveted or some-where else entirely. I don't want to bother her; I'll let her deal with this her own way.*

Finally, they get to our story. The images are familiar. The wall, the por-taledge, the outlines of the mountains and valleys. I'd been curious to register my response, and I find that I have none. It's as if it all happened to someone else.

The scene shifts. A woman is in a prison interviewing a man. They are speaking Kyrgyz; a voiceover provides the translation.

Beth and I both lean forward and hold hands. Finally, after months of in-nuendo and suspicion, we hear the words we've been hoping for, "Were you pushed or did you fall asleep?" the woman asks.

"They pushed me," he says.

Finally.

Finally.

I turn off the television. I just want to get back to living our lives free from the weight of suspicion.

Moving on.

The men pointing guns at our heads were members of the Kyrgyz military. They quickly realized that we weren't rebels. Within minutes they'd offered us warm clothes and food and water. The four of us devoured two tins of sardines. I'd never even tasted canned sardines before, but in that moment I kept thinking, *This is the best food I've ever tasted.* I brought my hands to my chest and then toward them, indicating my thanks. From their weary looks and gaunt frames, from what we'd seen and heard of the fighting, we knew they'd been worn thin from combat.

Within hours we were helicoptered from their small forward operating base to a large military complex, several hours by air from the capital, Bishkek. Once at the larger base we met briefly with the president of Kyr-gyzstan, Askar Akayev, and other officials. Because of the language barrier, our exchange with the president was brief. From his questions, he seemed mostly interested in the role his troops had played in "rescuing" us. I was so numb that it didn't fully register that we'd really rescued ourselves, and that his interest in our story was primarily for his political gain.

We boarded an airliner that took us to the capital. Once in Bishkek, we were taken to the American Embassy, a bunkerlike facility in a row of buildings guarded by gates and concrete Jersey barriers. We all took the first opportunity to contact family. It seemed to take forever for the line to ring on the other end. I wasn't sure if the static and hum was on the phone line or in my head.

"Mom, it's me," I said. "Is Dad there? Could both of you get on?"

"We got kidnapped," I began, haltingly, trying to measure what to tell and what to leave out. "We're okay. We escaped. We had to throw one of the guys off a cliff. But we got out."

It took so long for my parents to respond that I wondered if we'd lost the connection. The static crackled and the white noise droned on.

"I'm so sorry," they said nearly in unison. They kept repeating those same words over and over. I couldn't blame them. This had hit them out of the blue. They told me that they were glad that we were okay. Through my tears, I told them that I had to go. I'd be in touch to let them know when I'd be back.

I hung up. From another part of the office, Singer's excited voice recounted to his mom what had gone on. I felt as if I was listening to someone talking about an action-adventure movie, an old Jean-Claude Van Damme flick. A small part of me wished that I had Singer's gung ho attitude and ability to see this as a thrilling adventure. I was just sad that it had to happen at all. That I'd had to take a man's life. I just wanted to move on and get out of there.

At the embassy debriefing that followed, Singer monopolized the meeting. I sat silent, feeling the pit in my stomach gnawing and tearing my insides. Before being dismissed, we were told that we really should have registered upon arrival. We all nodded. The staff at the embassy treated us amazingly well. They helped us buy new, warmer, cleaner clothes. The next flight back to the United States from Bishkek wouldn't be for another week, so they assisted us in getting into Kazakhstan to fly back to California. Beth and I settled into our seats and our own little bubble. Dickey and Singer had opted to wait out the week in Kyrgyzstan for a cheaper flight. Beth and I dozed and whispered, grateful for the bit of rest, 35,000 feet above it all.

On August 22, Beth's parents picked us up at the airport for a tearful reunion. When we arrived at her house in Davis, a smattering of news trucks and reporters were out front. We ducked our heads and ran inside. We had no idea that our ordeal had spread in the press. We felt no need to talk to anyone outside our tight little circle. Still, the trucks sat there, the reporters clustered. I just wanted them all to go away.

We shuffled around the house in bare feet, wide-eyed. We flinched at loud noises. Beth's parents cocooned us. When reporters knocked at the door they'd put their arms around us and lead us to the back room. Beth and I would stand in the open doorway listening. Firm but polite, Beth's parents told reporters that we would release a press statement in due time. Beth and I were very grateful for their calm and support. They seemed to instinctively know how to handle us. Beth told me that years earlier her dad had nearly died of cancer; her mom and dad had already learned that paradoxical caretakers' demeanor: iron and velvet.

Like us, they didn't know how to handle the press. Clearly, they weren't just going to disappear. As much as Beth's mom and dad wanted to create an iron barrier between the press and us, those bars would also imprison us.

My parents soon arrived. My heart cracked when I saw my mom's lips trembling as she tried to control her emotions. We gathered in the living room. My mom sat on the white sofa behind me, rubbing my shoulders. Nobody knew what to say. It was all idle chitchat and awkward silences. My dad mentioned how nice the weather was. Everyone looked annoyed, not necessarily at him, but at the situation. For days we had talked in hushed tones. My dad wasn't shouting, but his voice seemed big enough to let the air out of the protective cushions her parents had inflated.

Beth got up, walked to her bedroom, and closed the door. The rest of us stared at the floor or out the windows. I waited a few minutes, then went to Beth's room.

"I can't deal with your parents right now," Beth said.

Everyone was hurting. I needed to be there with Beth, but I wanted to be there for my parents, too. I appreciated their coming. I needed their support. I was caught in the middle, but I sensed that in this case, Beth's needs outweighed my own and my parents'.

Two days of awkwardness passed. As before, my dad tried to make conversation, to normalize things, to make it feel less as if we were in a funeral parlor. Still, whatever he said or did seemed to agitate Beth. Even when my dad sat quietly working on a jigsaw puzzle, his muttered "All right" at finding a piece that fit seemed raucous. I'd watch Beth heave a sigh, as if she was moving heavy furniture. In fact, she wanted to move my parents out of there. My allegiances were torn, but I said, "Okay, I will tell them."

The thought of asking my parents to leave broke my heart. They'd just arrived. We went for a walk, the news trucks now all gone, strolling past white picket fences and flower boxes. The sound of birds chirping filled the air. The streets were wide and in a perfect grid pattern. I could tell they were trying to make no sound with their feet. I took a few deep breaths and started to speak.

"I am so sorry, Mom and Dad." Tears began pouring down my face. "It's too hard for you to be here right now. I'll come home as soon as I can. Don't worry about me. I'll be fine."

I wrapped my arms around both of them. We let it linger for a minute, then walked back. They gathered their bags, said good-bye, and drove away. I felt guilty about the relief I was feeling. At least now I wouldn't have to deal with Beth's discomfort around my parents. I'd been through enough conflict; I just wanted to do what she asked, hoping that she'd stabilize.

I also knew that my parents could handle it. And though my mother didn't say a lot to me, she never said anything inappropriate—the "it-could-have-been-worse," "you-should-be-grateful" kind of things that people sometimes say. I saw the hurt in her eyes for only a few seconds, before she recalibrated. I think she understood that I was doing this for Beth, this other woman in my life. Mom was willing, as always, to do the right thing, to put her interests aside to help me.

It didn't take long for me to feel out of place in Davis. Even worse, I didn't know how I *should* feel. I kept expecting a strong dose of emotion to arise and guide my actions. Should I be shaking with fear and trauma, or jumping up and down shouting, "It's great to be alive!"? Am I a hero for taking the action that got us out of there? I didn't feel like a hero. My days were laced with flashbacks. Blood pooling on the alpine tundra. Bullets slamming into the boulder then buzzing off into the hillside beyond. Shouts and whistles and screams. The sirenlike shrill of rocket-propelled grenades. The noise and the fear blurred fuzzy white, like static on a television. Hours passed in what seemed like minutes as I sat on park benches staring blankly ahead. Mentally I was digging holes as fast as I could, burying any sign of outward emotion while fixating on a single fact: I had killed another human being.

One moment Beth was crying, then she would be trembling in fear or staring blankly out the window. She felt certain that the IMU was going to hunt us down. She repeatedly asked what we had done to deserve this. During our six days of captivity there had to have been times of laughter, glimpses of lightness, but I couldn't remember any. The same was true of our return home. I experienced the discomforting sensation that as bad as the abduction had been, it had finite starting and end points. How long was our recovery going to take? How was I going to summon the strength to manage these stresses for myself and for Beth?

At night I would massage her back, and she would fall asleep. But that crucial elixir of human restoration never seemed to last long for her. She awoke constantly, startled by nightmares. Her parents and I did everything we could to comfort her. We ordered takeout from her favorite restaurants, told her repeatedly that we were safe, that nothing was going to happen to us here. But the horrors of those six days continued to haunt her.

Beth's parents figured we needed professional help and made an appointment for us with a psychologist. Within minutes the guy was comparing us to rape victims. I sat there for a few seconds, startled and stunned. This guy didn't know a damned thing about us or what had happened or how to help us. We hadn't been raped. But I wasn't willing to listen to anyone. More so, I didn't want to talk to anyone about what had happened. I understood later what he was trying to say: That we'd been traumatized. I had been trying to avoid deeper thoughts. I wanted to put a Band-Aid over a festering wound without cleaning it first. Beth was my confidante and the only one who could possibly understand.

I kept returning to a powerful moment back in Kyrgyzstan, after the military realized we weren't rebels. We sat against a wall in a hut, and though I held Beth in my lap she felt distant. I was happy to be alive but worried she might fear me after what I had done.

"Tommy," Singer had said, "if you want, I'll take the rap for pushing Su.

Or we can say the three of us did it. It's up to you." My head had tilted in confusion. Throughout our ordeal, Singer's mind had been so quick, always several steps ahead of the rest of us. Seeing my despair, was he genuinely offering to take the blame? Or, I wondered, was he trying to take the credit for our escape?

Initially we'd been vague about the specifics of the push. But our secrecy was beginning to feel wrong. Over the phone one day, I told Singer that I needed the truth to come out. He said he had been thinking the same, and then explained how he saw the mental state that led to my pushing Su.

"You know that song 'Jeremy' from Pearl Jam, where a tormented and bullied kid gets driven mad to the point where he bursts into his classroom one day and mows down everyone with a gun? I think that's similar to what happened to you," he said.

His words didn't sit well with me, comparing me to a crazy person lashing out, but I chose to keep quiet.

After we hung up, I put my focus on where it needed to be—Beth. She needed me, but not in the starry-eyed, head-in-clouds way I felt toward her. In her mind I was the only person who could truly understand all she'd been through. She asked me to stay by her side. There was no way I was going to push her away.

She was struggling, probably more than the rest of us, but she still wanted to support me in my promise to my parents that I'd come home. We headed to Colorado.

My dad is my dad, bless his heart, and he only knows one way of moving forward. He had been trying to help me since I was that two-year-old learning to flex, trying to be strong like him, trying to be tough and to never show weakness. "You gotta get back on that horse, son," Dad said one day soon after we'd returned to Estes Park.

Beth was furious. "How could he say that? Does he even know what we went through?" She insinuated that my dad's urgings were motivated by his self-interest, his selfish pride in my career. But I was alert to the pattern of others using our painful experience for their own interests, and I knew, deep in my heart, that my dad would never be one of those people. Yet also my mother's son, I felt Beth's pain and tried to be patient.

Inwardly I agreed with my dad. But again I felt pulled in different directions, and ultimately I sided with Beth. I can see now that I was so numb, so devoted to helping her recover, that I disregarded what was best for me.

We didn't stay long in Colorado. Beth needed her parents. That meant living at their house in Davis for an indeterminate amount of time. Even back in California, Beth's intolerance for my parents grew. Whenever I talked to them on the phone, she steamed. *How could they encourage me to climb? Isn't that what led to our lives being split in half?* It seemed she was indiscriminately lashing out at others; we needed time to heal. I needed to get Beth back to a better place.

The continuing media attention didn't help. From the moment we returned, we had been under siege. In that first week, we chose to entrust our story to Greg Child, an accomplished climber and author who was friends with Singer. Greg struck a deal in which he would write a story for *Outside* magazine, which he would then expand into a book. We signed a contract giving him exclusive rights to the story. (*Over the Edge* was published in 2002 and is a thoroughly researched book about our ordeal.)

Meanwhile, a woman who worked in public relations for one of my then-sponsors pitched the story of our kidnapping to *Playboy* magazine without our consent. They accepted her proposal. But we'd already signed the exclusive deal with Greg and *Outside* and were, if not legally then certainly ethically, bound to not cooperate with her. In turn, she thought we were trying to control the reporting, and then decided that we had embellished our story into something made for Hollywood. I was infuriated that she accused us of using our suffering for personal gain—especially when she and, later, her husband tried to do exactly that. And if we were making things up, why did she use our story, as we told it, in her pitch to *Playboy*?

The couple preached their conspiracy story everywhere. She even lined up a book deal (which ultimately fell through) for their grand exposé. Her husband became so obsessed that he traveled to Kyrgyzstan to investigate, and by the time they stopped he'd spent over thirty thousand dollars of his own money trying to prove that we'd perpetrated a hoax. He wouldn't let go. I still don't know what drove him. It would have been easy to dismiss him as a wing nut, but his relentlessness roused publicity, with controversy-hungry media outlets latching on like tabloid sharks.

One day Beth and I were standing in line at a gas station in California's Central Valley. Ahead of us, we overheard a couple discussing the details of our kidnapping.

"Did you hear about those four rock climbers who got kidnapped?"

"Yeah, crazy story. Did you hear that it turns out they made the whole thing up to get press? Crazy, what is this world coming to."

Beth turned and bolted for the car. I paid for our gas and by the time I got back she was a sobbing mess. We had been through hell and now we were being called liars.

I started ignoring my phone messages and stopped talking to virtually everyone. I craved the freedom that climbing had always brought me. But I also wondered about the deeper meaning of it all. Was it selfish to spend so much of my life on an activity that directly served no one but me? Yet isn't that what nearly all of us do, often while hurling accusations at others for being selfish? Most of us are just trying to get by, trying to connect with the people, places, and things we love; trying to live with individual purpose and meaning, and if we're so blessed as to live with a burning passion, then it's truly a gift. When I think of it all that way, climbing—or whatever makes you happy without harming others—needs little defense. Besides, at a simpler level climbing is just so damned fun; I love it. But for Beth, climbing had now come to symbolize terror. It was an activity tied to nightmares and death.

I craved the mountains, and again I felt torn. But the magnetism of our love for each other brought me back toward her. Before long, though, the idyllic bubble of suburbia began to grate on me. In moments of weakness—which were common—I couldn't help judging it. Nothing was real. Everyone talked about organic food and the best drive-through car wash. Meanwhile, each day I had to live with the knowledge that my heart contained the evil I so despised.

Everyone treated me with kid gloves. Were they afraid I would snap? Were my actions a matter of strength or of weakness? Ultimately I felt that I simply did what had to be done. I wanted to be treated as the same person

I always was, but I felt that I needed to act traumatized so people wouldn't see me as evil. If I didn't snap and if I wasn't traumatized, did that mean I was a cold-hearted person who cared little for human life?

Despite my internal unease, I still saw compassion and beauty in the world. In Beth's suffering I saw her strength. She was hurting and didn't pretend otherwise. I saw how the four of us had stuck together throughout those six hellish days, and how we cared for one another. I thought about how every one of us is a mix of both good and bad, even Abdul and Su and the other rebels. Many of their people had been oppressed and killed, and they probably believed their actions were noble, a fight against tyranny that would provide for their loved ones. So where do we draw our lines? For a while I doubted everything, including myself.

I spent a lot of time thinking about the human heart. Often I thought of Turat and his bravery as he was being led to his death, of his simple gesture of handing Beth a piece of candy and telling her not to cry, how his last actions on this earth were an attempt to reassure someone who was hurting.

For two months I lived with the knowledge that I had killed another human being. I'd always thought myself a gentle soul. I was the person who let other kids win in wrestling. Who cried at sad movies. And then one night, under the moonlight in a faraway land, just like that I took a life.

One day I got a call. The woman who had wanted to write our story for *Playboy*, and who, with her husband, had rededicated her efforts to proving us frauds, was reporting that Su was alive and in prison in Kyrgyzstan. My first reaction was disbelief, and then anger. Despite how I felt about people being essentially good, I believed this had to be a ploy to support their agenda. I called Greg Child, who investigated the claim and discovered that it was true—Su was alive. None of us could believe it. Dickey and Singer and I had seen him hit the ledge and then disappear. Nobody could survive such a fall. But somehow, Su did.

If you were to ask my parents today, they would tell you that learning of Su's survival was the moment I came back to life, but I remember it differently. I felt some relief, but it didn't change what gnawed away at me: I had the capacity to kill.

For months, Beth barely left her parents' house. I stayed with her as much as I could, but oftentimes when I would leave, her anger and fear would boil to the surface. She feared the IMU would seek revenge, track us down. She worried that people on the streets would recognize her and call her a liar. Sometimes all of it overwhelmed her and she would break into tears. Yet she saw me getting progressively more stir crazy in Davis, so Beth gave me her blessing to start making trips to Yosemite.

By March 2001, El Capitan had become my closest companion. Nonjudgmental and brutally honest. Challenging and always inspiring. I rediscovered Yosemite's splendor, and the beauty in feeling small. In the face of climbing something so massive and magnificent, my stress seemed to fade. I devised systems for safely climbing alone, self-belayed with a rope.

At first it was all about distraction, but gradually moments of simple euphoria, more intense than ever before, flowed through me like a form of rekindled gratitude: the damp smell of the forest as I walked to the base of El Cap, the cobalt-blue sky, the screech of a peregrine falcon. I wished I could put it all in a bottle and bring it home to Beth. I would return to Davis every few days, hold Beth in my arms as she fell asleep, and tell her she no longer had to worry. I loved her and would be there to take care of her for the rest of our days.

Beth and I had developed an unspoken understanding that the needs of the other were as crucial as our own. I accepted her need for sadness while she accepted my need to climb. When we were apart, we still talked on the phone often.

Come spring, she offered to join me on my attempt to make the first free ascent of a desperately hard aid route called the Muir Wall.

On the wall we got lost in the details of difficult climbing. This route was a notch harder than any of the others I had previously done on El Cap. It would be a new level for my climbing, and prove to others, and to myself, that I could still be a professional climber. I'd demonstrate that I was in control of my life again. Beth selflessly belayed and gave me endless encouragement. In the evenings she would massage my aching body. Like a mother, she tirelessly attended my every need. Surrounded by air and granite, it felt like the closest thing we had to home.

On our fourth day, a massive storm hit Yosemite. Suddenly the sky swirled with snow. We'd packed a specialized rain cover for our portaledge and strapped it on, battened down the hatches, and crawled inside. Through the occasional break in the clouds Beth and I could see other parties rappelling off. Matchbox-sized cars fled the valley. Silence settled around us. Darkness fell. The wind picked up. The portaledge, though anchored securely, rocked like a giant kite. Snow flurries fell steadily as we drifted off to sleep.

In the morning, we woke to a lull in the storm. A breeze blew, partially drying portions of the rock. We hurriedly threw on our rainwear, and I racked up. "Quick, put me on belay," I said to Beth. I raced upward, pulling on gear when needed. The wind picked up and wet snow fell hard again. The rock began to pour. A hundred feet from the top we climbed through a runnel of cascading water. Soaked to the bone, we pulled ourselves atop El Cap. Everything was still. I looked at Beth and was overcome with intense pride.

Even though I had not freed the climb we had weathered the storm with grace and even a little laughter. I put my gloved hands on the cheeks of her hooded face and gave her a quick, firm kiss on the lips.

"I'm proud of you, baby," I said.

We jogged down the trail with a confidence and lightness that we hadn't felt in a long time.

Beth could be unbreakable. It was the aftermath that sometimes sent her spiraling. In the following days, her feeling that we were doomed returned. She thought there must be a force in the universe out to kill us, that we must have done something terribly bad in a former life. Why expose ourselves to these potentially dangerous and painful experiences? She decided she needed a break from big wall climbing. In truth, she hadn't been able to flee the demons of Kyrgyzstan.

My reaction to the storm had been very different from hers. I felt no doubt, did no second-guessing. I just did what had to be done. Something was growing inside me. Something I couldn't quite put my finger on.

———

My best friend, Nick Sagar, was a sport climber, excelling on short, difficult, bolt-protected routes. We'd met in my post–high school years on the road. I initially liked him because of his ability to turn almost every conversation into a "That's-what-she-said" joke, but our friendship grew over time. We shared a devotion to climbing. He lived in a Toyota minivan with his girl-friend and two dogs, and I admired his willingness to sacrifice material wealth for a different kind of gold.

On a few occasions we had spent our last dimes to go sport climbing in Southern France and Spain. My stomach muscles gained strength as much from the laughter as from the climbing. Yet he was also one of those guys who seemed to possess a deeper knowledge. Just being in his presence felt like what I needed. Nick knew nothing of big wall climbing, but when I asked him to join me for another attempt to free the Muir he dropped everything. "I am *always* up to try something long and hard," he said, following it with the obligatory, "That's what she said." We laughed and I felt like a kid again.

There had always been a friendly competitiveness to our climbing. On sport climbs our abilities were perfectly matched. But El Cap was different. I was different, too. Once we started climbing, it was as if a switch had been flipped. I pushed forward despite nightfall, wet cracks, and storms.

"Damn, dude, you're possessed," Nick gasped at one belay. He was right. I was starting to recognize something that people close to me had already seen—a strength that I was only beginning to understand. I just smiled in return.

Even with Nick, I wasn't eager to talk about Kyrgyzstan. It opened a wound I wasn't ready to expose. Without my saying anything, he understood. He needed to be my friend and not my therapist. He was fully empathetic so he knew that I needed more time to process everything.

I did most of the leading and hauling, but Nick climbed brilliantly, espe-cially given his unfamiliarity with the big wall world. We both freed every pitch, on lead or while following, and succeeded in making the first free ascent of the Muir Wall. I was twenty-two years old. Kyrgyzstan was nine months in the past. This was my third independent free route on El Cap—more than anyone else at that time, even the legendary free climbers I so admired and to whom I still didn't consider myself an equal. Later, in the account I wrote for the *American Alpine Journal*, I didn't mention the kidnapping, didn't tout the Muir Wall success as any kind of comeback. I was still the same shy warrior and didn't talk about or revel in that sternly tested ability to endure. I wanted to treat the Muir as just another climb. I'd taken another step toward normalcy.

On one of our last nights on the wall Nick and I sat quietly on the portaledge, staring at the stars. For the first time Nick mentioned Kyrgyzstan. "The second I heard that you guys escaped because someone pushed the guy with the gun," he said, "I knew it was you."

Beth gradually returned to climbing. As long as I'd known her, she had always possessed a deep need to excel. She had confided that she'd once gotten a B on a test in high school. It created so much anxiety for her that she told no one—and it was the last B she ever got. As a former special ed student, it was hard for me to relate, yet with climbing I knew exactly how she felt.

We moved into my six-hundred-square-foot cabin in Estes Park, Colorado, surrounded by a thousand or more climbing routes on the nearby crags and mountains. We started training. As a professional climber Beth knew she had a duty to her sponsors, but initially she kept her return to climbing a secret. She feared exposing herself to any kind of ridicule. Normal concerns, such as not performing well in the public eye, were magnified in Beth's eyes after Kyrgyzstan.

On the surface, our life was a portrait of domestic bliss. Train, climb, eat, rest. The cabin was run-down and old, so I bought a few books on home remodeling and got to work. Beth covered the walls with framed pictures. When we were home, she scurried around the kitchen in her apron, baking cookies and pies. She would leave me loving notes—"Fresh batch of cookies in a Tupperware on the counter"—and hide goodies in my backpack for me to find when I went climbing. We would go on sunset walks, then settle into bed, her head resting on my shoulder, and talk for hours. She always wanted to discuss baby names. I would talk about places that I dreamed of traveling to.

Beth's public face was one of puppy dogs and rainbows, but the strains of depression and anxiety still lingered. We would go to bed feeling loving and hopeful. Overnight, agitation or skittishness would creep back in, like ghosts sneaking through the floorboards while she slept. She'd choose targets for her frustration: the smothering presence of my parents, the pressure of our careers, the conservative Estes Park locals. To me, her concerns seemed arbitrary. Alternately frustrated and feeling tender pangs of protectiveness, I rode the waves of her recovery as best I could.

The one thing that seemed to provide her with the most contentment was training. She took it on with a vengeance. We would spend the majority of our time hardening our bodies and fingers by lifting weights, or working out on the indoor climbing wall. Beth always chose the dark rap songs of Eminem while we trained. When I was tired and ready to call it a day, she would crank out a few more sets of sit-ups, grunting and screaming with each repetition.

At first, most of our climbing was bouldering—unroped on small rocks, close to the ground, with foam "crash pads" and spotters to break a fall. In bouldering, the whole idea is to try the hardest possible moves, so you're practically always falling. The endorphin high of pushing to exhaustion brought her satisfaction. She could control her ability to work hard, and that created stability, at least temporarily.

Beth's focus soon shifted to the hardest single-pitch rock climbs she could manage, in places where it could be just me, her, and the rock. We often returned to climbs I had established with my dad as a teenager, giving me a warm dose of nostalgia. Beth is slight and has impeccable balance, which combined with her toughness makes her an extraordinary climber. She, too, began to notice some beneficial aftereffects from Kyrgyzstan. At a high level, as in many sports, climbing is about pain tolerance. Our ability to endure had been completely recalibrated. That combined with her natural talent meant that before long she was once again climbing grades that only a handful of women in the country could match.

About a year after Kyrgyzstan she started asking me when I was going to propose. She had laid out a plan. Get married, have kids by the time we were thirty, secure ourselves as two of the best climbers in the world. I was all in.

More than ever, Beth's needs became my needs and my needs became hers. When she felt depressed, scared, or unsettled, I would experience physical pain. When I went on climbing trips with friends, she would call me in tears. I didn't fully understand the extent to which she needed my presence for emotional strength. We had become completely intertwined, like the strands of a rope. We barely noticed as our ability to live independent lives faded away.

In addition to training and climbing on the local crags, practically staring out our back door was the gem of the region: the Diamond, the famous big wall that I had climbed with my dad when I was twelve. There had been a buzz in the Colorado climbing community about when the first route rated 5.13 would be climbed on the Diamond.

My friend Eric Doub had been exploring just such a route. He'd spent something like forty days over three years trying to free climb it. In the climbing world, when someone's trying a new route it's customary to show respect by staying away until he or she nabs the first ascent. "It's a pretty wild spot, man, but a bit hard for me," Eric told me. "You should try it." He generously gave me not only his blessing but a detailed map of the route.

I'd been continually progressing, growing, since our ordeal the previous summer. It felt as if that potentially crippling experience had somehow manifested into a newfound ability to endure, and in more ways than I'd ever imagined. My first attempt was a flashback to my childhood, a chance to return to life as it once was. I went up with my dad, only this time, on this much harder route, it was me leading the way and him following behind. He had as much enthusiasm for the route as I did, but the chimney that had bombed us with ice that first time, a decade earlier, was dripping with water. The rock above was drenched as well. We only made it halfway up Eric's route.

What I'd climbed included clean, steep rock, devious cracks, thin faces, and pretty much everything else a climber dreams about. I hadn't been on the hardest pitches yet, and the inevitable Diamond combination of sudden thunderstorms and high altitude added up to an intimidating undertaking. For the next month and a half I thought of little but that climb.

Beth wanted to see the wall, too, and offered to come along as my belayer. After the three-hour approach hike, we scrambled to Broadway Ledge as first light hit the wall. The rock had dried since that first attempt with my dad, and we made good time up the opening pitches, me leading and Beth jumaring behind with a backpack of supplies.

My dad had hiked to an overlook adjacent to the wall, a place called Chasm View, and silently cheered me on through the early pitches. Soon I was into the heart of the route. My lungs seared. My forearms burned with lactic acid. In full battle mode, I struggled to keep control, breathing, relaxing, then powering through strenuous sequences in the thin alpine air. Beth's high-pitched shouts of encouragement echoed throughout the cirque. My feet skated on barely-there edges, but somehow, pitch after pitch, I stayed on.

It was an August weekend, 2001, and other climbers on the wall had gotten wind that I was trying the route. Some of them I knew, others I didn't. I climbed higher, redlining, barely managing, fluctuating between flailing and pulling it off. The other climbers joined in, shouting support. My dad's silence turned to booming cheers. Beth shouted so hard that I felt she was lifting me upward as I grabbed razor-thin holds and forced my quivering body to move with precision.

The only fuel I had left came from the two most important people in my life. I nearly fell countless times. After twelve hours on the wall we topped out. We'd done the hardest free climbing ever on the Diamond. I had been pulled in so many directions for so long that it felt wonderful to be simply moving upward, feeling an almost mystical newfound power.

Eric wanted to name the route The Honeymoon Is Over. Purely out of respect and gratitude, I kept the name. At the final belay, as Beth joined me with a kiss, and the landscape of my youth spread out along the horizon, my shouts of joy were carried away by the wind.

CHAPTER SEVEN

I recognize the worry in the young woman's eyes. I have been in the hospital for two weeks, long enough to read the various nurses and long enough to develop bedsores. Not so long that I don't still press the button to dispense another dose of morphine. I'm numb with boredom. My stomach is in knots with worried exhaustion.

They've pumped me full of drugs and blood and cut and sewn me like I'm one of my stuffed animal creations. At night they come in and harvest my vitals and steal my sleep. I'm both weary and wary, frazzled and frustrated; what passed for my former life now feels like the bits of paper I used to cut up. I see a mosaic of memories in my drugged haze.

"Sometimes when people lie in bed for this long their lung capacity goes down," the nurse says. She hands me a plastic contraption that looks like a measuring beaker with a hose coming out of the bottom and a red plastic ball trapped inside.

"Now, blow into the tube as hard as you can. If the ball rises to the number four that's really good."

She holds it out, and I give it a try. The ball shoots to ten in an instant.

"Wow, are you some kind of athlete or something?"

I have to think of how to respond.

I look to my left where my bandaged hand rests on a raised tray. My index finger is unwrapped, and looks like a hot dog left too long on a grill. That is, if the hot dog had metal pins rising from it, as if from a specimen to be dissected.

"I used to be," I say. "I mean—I am. Hope to be again," I'm like a beginning pianist trying to find the right note to play in a song I thought I knew by heart.

"You are an athlete," Beth says, staring intently into my eyes. "You are."

A half hour later, the door opens and a pale, sad-looking doctor walks in.

"I'm a climber, too. And a hand surgeon. If you'd been brought in a few hours later, I'd have done the first of your surgeries."

He looks from Beth to me. He tells me that he's been keeping track of my progress. I hear the beeps on the heart rate monitor; it's no longer a slow, steady metronome. It's as if my heart is beating out an urgent message. Please give me some good news.

He looks at the floor, then back at me, and says, "Tommy, things aren't looking good. You're going to lose your finger. You better start thinking about what else you want to do with your life."

"Okay," is all I can think to say. The doctor lowers his head and walks out.

Beth has risen and is standing alongside the bed. Her expression is stern with resolve. "Fuck that guy," she says as the door shuts. "How can he have so little faith in you?"

My love for her soars.

In the fall 2001 climbing season, I formulated a plan that might help me rise to the level of the people I most admired, such as Lynn Hill and Dean Potter. After dropping Beth off at her parents' house, I returned to Yosemite. I desperately wanted to explore the limits of my physical capabilities. Although I had experienced success in free climbing many of the walls, therein lay a problem. It no longer felt impossibly huge to free climb these routes in multiple days. Early in my climbing career, success came from improving efficiency, not pushing through preconceived limits. Then in Kyrgyzstan I got a glimpse of the other side. I discovered that in those moments when all seems lost, when you feel that you can go no further, sometimes a survival instinct kicks in. Your body is flush with energy and you feel as if anything is possible. It must be built into our genes, a part of human evolution since the dawn of time. I was desperately curious about the edge of human capability. I knew I could do much more.

I decided I would have to free climb El Cap in a day.

First, I would need to learn how to go fast. So, when I returned to Yosemite, I asked speed climbing guru Hans Florine if he would teach me his secrets. Speed climbing is a game without rules. The goal is simply to climb the route as quickly as possible. Sometimes that means free climbing, other times you resort to aid climbing. Most of the time it's a combination of the two. Hans had literally written the book on this style, coming up with all manner of logistical tricks. I wasn't interested in setting any speed records, but knew that I could learn from the craft.

He agreed to be my teacher. We ran up the Nose in four hours and twenty-two minutes. When we got to the top, Hans asked if I wanted to go throw a quick lap on Half Dome, too. I declined, not believing that I had it in me. I was still wrapping my head around the idea that El Cap might be just a crag, not a monster whale. The experience blew my mind.

Soon after, fresh off our speed ascent of the Nose, Hans offered to belay me on an attempt to free the Salathé Wall in a day. We started at first light, me leading every pitch and Hans jumaring behind. I climbed as fast as possible and the pitches flew by. We reached the headwall, twenty-eight pitches up, in just nine hours. In the blazing sun I quickly reracked and started up the 5.13 endurance pitch.

As I climbed, my forearms swelled. My head pounded from dehydration and my focus faltered. Five feet from the end of the pitch, I pumped out and sagged onto the rope. I lowered back to Hans and pulled the rope. On my second try I fell just thirty feet up. "All right, body, here it is. Time for that reserve of energy to kick in," I told myself. I tried two more times. My forearms gave out completely. I could barely hold a cam, much less free the Salathé headwall. Hans took over the lead, and we speed climbed to the top.

I had failed, but, as I would later realize, I had also learned what it took to free climb El Cap in a day. More than climbing fast, I needed to conserve energy. I had been so concerned about going fast that I forgot to relax. Through my disappointment, I knew what I would do differently next time.

That winter Beth and I returned to Estes.

Much as I'd have liked to, I couldn't train 24/7. The body needs rest. One day, I was building a platform for our new washer and dryer. The cracked and slanted concrete floor needed to be shimmed to make it flat. Instead of buying shims I decided I could make some by ripping two-by-fours with the table saw. I gathered a handful of one-foot lengths and headed outside, feeling good about solving the problem and not having to make a trip to the lumber yard.

As I fed the pieces lengthwise, a two-by-four shot from the table into the hillside like an arrow. I switched off the saw and noticed a few drops of liquid on the table's black surface. I raised my left hand. Blood burbled up from the stump of a finger like water from a leaky drinking fountain. I saw the white bony stub of my index finger, the lower joint above the knuckle, some jagged flesh, and what must have been a tendon or ligament. My hand and arm tingled.

Panic flooded my mind: *How can I climb without a left index finger?*

I started to feel faint, my vision swam for an instant, but I blinked and took in a deep breath. I had to find it. I scanned the saw table, scrambled around the side, careful to keep my hand above my heart while searching the ground. Not wanting to distress Beth, I turned toward the house and called to her, voice steady, "I just chopped off my finger. Please come out here." I couldn't find my finger, so I took a step in the direction of the hillside, where the wood had shot. But my legs wobbled and I thought better of it.

Beth came running and found my finger lying beside the saw. She snatched it out of the pile of sawdust and rushed inside. I stood confused, shocked. She returned in a flash with a Ziploc baggie, the severed part of my finger floating in water. She handed me a dishtowel and wrapped it around my hand. Then Beth sped our little Honda like a race car, tires squealing, to the hospital in Estes Park. No more than five minutes elapsed from the time of the accident to when we arrived. The doctor was calm. We weren't. He injected Novocain into the nub. Then he packed the finger in ice and sent us down the hill to the big hospital in Fort Collins. He told us to drive slowly. Beth didn't.

No matter how fast she drove, she couldn't outrace my anxiety.

Tears streamed down my face. I thought about the glistening granite of Yosemite. I remembered the way I felt when I was focused on nothing but the moment, high above the ground. Would I ever again be able to do the thing that I love most, the thing that both drives me and brings me peace? I felt exposed. I had no backup plan, no skills, no dreams beyond those that climbing provided. Would Beth still love me if we no longer had the connection that had brought us together in the first place?

In the next two weeks, between the accident and three surgeries, I lost nearly a third of my blood volume. I spent my days lying motionless in a sterile hospital room, connected to a morphine pump that I pushed endlessly, even though I knew it would only send the allowable dose. I wanted the drug more to numb the psychological trauma than for the physical pain.

I had likely just ended my climbing life.

I thought of what Beth had said, that there was some force at work in the universe that seemed to have it in for us. I'd dismissed it at the time as her depressive state speaking up. Lying in that bed, I had to wonder. First the abduction, now the finger. Had I done something to deserve this? I was so used to living a life that was bound by this equation: Effort equals results. Luck didn't play a part in climbing. You got what you deserved. Did I deserve this? I knew that ripping a two-by-four without using a push stick—a device that would keep my hands away from the blade itself—wasn't the smartest way to operate. Still, having the wood kick back and jam a finger might have been punishment enough.

Had I been in too much of a hurry? Had my newfound emphasis on speed on the walls crept into the rest of my life?

The drug-induced haze bent hours into days and then weeks. My doctors reattached the finger by pinning the bone and patching together the nerves. Then they tried to sew together the tiny veins, an exceptionally delicate task. The finger kept congesting with blood. To relieve the pressure they removed the fingernail, cut and drained my finger through the nail bed, and applied medicinal leeches. My fingers are fat from climbing and have such high blood flow that the congestion was massive. They had to relieve the pressure so often that I bled profusely, resulting in more transfusions. They did everything they could as I drifted in and out of consciousness.

When I was awake, my emotions fluctuated from severe anguish to numb acceptance. But through the fog, I thought about two things: Beth, who was always beside me, and climbing. I wanted to stay strong for her, and held at bay the questions that plagued me when visiting hours were over. The lights and sounds of the monitors, the laughs and chatter from the nurses' station, all combined to imprison and torture me.

During the day, when friends and family were around, I felt very loved. My father volunteered to donate his finger for a transplant. He showed up several times with magazines that featured my accomplishments as a climber. He wanted to convince the doctors to take special care with me. That my hands were my livelihood and climbing was my life. I knew that part of his identity was tied to mine as a climber, but I lay there humbled and awed by the lengths he was willing to go for me.

He wasn't alone in expressing his support and concern and love. Beth's mom was like a hawk soaring above the hospital, swooping down any time she spotted my doctors. Given what she'd experienced with her husband's cancer treatment, she knew her way around a hospital. Everyone in my family asked countless questions and urged my doctors to do their very best for me. And, of course, Beth remained steadfast in every possible way. She would lie in bed with me, stroking my hair and telling me how much she loved me. She read to me, helped me eat what little I could stomach, and spent nearly as much time in that hospital room as I did.

My mom gracefully retreated into the background. She saw that I was well cared for, and another voice in the chorus would only get lost or prove irritating. Once again, I felt that silent connection between us, the energy she was sending me.

Still there were those nights, those doubts, the wondering if I was letting Beth down and ending my father's dreams for me. I couldn't wait for sleep to overtake me, to ease the pressure of the expectations and obligations that I imposed on myself.

Two days after removing the faltering reattached length of my finger, the doctors sent me home. The index finger on my dominant left hand was now a throbbing stump, two-thirds of it missing. The skin was stitched around the bone, edges protruding like a tiny calzone. Looking at it nauseated me.

———

Beth set about finding me the best physical therapist. I couldn't do any more damage, and to mitigate the risk of an overly sensitive stump I needed to condition the nerves. "Basically, beat the hell out of it," the therapist said. She gave me a set of nerve retraining and desensitizing exercises and told me to do them each day for an hour. I did three. One was to reaccustom me to temperature. Hot water, cold water, repeat. Then texture, running my finger through different substances. First rice, then lentils, then dry macaroni, then sharp star-shaped pasta, getting progressively more aggressive as I went. I would beat on the stump with the eraser end of a pencil. Next up: dexterity. We'd dump a jar of pennies on the carpet and I had to pick them up one by one with my nub and thumb or other digit. I focused on every penny, trying, fumbling, flailing but not quitting until my brain synchronized the nerves and muscles to perform these fine movements with my new and different finger. And then, I iced it incessantly.

Beth drew up a schedule and directed my training, charting my progress and instructing me on which exercises to do in which sequence for how long, on which days. But the most powerful support she offered was her belief in me. Never for a second did she doubt my ability to recover. She would look me straight in the eye and say with tearful but stern conviction, "You are going to do this."

Beth nursed me back to health. Deep down I had always wondered if she truly loved me, or if she just needed me after Kyrgyzstan. Now I knew. She cared for me when I needed her, and I felt her love.

In time, I realized my mind was the only thing holding me back. Not long after my release, I started training again. My dad welded up a finger-strengthening machine and I used it constantly. Eventually I outgrew the capacity of Dad's homemade contraption and he had to weld wings onto the sides of it to hold more weights. I did pinch-strength training by gripping stacked weight plates. I went for runs in the snow, figuring extra blood flow would enhance the healing. My energy soared. I felt my power returning. Training in my parents' dingy garage, my inner fire raged while the winter winds raced down from the Continental Divide.

For a long time I dropped things, mostly smaller items like car keys. My hand was sore but I also suffered from phantom pains. The tip of my finger itched even though it wasn't there. I forgot about the finger at awkward times. Weird things would happen, like I'd get in an elevator and someone else would enter.

"Which floor?" I'd ask.

"Four."

I'd reach out, press four, and wait for the elevator to move. Nothing. The person would stare at me. I'd return a polite smile. He'd raise his eyebrows. Smile. *Shit!* It would hit me. Two inches short of the button, half a phantom finger.

When I started climbing again, I felt a surprising amount of exhilaration. My focus and direction were crystal clear. I realized that it wouldn't help to dwell on what went wrong. I told myself that pain is growth. That the trauma would enhance my focus. My ability to quickly shrug off exhaustion surprised me. I assumed that no one outside of my family truly expected me to make a full comeback, an idea I found strangely liberating.

Three weeks after my release from the hospital, I entered a local bouldering competition. My hand still felt weak but I climbed passionately and surprised myself by placing third. I keep working.

I noticed that, while climbing, at first I grabbed all of the holds as if I still had my finger. The tendons in my palm needed to readjust, and climbing ballooned it with inflammation. I had to learn to correctly position my nub to prevent the swelling. Over time, this pushed me more in the direction of vertical, highly technical, cerebral climbing—like on El Capitan. Still, I knew I had to address my weaknesses. Hard sport routes, which are usually much steeper than traditional climbs, were a far greater problem with a missing finger.

In early spring, to measure my progress I began repeating local sport climbs that I had developed in earlier years. I needed to learn to climb with my entire being, rather than relying so much on finger strength. To shift my weight more to my feet, to use core strength to keep me close to the wall so I could use my legs and spare my arms, to refine my technique so that I wasn't only pulling for upward progress. Just three months after leaving the hospital I reclimbed Grand Ole Opry, a local route rated 5.14b. Through the crux sequence, I rocked my foot onto a minuscule hold and turned my hip just a few degrees, perfectly positioning my body to take advantage of the power in my legs instead of pulling hard with a finger I no longer had. I was held to the wall by mere millimeters of skin and rubber, and yet the moves flowed together, feeling even easier and more natural than when I'd done them years earlier.

But those were small routes. I needed to work harder, think better, adapt myself for the rigors of big walls.

I also thought of my new and different finger as a fresh start. Early on I easily exceeded my own, and what I assumed to be others', expectations about my ability to climb with a severed digit. I loved the feeling of progress. I had enjoyed the problem-solving aspect of climbing for my whole career; now I had a new problem to face. For example, pinch holds were exceptionally difficult, so I compensated by strengthening my shoulders—now, rather than pinching holds, I could place my fingers on the inside of the hold and push outward with great force. The loss of the finger wasn't as crippling as it might have seemed to outsiders because often on the harder climbs, the holds are too small to grab with all four fingers anyway. I excelled on these smaller holds—the two- or three-finger holds—because that's all I had on my left hand. I'd always thought of vertical climbing as a kind of dance, while overhanging climbing is more of a wrestling match. Strength is relatively easy to build, and many climbers rely on it to compensate for deficiencies in skill. Due to my injury and my general inclination, I focused more and more on technique. I began to think of myself even more as a cerebral climber.

At a remote, beautiful cliff in western Colorado called the Fortress of Solitude, the year before Kyrgyzstan, I had established a 5.14d route named Kryptonite. At the time it was the hardest sport climb in the country. A hundred feet to its right I'd started working on an even harder route, which I was calling Flex Luthor, a play on the name of Superman's archenemy. The spectacular line traces its way up 120 feet of wildly overhanging limestone. It could certainly take the informal title of the hardest single pitch in the

United States, but was not the sort of climb favorable to the new me. Flex Luthor became one of my goals.

My primary goal, however, was to return to the first route I had freed on El Cap—the Salathé Wall—and try to free it in a day. The same goal I'd failed on with Hans Florine the previous autumn, before chopping off my finger. The only person to have freed El Cap in a day was Lynn Hill on the Nose. A year after her visionary four-day first free ascent of the route, she had returned and upped the ante in just twenty-three hours.

I couldn't get it out of my head. The way I saw it, if I could free the Salathé in a day, I would prove to myself that I still had what it took.

Stars shimmered in the Yosemite sky as Beth flaked the rope below the first pitch of the Salathé Wall. It was one o'clock in the morning, a day shy of six months since I'd lost my finger. Beth had been by my side every moment.

The moon had yet to rise. I tied in, tightened the laces on my rock shoes, and chalked my hands.

"Knot good?" Beth asked.

I shined my headlamp down to my figure-eight tie-in knot. "Yup."

"C'mon, Tommy, try hard," she said. *Try hard.*

I concentrated on relaxing as much as possible. The darkness narrowed my focus to the beam of my light, and I watched with detachment as startled silverfish scurried out of the cracks. I thought of nothing but the next move. Even my breathing was slow.

By the time dawn glowed on the horizon, we were nearly halfway up. The sun hit the wall, warming us like a familiar old friend. The opening eighteen pitches floated by. I continued for a few more hours until we reached a comfortable ledge, then decided to wait out the midday heat. I lay on the ledge, my head on Beth's lap. She put her hand on my forehead and whispered, "You can do this, baby." I tried not to think about what waited above and dozed off for a couple of hours.

A cool breeze woke me from my nap. I rubbed my eyes, took a deep breath, and stared upward, tracing the line through the crux headwall. The valley had come to life. I could see cars on the road and people lounging in the grass of El Cap meadow, watching the climbers.

The architecture of this portion of El Capitan looked as immaculate as when I'd first been there with my dad five years earlier. Cracks and corners, golden and pristine, soared into the sky. The headwall begins with a twenty-foot roof and then continues, gently overhanging, up a flawless crack that gets progressively thinner, steeper, and more strenuous the higher it goes. The difficulty builds to a crescendo with a few powerful, boulder-problem-like moves that end with a lunge to a perfect pinch hold.

Excitement welled in my chest. I was rested and well hydrated. I could see a fixed sling flapping like a flag. The conditions were perfect. I knew I had to move smoothly, and rely on emotion only if I needed an extra push. I lazily climbed the initial corner and out the headwall roof. Atop the pitch, the wind howled. Loops of rope blew and tangled into knots as Beth ju-mared toward the belay. When she arrived, I restacked the rope in tiny coils and tried to calm my nerves. The crux pitch was next. I racked the gear on my harness in the order I would need it and rehearsed the moves in my head. Then I started climbing.

I took long, slow, deep breaths. I thought about precision and wiggled my fingers deep in the crack. Near the end of the pitch, as my forearms fatigued, I reached a section of insecure, flaring hand jams. I positioned my feet and relaxed until barely enough tension held me to the rock. Anything less and I'd sail through space. I closed my eyes and rested for several breaths.

On my previous attempt I had gotten desperately pumped here and was unable to recover. This time was different. I was different. I knew what not to do and what to do. I'd started earlier in the day. I'd climbed more slowly. I'd conserved my energy for the crux pitches at the top.

Above, the crack pinched down to the width of a finger, while flaring outward, making for insecure jams. With one hand I removed the remaining gear off my harness and clipped it to a cam to reduce my weight. *Breathe, breathe.* Beth's encouraging voice rose up from the belay, that same voice from so many climbs and from every rep in rehab. I thought about my time in the hospital. *Exhale, relax.* I had been so weak. *Just breathe, calm. . . .*

Now I was here, near the top of El Cap, only fifteen feet from realizing a goal that had seemed distant, impossible. I exploded into the section above, shoving my fingertips hard into the thin crack. Stepping my feet high onto clusters of jagged crystals, I placed no gear and flew through the boulder problem, lunging and latching onto the final hold with a scream. I raced up the easy climbing that remained, anchored myself, and fixed the rope. And then I sat, panting, smiling, but not moving as the wind blew through my hair and across my face. I stared at the grand expanse of the Sierra Nevada.

When Beth arrived she smiled warmly, then leaned over and wrapped her arms around me. The craziest thing was, the climb had almost felt easy.

CHAPTER EIGHT

I crack open the window and feel the warm California air on my left hand. I let it dangle outside the van. I turn right onto California's Highway 120, a freshly repaved black ribbon of tarmac that rolls through the high desert. A few miles on, we rise and fall over a series of whoop-de-doos, feeling more like we're on a carnival ride than a public road.

I look over at Beth. She's curled up in the passenger seat, forming a neat comma of nylon and fleece. Her ability to sleep as we curve and dip is a by-product of many nights on a portaledge. Her trust in me—the trust we have in each other—amazes me. I don't want to disturb her, so I drive without the radio on. The sun rises more fully behind us and my mind drifts, just like my hand in the currents of the wind. Dust devils blow across the surface of Mono Lake to my north and my mind flashes to a moment from my childhood.

I am nine and my dad and I are a few miles into a ski-touring adventure. It's snot-freezing cold.

The wind howls, the lodgepole pines bend and twist. We reach Mills Lake. Spindrift tornadoes skim along the frozen surface. We skirt the snow-ice junction. Through a break in the trees a blast of wind lifts me onto the lake's surface. I weigh maybe forty-five pounds and now I'm a forty-five-pound iceboat skimming on my skis across the lake. I cant my legs and feet, hoping the steel edges of my skis will slow me. I dig the plastic points of my poles into the hard surface. I pick up speed. I'm momentarily seized by fear. A moment later, I back off the edges and surrender to the wind. I spread my arms out, increasing the sail effect of my slender body. Sheer joy and the pleasure of speed and *freedom move through me. Moments pass until I slide gently into a snowbank on the opposite side of the lake.*

I stand there grinning and giddy. From across the lake, I hear my father calling me, "Tommy!" I wave to signal that I'm okay. A moment later, I see his bulky figure shift and he heads toward me. The wind catches him as well, the ice is nearly frictionless and he careers toward me, laughing and hooting.

I look again at Beth, still curled in a ball on the passenger seat. My mind carries me to our future. Dazzling sunlight flares in my eyes and then my vision clears. A little boy run-stumbles toward a rough-hewn playground set. He pats the seat of a swing then thinks better of it. He looks back, eyes wide, his face slit by an even wider grin, his brown-blond curls backlighted and haloing his head. He toddles toward the jungle gym and climbs its ladder. Without a pause, he jumps for the first handhold, a tree branch doweled in a row with others. He kicks his legs and goes hand for hand forward, giggling and giddy. I walk toward him, offer to help him down. "No, Daddy, me do," he says. Beth comes striding toward us, a beribboned little girl on her hip.

"The apple doesn't fall very far from the tree," she says.

"This guy doesn't fall at all," I reply.

Past the dips, the road levels out. We're hours from Yosemite, hours from our home away from home. I accelerate, eager to get to that bright future, eager to make it real.

I don't know why it took me so long to ask Beth to marry me. She was my first serious girlfriend, and maybe my insecure nature didn't allow me to believe that she loved me for who I was. Over time, however, I saw that our bond was too tight to break, and I finally proposed. Eight months later, on an unseasonably warm spring day in 2003, we wed in her parents' backyard. As she walked down the aisle of green grass, I had no doubt in my mind that I would be with this woman for the rest of my days.

In terms of the passion for climbing we shared, Beth was slowly beginning to feel more comfortable being in the public eye again. When she was on, she was nearly unstoppable. In 2002 she'd made a free ascent of a route in Yosemite called the Phoenix, probably the hardest-ever onsite (climbing the route clean, first go, without any prior inspection or knowledge of the moves; the purest form of ascent) of a traditionally protected crack climb by a woman ever. Then she became the second person, male or female, to climb a 5.14 route called Sarchasm that I'd established at 12,000 feet in elevation in Rocky Mountain National Park.

As for me, just over a year after my accident I'd returned to that project I thought I'd never have a chance to do with a missing finger—Flex Luthor—and pulled it off. It's widely considered America's first 5.15, though nobody's successfully repeated it to confirm the grade. Today, some of the younger climbers who've attempted it think that I may not have rated it high enough. That's all conjecture, of course, until someone else climbs it. For me it was less about climbing a big number grade and more about quantifying that I'd made a full comeback from the finger injury.

Sending Flex Luthor, though only a sport climb, solidified my desire for a bigger form of adventure. Part of the appeal was that the route was not your traditional roadside sport climb. To get to its location we had to hike through knee-deep snow in January's subzero temperatures. The climb itself sits in a large limestone depression that acts as a naturally occurring solar oven in the winter. The ambient temperature inside the cave is often forty degrees warmer than the exterior. Limestone tends to seep water, so as a result, at night giant icicles formed around the climb. At just about the time I arrived each day, the icicles crashed down.

The climbing was very steep and physical—more of the wrestling type than the dancing type. Powerful boulder problems separated by strenuous rests that required me to jam my knee in overhanging corners to hang upside down. Different from the kind of climbing I later became known for, but no matter.

We were back.

It seemed time to return to more faraway journeys together, so in the summer of 2003 we traveled to a remote group of rock towers in Canada's Northwest Territories called the Cirque of the Unclimbables. Beth's sponsor, The

North Face, had suggested the trip and she agreed. I took her choosing to venture to such a remote climb as hugely positive. We chartered a floatplane and flew for hours through desolate, bear-infested wilderness to a small lake. Then a helicopter shuttled us to a blissful meadow, well above tree line and surrounded by needlelike spires. We set up our tent beneath a house-sized boulder, and for two weeks storms raged. We huddled inside, mostly sleeping and playing cards, as the rain came down in sheets.

Some other climbing teams had come to the same spot. One of the guys had discovered a sack of flour in an ammo can, stashed and abandoned beneath the edge of a boulder by a previous climbing team. We baked bread and played Scrabble. When the rain fell at its heaviest, the mountains would come alive. Earth-trembling rock falls cascaded down around us. We'd leap up from the camp stove or Scrabble board and gawk at the awesome spectacle.

I immensely enjoyed the primal nature. In my mind we were cavemen and women (except we weren't scratching out our Scrabble words on the walls) and the rain was like a version of a saber-toothed tiger trapping us inside. When we weren't hanging out, Beth and I stayed in our tent, reading. I enjoyed the forced hibernation, but Beth didn't see our adventure as fun. She was understandably cold, tired, and scared. Perhaps she was just going stir-crazy from the inactivity. I later realized that being in such a remote and wild place had stirred up memories of Kyrgyzstan.

On our fifteenth day a patch of blue sky opened, and we hurried to the base of a cathedral-like 2,000-foot formation called the Lotus Flower Tower. The rock seemed sent from the heavens, stretching toward the sky. I wanted to scream with joy. Beth barely spoke.

After the climb we called the floatplane pilot on a satellite phone, then loaded all of our remaining gear into two massive packs and started hiking back to the lake. If we could avoid the helicopter shuttle, we would save a thousand dollars. Beth looked like a third-world child laborer, hunched under her bulging backpack, but she toughed it out. For half a day we balanced across loose scree and battled through thick brush.

By the time we made it to the lake, Beth had a sharp pain in the ball of her foot. A doctor's visit when we got home revealed that she had broken a sesamoid bone, a small bone with poor blood supply that is notoriously slow to heal.

Her injury pulled Beth away from the one thing that brought her contentment: climbing. When she couldn't climb her view of our lives darkened. She worried incessantly about the future. Professional climbing has a limited life span. What would we do when our fingers and bodies no longer had their youthful strength, when we were no longer of use to our sponsors? What would happen when we could no longer keep pace with the up-and-coming generation? To be injured at age twenty-three, just when she was regaining her climbing prowess, was a huge setback.

I tried to buoy her with genuine enthusiasm. I knew I was being a bit like my dad, but that was the only way I knew to approach such things. I'd seen him do the same with my mom and my sister and me, but what the hell? We were alive and had the ultimate freedom. We got paid to spend our time playing in the most beautiful places in the world. We were deeply in love.

Our partnership had gained some notoriety in our little world. People started calling us the First Couple of Climbing. As a result of the publicity, we got increased corporate sponsorship. Beth recognized that when she was out of commission I could pull the weight for the team. Becoming the best climber I could be had become more than a selfish pursuit. We wanted kids someday, and the plan was for me to eventually become the primary breadwinner. I figured I'd better perfect my craft. After all, it was the only thing I was good at.

By early 2004, Beth's foot had still refused to heal. She sat out the spring climbing season and stayed with her family in Davis. I spent a month alone in Yosemite working to free climb another El Cap aid route called the Dihedral Wall. On this one the cracks in the dihedrals (corners formed by rock walls) were flaring and thin, often petering out completely. Tiny face holds sometimes appeared outside the closed-down cracks, offering the only chance for upward progress. As my climbing ability improved I was venturing onto more and more unlikely terrain, driven by the allure of routes that had once seemed impossible.

I would start each day at 5:00 a.m., attach myself to my self-belay system, climb from the ground to the end of the last hard pitch, 1,800 feet up, then rappel back to the ground by noon, eat lunch, and boulder till dark. I pummeled myself into such blissful exhaustion that sometimes, as the sun set, I fell asleep while talking to Beth on the phone. I spent each day alone amid the arc of sunlight and shadow, the sweep of stone and the dive of swallows. The Dihedral Wall was the first time on El Cap that I truly felt as though I had faced my physical limitations. I climbed alone and unwatched, privately sensing that I could be pushing big wall free climbing farther than it had ever been pushed. I combined everything I'd learned and all I'd trained my body to do. I loved living in my own little secret world. My body responded to my commands as never before; I kept nudging my limits, hour after hour, day after day, requiring—*demanding*—that my body accept less sleep, food, and water. Each night I slept soundly, drifting off with a satisfied smile, pleased and surprised at just how little and how much my body could take. Working to unlock the incredibly difficult sequences, making incremental progress, I climbed until my toenails fell off and the skin flaked from my fingers. I came to love the silence, and began to embrace the hunger for progression that was the base on which nearly everything in my life had been built.

My heart ached for Beth, yet when climbing I felt freed from the weight of her darkness and her worry. My energy level rose, my view of the world brightened. I felt alive. El Capitan had once again become my dearest friend.

One day in the valley I ran into a great climber named Adam Stack. We went way back—my dad, his middle school gym teacher, had gotten Adam into climbing. He was fresh off a free ascent of the Salathé, and I invited him to join me on the Dihedral Wall. From the outside, big wall climbing seems like a serious endeavor. And yes, you have to learn to negotiate the risks. But climbers are ultimately little more than overgrown kids playing on nature's grandest jungle gyms. The ability to laugh through the good and the bad is an essential quality in a first-rate partner.

Adam joked incessantly. He declared that the Homestead Act of 1862 meant that he had "squatter's rights" to any place where he spent enough time. I'd be ready to climb, and notice a rare stretch of silence. I'd glance over and see Adam squatting on a tiny ledge, a huge grin on his face. "Dude!" I'd say. "You do NOT own that piece of granite. Get your butt over here and put me on belay!" Every time Adam linked together a hard sequence or freed a section, he'd say, "Do you smell something? Oh yeah, I'm the shit!"

I wanted Beth to experience this playful back-and-forth, too, a world of lightness and beauty. Yet it was starting to feel as if we were two very different people.

Every week I'd return to Davis to spend a few days with Beth. She wondered how I could look at life with such hope while she saw mostly pain and darkness. Despite our differences and her injury, she wanted to support me. "I love being up there with you," she said. In May 2004 I felt ready to attempt a continuous ground-up push on the Dihedral Wall. I'd have to pull it all together and free climb the twenty-five-pitch route from bottom to top. If there was one tiny section I couldn't free, I'd fail.

The rules of the game might seem arbitrary to an outside observer. No governing body oversees big wall free climbing, or indeed any other form of outdoor climbing. The rules, such as they are, are established by consensus within the community. The people pushing the boundaries and establishing the hardest routes in a particular era define what constitutes a successful ascent. On the Dihedral Wall, my rehearsals mirrored the process of working a sport route: You can aid climb through sections and practice the moves all you want, and you can try a pitch again if you fall. But in order for the eventual ascent to be valid, you have to climb each pitch completely free, without falls (though you can try a pitch repeatedly until you get it, before moving on to the next), in one sequential effort, starting on the ground and ending on the summit.

Adam insisted on helping but he had only two days free. Beth figured that a big mountain boot would make an adequate replacement for the walking cast her doctor had prescribed. Both of them would belay and follow behind on jumars.

I started the route strong, climbing well. Yet as I moved into the harder terrain, my body began to tremble under the strain. The heart of the route, culminating nearly 1,800 feet up, involved ten straight pitches of 5.13 and 5.14. As the difficulty increased, I felt as if I was trying to pry open an increasingly heavy door. I constantly teetered on an invisible line between success and failure. Adam's and Beth's voices went hoarse from urging me on. I took repeated falls on most of the harder pitches, sometimes huge ones, each time lowering to the anchor, pulling the rope, resting, and trying again. It was like rehearsing a high-level gymnastic routine over, and over, and over again, until you got it right. And then there's another one, just as hard, rising above. And another after that, and after that. At night on the portaledge my body trembled in pain, and doubt crept into my mind. Beth would massage my tired muscles while Adam rambled on about riding grizzly bears into base camp and all manner of hilarious antics. Love and laughter, laughter and love. The ultimate combination.

By the third day, Adam headed down. I had freed the first two-thirds of the wall, and only one desperate pitch remained—the final ten to the top were comparatively easy. But my energy had waned. I was ready to stop for the day, to rest until morning. Suddenly our radio crackled. "Nice job, dude!" It was Adam. He'd been watching through binoculars from the meadow below. He wasn't alone. "I've got a whole crowd of people down here waiting for you to send the last hard pitch!"

The solitary nature of the challenge is one of the things that draws me to big wall free climbing. You exist in a different world, without that group energy you get cragging. Except for this time. I managed a laugh, closed my eyes for a moment, and racked-up. Exhale. *It is almost over. One more.* As I started climbing, my whole body quivered with pain and fatigue. I had been concentrating for three days straight and my mind was tired. I climbed higher, moving from a shallow groove to a small layback crack that marked the last ten feet of hard climbing. I paused at a strenuous stance, gritted my teeth a little harder, then willed my feet to stick and started pulling. If I fell here, a fixed pin that was at least twenty years old, and driven into a rotten flare, would, I hoped, catch me. I pressed my bloody, swollen fingertips against a tiny sidepull and smeared my feet into a glassy dish. Just as my fingertips reached the next hold, my foot slipped. Panicking, I desperately re-smeared my foot and shot my hand into a bomber jam above. The remaining thirty feet of the pitch was the most carefully climbed 5.11 I have ever done. When I reached the ledge I heard faint cheers from below. I turned to face the crowd, threw my hands in the air, and screamed as loud as I could.

When Beth and I first met, she had one aspiration above all else: to free climb the Nose on El Capitan. In the first months of our relationship that dream fueled much of her drive. Then Kyrgyzstan drained her ambition for the climb.

But over the following year, her days of depression and darkness seemed to be slowly coming to a close. Her injured foot was healing, and her motivation returned with a vengeance. I hoped that Beth's decision to return to big walls symbolized the end of an era of fear. And I'd be lying if I didn't acknowledge my desire for her to re-embrace big-route climbing. She didn't like my leaving and I didn't want to stop big wall climbing. This way, we could both get what we wanted.

As I supported Beth's training for the Nose, I, too, had a goal that I kept largely to myself. The next step on El Cap would be to free climb two routes in a single day, a seemingly absurd proposition. People had theorized that it would require next-level tactics, like BASE jumping from the top to save time. But I'd worked it out in my head. If I could free the Nose in eleven hours, I could run down in an hour, then climb another free route called the Free Rider, also in eleven hours. That would leave an hour to spare before hitting the twenty-four-hour mark.

Only Lynn Hill had freed the Nose in a day. I secretly schemed, rarely mentioning my idea, telling Beth that I simply wanted to see how strong I could get. I started with a power base: three weeks of the hardest boulder problems in Rocky Mountain National Park. Then I added high-end sport climbing to my routine, climbing a half-dozen pitches a day, between 5.12 and 5.14. I began endurance training, too. Every few weeks I piled on a new element. Climbing, weight lifting, campus board training, and, near the end of summer, three-hour bike rides, gaining 4,000 vertical feet and topping out at 12,000 feet in elevation. My training days often lasted fourteen hours. My goal was to enhance my stamina, my capacity for taking abuse, and my overall toughness.

By the time we went to Yosemite for the fall 2005 season, Beth was climbing up a storm, and I was in the best shape of my life.

The warmth of the sleeping bag made me linger. I lay lazily on a shelf of clean gravel beneath branches of an ancient cedar tree, surrounded by fragrant manzanita bushes. A few feet to the south lay slabs of perfect white granite, the exposed summit of El Capitan. The wind was calm. The clank of a cook pot and the hum of a butane stove made the only sounds. I watched Beth's little bowed legs scurry about, readying our gear for the day. She came over, handed me a cup of hot coffee, slipped into her sleeping bag, and leaned into me, resting her head on my shoulder.

"Good morning, love, did you sleep well?" she said, pulling her sleeping bag tight under her chin.

"I did," I replied. "Aren't you excited to get this project under way?"

For ten minutes we watched the sun crest the horizon. For the moment, nothing was out of place.

We planned to lower ropes from the top of the wall, and rappel in to practice the crux upper sections of the Nose, bettering our skills with each rehearsal. After a while we put on our harnesses, then I tied the end of a six-hundred-foot rope to a tree and walked to the edge. I looked at Beth, standing a few feet above. She smiled.

I eased over the lip. A cold breath of air rushed upward from the valley below, making me shiver. Within seconds the wall in front of me was too far away to touch. I spun in a slow circle, looking down 3,000 feet to the valley floor. The exposure had become comfortable, like mounting a fast motorcycle and then taking it for a slow spin. The feelings of fear had passed years ago, replaced by only a twinge of excitement. High on the walls is my rightful place in this world.

Fifteen minutes later I looked down to see a flat, ten-by-ten-by-ten-foot triangular ledge. Two men sat upright in their sleeping bags, staring out. As I got closer, one of them looked up.

In the nearly fifty years since its first ascent, the Nose had become the most sought-after big wall climb in the world. It's a striking, historic line with perfect rock. And although it's nearly impossible to free climb, the aid climbing is relatively straightforward. During the high season there might be as many as ten parties attempting the route at any given time.

As the crowds have increased on the wall, a micro-community has emerged. People from around the globe come to El Cap to live their dreams, bonded through a shared love of climbing. It's colorful and a bit nutty, with people doing drugs, playing music, having sex. There is life and death and countless stories of close calls. The physical and psychological intensity of a big wall tends to bring out either the best or the worst in people.

"G'day, mate," the guy said.

"You don't mind if we have a go at free climbing this section while you guys get ready, do you?" I asked, as I joined them on the triangular ledge.

"Free climbing?!"

"Well, trying."

"Not at all, mate, I'd love to see that. Is that a sheila with you?"

"Yeah," I said. "She's my wife."

"Goodonya, bringin' your wife up here."

A few minutes later Beth joined us on the ledge. She was all bubbles and giggles. "Did you guys have a good night's sleep?" she asked. She always looks as if she just got out of the shower. Something about the texture of her skin, the silky nature of her hair, the way she doesn't produce body odor.

When she turned to anchor herself in, one of the Aussies patted down his hair. Large yellow crumbs lined his tear ducts. Swollen red fingertips shined like beacons from his cut-off leather gloves, which he'd obviously been too tired to remove before falling asleep. They were on day four of their aid ascent of the route.

Beth slipped on her tiny climbing shoes and started tiptoeing up the rock above. She moved gracefully between two cracks, silently pressing each foot into the grain of the rock, daintily slotting her hands into the openings. After eighty feet she reached a spot where the cracks end. She made a full arm reach to a shallow groove, pulled herself in, and started inching her way higher. Her arms and legs pushed in bizarre contortions, her limbs weaving themselves in and out of one another with rhythmic precision. It was like watching a spider climb a piece of glass as she pushed into opposing walls, inching her way up a nearly holdless ninety-degree corner.

The two Aussies stared up, mouths agape, as if they had just seen an angel. "I can't imagine how you free climb up here," one of them told me, shaking his head. "I can barely get out of my sleeping bag."

For the next hour Beth climbed up and down, trying to commit the subtleties of each move to memory. She was on the Changing Corners, the hardest pitch of the climb. She would climb a few feet, hang on the rope, lean her face close to the rock, run her palm over the surface. As if reading braille, she was looking for the rough spots where climbing shoe rubber would stick ever so slightly better. She would mark those sections with dots of gymnastic chalk and map out a sequence, like a puzzle with the inter-locking pieces of her body and the undulations of the rock. And then she'd try again.

I chatted with the Aussies. "How's it been?" I asked.

"Oh, mate," one said, shaking his head. "Such a bitch." On their second day they'd caught up to a team of Irish climbers, but somehow their ropes had gotten entangled. The Irish guys' haul line was running right over the Aussies' climbing rope, sawing into it as the Irish hauled their bags while the second Aussie was ascending the rope.

They paused so as to not cut the rope, but at the belay the four exchanged harsh words. One of the Aussies unclipped the Irish team's haul bag and threatened to toss it off the wall. By the time they got climbing again the day was half over. The wind kicked up, tangling everyone's ropes into knots, add-ing to both teams' frustrations. The Aussies had gone ahead, and late in the day one of them had to defecate. While hanging in a harness in high winds, he held a brown paper bag below his butt (a standard protocol; you deposit the bag in a "poop tube" that you empty upon getting down). Just as the wind abated, one of his turds missed the bag completely, taking a spectacular two-hundred-foot free fall and splatting squarely onto the Irish team's haul bag.

Both teams spent a sleepless night hanging upright in their harnesses. The next day, they continued up in tandem, reaching a small ledge halfway up the wall by nightfall. As a peace offering the Irish pulled out a bottle of whiskey, and the four of them got drunk and howled at the moon. The two teams had merged into one. By the time we saw the Aussies, on their fourth day, they were still six hundred feet from the top. They were basically out of food and had less than a gallon of water.

"So what happened to the Irish guys?" I asked.

"Oh, they're sleeping on a ledge a hundred feet below." As he said this, the other Aussie peeked over the edge and shouted down. "Hey, you fuckers! Wakey, wakey, hands off snakie!"

Over the past four days these previous strangers had nearly killed each other, shat on each other, gotten drunk together, suffered together, and were now recounting stories like long-lost buddies in the pub, drunk on the humor of their adventures.

For the next month we mostly lived out of our little camp atop El Cap. Each day we rappelled down and worked on sections of the climb. Every third day we rested. We'd hike through magnificent forests of giant sugar pines, cedars, and redwoods, their trunks covered in fluorescent green moss. Shafts of light penetrated the high canopy and reflected off the small river that disappeared a quarter-mile downstream over the tallest single-drop waterfall in North America, Ribbon Falls. We would bathe in the ice-cold waters, giggling and splashing each other, goosebumps rising from our skin. We'd note evidence of bears hiding in the woods, see their footprints and their steaming fresh scat alongside the riverbank.

Eventually the pieces seemed to be in place, so we returned to the valley floor and made preparations for a four-day free attempt. We had stashed a camp halfway up the climb. Our first day would be a big one. We set off at 1:00 a.m. under a nearly full moon. Nighttime on El Cap brings a calm not felt during the day, when noise from the traffic reverberates and thermals create wind. At night you can nearly whisper to each other from a hundred feet away. At the belays, I would switch off my headlamp and the world would expand into a dreamscape. The giant walls cast eerie shadows across the valley floor and created a half-sky view of the stars. The western horizon glowed faintly from the millions of buildings and cars in San Francisco. An hour before daybreak the moon dropped and we continued to climb in the pitch black. By the time full daylight arrived we were already a thousand feet up the wall.

Our systems were firing, and we climbed quickly. I could feel a building energy and momentum. But at the end of the sixteenth pitch I caught Beth grimacing.

"Are you all right?"

"I'm okay."

Despite all of the time she'd taken off, the broken bone in her foot hadn't fully healed. The doctor had told us that surgery was an option, but could create problems down the road. Pain had become a constant part of her life. Beth climbed tentatively, yet still freed the last few pitches to our stashed camp.

We put up our portaledge and settled in. I removed Beth's shoe and sock and gently massaged her foot. An early fall wind blew, chilling my spine. I slipped on a wool cap and a jacket.

As I rubbed her foot I wondered. *What if everything I do is built on my own selfish need to be loved by her, my insecure need to be cherished? If her happiness is dependent on my being there for her, and my happiness is dependent on her loving me, is that real love? And if she fails on this climb, will she spiral into depression? No, that won't happen. If she succeeds she will be happy. And so will I.*

The next morning the pain in her foot had mostly subsided. Or so she said. Immediately overhead was the Great Roof, one of the most iconic and intimidating pitches in the world. For a decade this section of the route had shut down every climber who attempted to lead it free, except for Lynn Hill.

A massive ceiling of stone, extending nearly twenty feet horizontally from the vertical face of the Nose, the Great Roof is a staggeringly beautiful feature. From below, it sticks out like the overhanging eave of a house. Only this roof is 1,800 feet in the air. At some point in time, a large section of rock below the roof must have sheared clean off, leaving that flat, nearly horizontal ceiling, with a nearly featureless surface beneath. Featureless aside from a single weakness: A 150-foot-long crack runs up the wall and arches overhead, continuing into the underside of the Great Roof. To climb it, you first power up the vertical crack, reasonable climbing, until arching into the horizontal section, where the crack pinches down into only a tiny seam, with nothing but slippery dime-width edges for feet.

Beth started up the pitch. I noticed her trying to climb on the outside of her foot, to avoid flexing her big toe in a way that caused pain. And as she climbed I sensed a slight unraveling. I chewed on my fingernails. I was desperately afraid of what would happen if she came crashing down. I wanted this so badly for her. About two-thirds of the way across she slipped off and sailed through the air, the rope catching her.

She was silent as I lowered her back to the anchor. She clipped herself in and untied. "Just pull the rope and put me back on belay." Next try, she sent the Great Roof clean, no falls, and with so much joy that I felt it on the other end of the rope.

Above, we continued up perfect steep cracks, making for efficient progress to a large bivvy ledge. We planned to rest there for much of the next day, in preparation for the hard climbing that remained.

Although my primary focus was supporting Beth, my own aspirations lingered in my mind. When, six months earlier, I had mentioned to her my goal of the double—freeing the Nose and Free Rider in a day—I downplayed it, not wanting to distract her. During my exhaustive training, as well as on the wall with Beth, I daydreamed about ways to bring it closer to reality. By the end of our rest day on the ledge, ambition overwhelmed me.

"Hey, baby, do you mind if I give a go at the Changing Corners pitch tonight?" I said. "That way you can have the cool morning hours tomorrow to yourself."

The Great Roof and the Changing Corners are the two cruxes of the route. They're the ones that shut down even elite free climbers. You need cool conditions so your shoe rubber sticks optimally and doesn't roll off the granite. It's all the more essential in the Changing Corners, since there is nothing to pull on. You climb partway up one corner that is absolutely blank

146

for handholds, then, as that corner disappears into the smooth wall above, you continue by transferring to your right, into an adjacent corner. It's all body position and pressing against each side of the corner, using opposing outward forces that you create with your palms and the friction of your climbing shoes, contorting your body to maintain a baffling sort of tension that magically holds you on.

Strength has nothing to do with it. The ability to do a hundred consecutive pull-ups does not help you one bit. The only thing that allows anybody to free the mystifying Changing Corners is technique and a prayer. It's Houdini climbing.

"Uh, okay, I guess," she said. I racked up the gear and she put me on belay. After two false starts, I tried again. Thirty minutes later it was over for me. The rest of the climbing to the top was comparatively easy. I'd let my ambition get the better of me, and unintentionally added pressure. Now it was all riding on Beth's shoulders.

I woke the next morning to Beth sitting upright in the corner of the portaledge, eyes closed, breaths deep and steady in the crisp morning air. When I tried to talk to her, her replies came in quick clips. I quietly prepared everything for the day, afraid to say anything but the essential. I was nervous. I couldn't imagine what Beth was feeling.

As the sun cast soft rays of light onto the towering pines far below, she started up. With each exhalation she made low guttural growls, like a steam engine starting its steady chug.

She climbed higher and the growls turned to heavy breaths. Over the past month as we'd practiced this pitch, she'd worked out all of the individual moves, but hadn't been able to link them together in the continuous manner required to free the pitch. Now, when it mattered most, she had to climb better than she ever had in her life. The sun crept ever closer; once it hit, all possibility would vanish on the glassy rock. She got to a tiny perch halfway up. Through creative body positioning she turned it into a rest stance. Sparrows swirled around, chasing each other like tiny fighter jets. Beth shifted her weight delicately back and forth for ten minutes, recovering, then pulled into the adjacent corner. She pushed her palms and fingers hard into the opposing walls, contorting her body into precise, awkward, and powerful positions. As she neared the end of the pitch her grunts became little screams. When she passed her previous high point her little screams became full kamikaze shouts. As she pulled the final hard moves tears welled in my eyes. Beth sat in the small stance at the end of the pitch, not saying anything for several minutes. Then she yelled, "Off belay!"

I scampered up the pitch as fast as I could and when I got to Beth tears were streaming down her face. It was as if someone had hit a five-year pressure release valve. "My foot hurts so badly," she said between sobs.

"You did it, baby, it's just hiking from here," I said, using climber lingo for easy rock. It was still elite level free climbing terrain, but for Beth, the equivalent of the proverbial walk in the woods.

I held her and stroked her back. But we didn't linger for long before continuing. Watching her climb was like watching a deer limping along after being clipped by a car. She had toughed it out as long as she could. Now her fear and pain came flooding out.

A few hours later we crested the top of the wall. Beth sat on the flat earth atop El Capitan, staring through glassy eyes.

I think Beth had hoped that free climbing the Nose would bring her happiness, that it would help her heal. She'd realized a dream from so many years earlier, when she'd hung that poster of Lynn Hill on her bedroom wall. But as she sat atop El Capitan, she was still the same person she had been when we started. Scared, hurt, searching for something more. We were both hoping for an epiphany, but none appeared.

"So, when do you want to climb the double?" she asked in a monotone.

I didn't know what to say. Perhaps more than most pursuits, climbing is self-glorifying and self-serving. As we ascend, we risk becoming our own gods. But I wanted this to be her moment, a time when happiness and contentment crystallized before her eyes. The sweet smell of pine drifted in the wind, invisible in the crystal-clear Sierra sky. We shouldn't be thinking about what comes next.

Regardless, I suppose my project of the double wasn't purely about realizing a dream, either. There was a growing paradox in our relationship, one that we had never discussed. My life felt richest when I was exploring my limits and embracing the unknown; Beth increasingly sought stability and consistency. It's an issue common to the climbing world, one that simultaneously builds and destroys romantic relationships. I didn't recognize it at the time, but part of me wanted to fill the growing hollowness inside, to provide a distraction from the knowledge that life with Beth would never be the fairy tale I had hoped for. I'm no different from most climber dudes, I suppose: I want the romance *and* the adventure.

"I guess I could try next week," I said, forcing a smile.

We just jumped into the next thing. We didn't celebrate or bask in a job well done. I think Beth felt that it was her turn to offer loyal support as I had for the past month. Climbing in rock shoes hurt her foot; jumaring in mountain boots was fine. As I shifted my focus from Beth back to my own goals, my excitement emerged.

Three days later I freed the Nose in twelve hours, leading every pitch. Just two days afterward I did the Free Rider in similar style, taking just under twelve hours. Four days after that I climbed them both, running back to the base in between routes, freeing 6,000 feet of El Capitan granite in a little over twenty-three hours. Another friend, Chris McNamara, also assisted me. By the end of this massive day my arms had gone numb. I was exhausted, developed mysterious headaches, and for the next month I couldn't straighten my left elbow.

Beth and I knew this was a shared success, even though the public acclaim for the double trumped her climb of the Nose. People saw the Nose–Free Rider linkup as a giant leap forward in its combination of difficulty and endurance. The recognition felt good, and the feat has yet to be repeated. Still, Beth never expressed a shred of jealousy that most of the notoriety fell on me.

Yet as satisfying as the double had been for me, it paled in comparison to the experience of climbing the Nose with Beth. The climb had been a lofty goal for us both, and we had done it as husband and wife. Together we had become stronger than we ever could have been individually. Part of our vision for the future included moving full time to Yosemite, and earlier in the year we'd pooled all of our money to purchase a piece of property just outside the park boundary. Now we could carve out some time to build our house.

But in the peaceful moments of exhaustion following our climbs on El Capitan that fall, I didn't ponder what came next. I just remember thinking that as long as Beth was with me, I could die a happy man.

CHAPTER NINE

Readying for the next rappel, I pull the ropes. They twist and tumble toward me, alternately joining and separating. Topher Donahue stands stock still on the little ledge for a moment, looking up, considering something. Vertical granite disappears into the glacier below.

It has been years since I tended fires and played Wild West with Topher's younger brother, Tobias. In a sense, the Donahue family and I are like these ropes, together yet traveling different routes that sometimes cross. Topher is eight years older than me and a highly regarded alpinist. When he called to ask me to join him on this trip to Patagonia I was both psyched and a little saddened. If things had been better, I wouldn't be here at all.

Topher stands and rubs his eyes and his face. He slips off his pack and reaches into the top zippered pocket. He holds up a clear vial for me to see. Spires, lakes, glaciers, and grasslands rise, fall, and spread in every direction.

"He was with us the whole time," Topher says of his father.

I had no idea this was part of our mission, but I'm glad it is. This was to be a father and son trip. But brain cancer, sinister and swift, took Mike Donahue only two months ago, at age fifty-nine. I can still hear his hearty laugh, see his huge grin and his squinted eyes in his frequent expressions of joy.

With a faint smile, Topher twists open the vial and shakes out his father's ashes. A tiny gray cloud swirls for an instant before the wind carries it away. Mike's relationship with nature ran deeper than that of anyone I have ever known, rooted like an old oak tree. He always talked about the seasons, the cyclical nature of life, the impermanence of "bad conditions" in the *mountains, and how if we accept nature's seeming indifference to our fate, we will find comfort and strength. I can only hope that I will carry with me the rest of my days some of his spirit, his abundant love of the mountains, his joyful embrace of whatever came his way, his recognition of his place in the universe.*

The bus rattled along the washboard road in the austral summer of early 2006, raising a cloud of dust that blew to the distant hills. I was twenty-seven, but in this enchanted landscape I felt like a child. Framed through the windshield were the mountains of Argentine Patagonia's Chaltén Massif, rising from the rolling pampas like towering monsters wearing white, fluffy hats. Everywhere else, lazily grazing sheep dotted the vast expanse of grasslands.

Despite twenty hours of travel, I couldn't sleep. We were almost there, to one of alpinism's most storied arenas, where the wind scours the landscape with unimaginable ferocity and even the easiest summits require sustained technical climbing. It was as if the gods had made this place as a playground for alpinists.

The only problem: I wasn't really an alpinist. I was mostly a rock climber.

"If the weather is good when we get there," said Topher, "we're going to have to head straight into the mountains and start climbing." The oldest of Mike and Peggy Donahue's sons had grown into a Patagonia veteran. Even more eager than I was, he was already dressed in ratty synthetic pants and a polypro shirt, his gear packed and ready to go.

For a while, a deepening desire for ever-greater adventures had been growing inside me. With my Yosemite thirst temporarily slaked, I felt the need to up the ante once again. I thought the mountains of Patagonia—big and harsh and beautiful—would be the perfect venue for my continued self-exploration. I studied the stories and stared in awe at the photos, daydreaming of battling through exhaustion and of the region's legendary storms. Some of my most powerful experiences in nature had been in bad weather. I had also read books about Arctic explorers like Ernest Shackleton who had survived incredible and often horrific ordeals. These old stories connected with me; they ignited buried yet familiar memories of pushing through great odds and discovering what lay deep within. In the realm of mountain endurance, I had only begun to understand my limits. I wanted to know more.

Although the Chaltén Massif's technical difficulties were predominantly on rock, I knew that Patagonian alpinism would challenge me in new and different ways. The uncontrollable variables of technical climbing in the mountains—the mixture of snow, ice, loose rock, and sudden storms—added an element of wildness I didn't encounter when focused on the hardest moves on solid stone in stable weather. You can't control those objective hazards, so you just deal with them. In many ways I was out of my league. But Topher knew me and my love for new challenges. He seemed to think I had the right skills and attitude, but still I wondered if my experience in sunny Yosemite would translate at all. Either way, I was eager to expand my horizons in Patagonia—especially since the place wasn't on anybody's terror alert list.

Beth understood my ardent desire for the trip, but she didn't want to climb big mountains, and we couldn't imagine spending an entire month apart. Our savings were meager, and so was our income. We lived as frugally as possible, but this was the kind of thing we scrimped and saved for. So we traveled to Argentina together, accompanied by her dad. While Topher and I threw ourselves at a mountain called Fitz Roy, they would trek around its flanks.

I could hardly wait. But I also recalled the words of one of my heroes, Tom Hornbein, a renowned physician and climber on the first American team to summit Mount Everest, in 1963, back when it was still wild and remote. His book, *Everest, The West Ridge*, provided me with endless inspiration. "Maybe we can view risk like we would a drug, beneficial to the organism in the proper dose," he once wrote. "Too much or too little may be harmful."

Fitz Roy's summit soared 10,000 feet above the tiny village of El Chaltén. Trails wove from town through *lenga* groves stunted by the wind, across rivers, around lakes, and onto tumbling glaciers, all in surreal contrast to the surrounding plains. The never-ending wind blew plumes of dust along the dirt streets.

We pulled our collars over our noses and dragged our duffel bags past a few scattered buildings. A gaucho rode by on his horse, and we hired him to help carry our gear to the Río Blanco base camp. We hiked along for two hours to a goblins' forest, sheltered from the wind. For the next month, we mostly festered in damp tents while keeping watch on our barometer. When the pressure started to rise it was time to head into the mountains. Before leaving I would kiss Beth on the cheek, and she would say, "Promise me you will come back alive. I can't live without you." I'd set off up the trail with a tear in my eye.

I hated worrying Beth or anyone else with concerns about my safety. From my first mention of the possible expedition, she had expressed some trepidation. As a climber herself she understood that Topher and I had looked at the risks and believed they were reasonable. We'd be on clean rock. We'd be on a route free from avalanche hazard. We'd be roping up on the glaciers. Topher was experienced and cautious. All of that was true, but I was about to undertake more climbing risk than I'd ever experienced on El Cap or elsewhere.

Topher and I had set our sights on a route called Royal Flush on Fitz Roy's sheer, 4,000-foot east face. It rises straight out of the glacier, emerging from the flat white snow and blue ice. We set out from base camp at two in the morning. The light from our headlamps bounced in front us, illuminating a steep and dusty trail. Soon the dust turned to ice crystals as we made our way along a disintegrating glacier. We wove between the crevasses—in some areas, they appeared to be little more than shadows against the lighter ice. I even fell into one waist-deep.

After many hours and several thousand feet of elevation gain, we reached the bottom of the vast rock monolith we had come to climb. It looked impossibly huge and intimidating, complex and scary. It reminded me of Mount Doom from *The Lord of the Rings*. I could hardly fathom a possible route to the top. Bright light outlined the jagged lacerations along the horizon as we reorganized our gear. Before we set off, I looked up and tried to avoid thinking of what Beth had said about not losing me. I took several deep breaths to clear my head, then began climbing.

Frigid water dripped down the rock, and before long our fingers and toes went numb, while the distant wind made a nerve-tweaking roar that we heard more than felt. Keeping in mind Mike Donahue's mantra about bad conditions simply being a part of the larger cycle of nature, we continued, our route relatively protected, though we watched chunks of ice fall and explode onto the glacier below as the sun warmed the wall. The conditions evoked both anxiety and excitement; my senses sharpened, each breath like a bellows stoking an inner fire.

The day passed and we couldn't push any higher. Nearly 2,000 feet up the wall we came upon a small perch atop a detached flake, some sixteen inches off the rock face and three feet wide, with snow and ice caked into the narrow gap. This would have to be our bivvy. We packed more snow to level the surface. Backs to the wall and sitting upright, feet and legs stuffed into a lightweight two-person bivvy sack, with no sleeping bag, we tried to rest. I ran slings around my upper body to lash myself to the rock. I clipped my helmet strap to those lines to support my head. I was like an insect caught in a spider's web.

Dusk spilled spectral red, yellow, blue, indigo, and violet, all stacked and blended together, across the western sky. The wind had exhausted itself and lain down. All was still, all was surreal and utterly beautiful.

Only when I closed my eyes and the natural wonders went dark did a lance of cold and fear pierce me. Teeth-chattering, flesh-stinging cold had me rattling against my web of slings like a shivering puppet.

Why the hell would anyone put himself through this?

I beat my heels up and down, trying to stir blood flow in my wooden feet. The cold had seeped into my brain and I kept thinking that I was going to lose my toes and my fingers. I thought of Beth and of lying nestled against her, her body radiating heat. I thought of campfires and running around with Tobias. I had visions of the black and withered toes and fingers of frostbite victims that I'd seen. Finally, first light crept in. As high as we were, on the highest mountain in the range, we stared at the sliver of sun, awaiting its warmth. Grateful that we were now in some kind of purgatory, not quite heaven but no longer a frozen hell, I began untangling from my web of slings.

We rose and continued climbing, but our pace slowed. Seeps of meltwater, left over from the last storm, had frozen, leaving the face coated in a treacherous veneer of verglas. Clouds built overhead. We could hear the wind coming from the west like an enraged beast.

Though Topher and I were protected on the east face, I could see massive chunks of ice flying from the summit and landing a mile away on the glacier. I was strangely at peace as the mountain came alive and the sky turned dark. We were some 2,500 feet above the glacier when we began a hasty retreat. The storm blasted in with alarming suddenness, growing as we descended, leaving us soaked and shivering.

We stumbled down the glacier, protected by Fitz Roy's hulking mass. When we emerged from the sheltered side, the wind threw me to the ground. I knelt on the glacier anchored by my ice tool, and I tucked my head to avoid the flying shards of ice. Soon after, I lost hold of my helmet and watched it blow into the sky and over the horizon.

Despite the storm's fury, soon the wind calmed and the skies cleared. Different sounds then emerged: the rumble of collapsing seracs, the crunch of crampons in the snow, the rhythm of our breath. Rocky summits glowed crystal clear. There was beauty as peaceful as anything I had known. Back at camp, I hugged Beth and lay in our tent, overtaken by utterly satisfying exhaustion. Something in my soul had been stirred.

We lounged in the forest and recovered. From time to time we'd hike to town for groceries, steak, and cervezas. Beth and her dad headed home after two and a half weeks, leaving Topher and me to our own devices.

Between intermittent bursts of sideways-blowing rain, we could see the mountains rising above. The memory of our failed attempt consumed me. The knowledge of an uncertain outcome seared itself into my mind. I wanted to be up there.

The days passed and the time to fly home neared. Then the barometer crept upward again, and in the predawn darkness we started the seven-hour hike back to Fitz Roy. A friend named Erik Roed joined us; while he wasn't as seasoned as Topher and I were, he was strong and tough, an unflappable ex-marine who reminded me of a teddy bear.

This time we decided on a different route, a little to the right of Royal Flush, named Línea de Eleganza. It had first been climbed two years earlier by an Italian team, the culmination of several attempts using extensive fixed ropes and aid climbing techniques. In our brave daydreams, we hoped to free the route in a single push, but our only information was a sketchy topographic map Erik had found. We figured it didn't matter. Our chances weren't great or even good, and Patagonia had already delivered us a series of ass kickings. What was one more?

When we stood again at the bottom of the Fitz Roy's towering east face, I was infused with newfound confidence. The clouds burned off and the sky turned orange. In the daylight, we realized that we had even less info than we'd thought—we'd lost the slip of paper with the topo. But at least we were light. We hadn't brought any bivvy gear, not only to save weight, but because we were sure we'd fail.

We flaked the ropes, tied in, and started climbing.

The first thousand feet flew by as we found our way up an exhilarating blend of cracks and corners and face holds. Then we hit an overhanging section. Our pace slowed. Topher was on lead. He grunted and fought while staying calm and smooth, as he always does. But suddenly the rock spat him off and he flew through the air. He lowered to the belay, panting, and suggested I try.

Breathe, stay relaxed. As I climbed I alternately held on with one hand and blew onto the other to warm my fingers, then continued, trying to tell myself that I was only on one of the crags back home. The terrain fell away below my feet. Pitch after pitch, the glacier grew smaller and the horizon larger. Day became night and we navigated by the beam of our headlamps. We pushed on, climbing into the blackness. I was too cold to stop. Topher battled through a desperate five-hour lead, climbing by headlamp in a corner partially covered in a veneer of ice. His frozen breath drifted into the dark. Well above his last protection, he paused in precarious balance, pulled out his ax with one hand, and tapped into the verglas. He pulled on fragile flakes with his other hand, delicately stemming his rock-shoe-clad feet around the ice. Tiny shards rained down. Erik and I shivered, rocking back and forth and shouting up encouragement. Topher finished the pitch—it was a display of absolute climbing brilliance—and slumped over at the anchor, exhausted. I continued above, following the beam of my headlamp on barely-there holds. Soon, the features blanked out. I tried to unravel it but pitched off, skittering down the wall and sailing past the belay.

Unable to find the way, we stopped and huddled on a small patch of ice 3,000 feet up. I was confused and too tired to think. We seemed stuck, and there was nothing and everything to see, so I switched off my headlamp and stared into the darkness, breathing slowly and marveling at the stars. We dozed off in short spells only to wake shivering, our eyelids burning from fatigue. Eventually we pulled out the stove, scraped ice and snow from the ledge to melt, and warmed ourselves with hot drinks.

First light glowed on the horizon. I stared down to the churning glacier, my gaze shifting to the forests and rolling pampas in the distance. The world looked as though it was both falling apart and coming together. The new day brought strength and when we craned our necks overhead we laughed. Tricked by the darkness, I'd launched onto the steepest part of the wall. Easy free climbing lay just to the right. Alternately hyperaware and randomly delirious, we veered between leading and dozing off in our harnesses, climbing and resting, resting and climbing.

As the sky transitioned into hues of lavender, we wandered up steep corridors of translucent ice. Clouds crept across the sky like white flying saucers blowing in from the Pacific Ocean some thirty miles to the west. The wind began to rise. Runnels of ice transformed into lower-angled snow. Can this really be happening? It all seemed surreal.

Suddenly, almost out of nowhere, the summit of Fitz Roy was beneath our feet. To the east, the arid grasslands seemed to stretch forever. To the west, between us and the sea, was a dreamscape of white: the enormous Southern Patagonia Ice Cap. Clouds roiled over nearby peaks, as if a stove had started to simmer. The wind grew stronger.

During our rappels the sun set once again, casting flames of light upon the range. We staggered across the glacier, down the trail, and through the night. Winds alternately whipped and whispered. Eventually, a kind of preternatural calm descended, an acceptance. *This is what I've chosen. This is what has been chosen for me.*

Just before returning to camp, we watched the sun rise for a third time. We'd been on the go for fifty hours. Sleep deprivation and hunger shrouded everything in a dreamlike fog. Sounds became muffled. Only the pain in our worn-out bodies felt sharp and real.

As we descended past turquoise lakes, groups of hikers stopped and stared, looking like ghosts, silent and lethargic, their ski poles clanking with every step.

Through the struggle and bone-pulsing exhaustion a profound clarity had emerged, as if I had tapped into a place inside too often forgotten, where you are stripped bare and granted a glimpse into who you truly are. A place where you could look at the impossible and make it real. I'd never been so alive.

CHAPTER TEN

Stripped down to running shorts and a chalk bag, I sit on the top of a detached granite spire called the Rostrum. This rock's disconnectedness from other formations suits me. I crave simplicity.

Below me the low roar of distant waterfalls floats upward. Speckled white granite digs into the skin of my bare feet. I sit on the lip and stare eight hundred feet straight down to the forest. Wispy clouds swim through the valley. I need to peel away the mess my life has become, wipe clean the drama and ugliness.

A friend once told me about finding the body of a BASE jumper. The man's parachute failed to open and he fell to earth from 3,000 feet. His skin remained intact while his insides had imploded. Something about that jumper's fate seems okay to me; I only want a release from the thunderstorm roiling inside my head.

I hold my rock shoes in my hand and let my feet dangle over the void. I look out across the landscape, thinking back over the last six months. I watch the contrail of an airliner pass overhead, see its slow dissolution from line to smear to nothing.

The summer and fall of 2008 was the darkest period of my life. A tornado of depression has engulfed me since that beautiful May day on Magic Mushroom. Though she hasn't spoken the words, I know that Beth is trying to leave me. I'm haunted by nightmares, visions of my dad falling off El Cap, of dying myself. What brings you to a place where you dream of your own death?

———

As far back as 2001, Beth thought she had the plan all laid out: We would get married, free climb the Nose, and have kids before the age of thirty. We had made one addition: build a house in Yosemite. With two of the four checked off the list, we were eager to complete the rest.

We had lucked into a heavenly quarter-acre lot for an absolute steal: an unheard-of forty-two thousand dollars. It sat on a steep hillside with a canopy of hundred-foot cedar and sugar pine trees, in an area called Yosemite West, a small pocket of private land inside the gates of Yosemite National Park and only thirteen miles from El Capitan.

Yosemite was practically our office, so building a house there felt like the next logical step. We had saved a little money from the book deal about our Kyrgyzstan ordeal. We were thrifty, spending our meager earnings only on climbing trips and food.

As climbers we devote ourselves to living in the moment. Beth and I had spent hundreds of nights illegally camping in Yosemite, and many years dirtbagging in climbing areas around the world. But you can't really raise your kids in a van, poaching campsites, and a climber's paycheck is barely enough to cover food, gas, and travel, much less provide a stable home, college tuition, and retirement income. We knew we'd eventually have to reconcile the freedom we enjoyed with the responsibilities we planned to take on.

With the help of an experienced climber and homebuilder named Lance Lamkau, we'd make our vision of a life in the forest a permanent reality. We would live and raise our kids free of distractions, and we would focus on each other, on climbing, and on our growing family. We would have our own little paradise nestled in Yosemite. Everything would be within our control.

By late summer of 2006 Beth and I had temporarily traded our climbing gear for work boots, a miter box, and other power tools. Lance became my teacher, and with his expertise and our drive, the house began taking shape. We put in thirteen-hour days.

Beneath cloudless skies, I shuffled up and down the steep hillside lugging lumber, challenging myself to see how fast I could move a twenty-sheet stack of plywood. Beth stood at the saw, cutting two-by-sixes to stud length. Lance read the blueprint and laid out the walls on the plywood decking. I came to love the smell of fresh cut lumber. The feel of the nail gun in my hand. The deep satisfaction of creating something tangible. When building, you make progress every day. I loved the problem-solving nature of home construction. In climbing and carpentry, you had to think strategically, mechanically, to find the most efficient ways to do things. I reveled in the physicality of the task—a new focus for what I'd come to think of as my obsessive nature.

Beth and I took breaks to walk around the framed walls and talk about our future. She seemed happy; therefore, so was I. My mood, my mental well-being, was completely tied to her. Together we were strong. But part of me feared the return of darker days.

One evening after working on the house, I got a call from Nick Sagar, the guy I'd climbed with on the Muir Wall, nine months after Kyrgyzstan. Nick had written a book on training for climbing and started a coaching business. One of his clients was a man named Jim Collins.

"You mean the Jim Collins from Genesis, in Eldorado Canyon?" I asked. "And now he's a business guy?"

"Yeah, that's the one," Nick said.

It was impossible to have grown up as a climber in Colorado and not have heard about Jim Collins. In 1979 he'd made the first ascent of a route named Genesis, at the time Colorado's hardest pitch of free climbing. Rumor had it that he'd also free soloed the Naked Edge, a six-hundred-foot-tall prow that's one of Eldorado Canyon's most famous routes. Apparently he wasn't proud of it, though—too much risk, as he subsequently reflected—so he kept it quiet. His real fame came later in life, as a business consultant and author. After a teaching stint at Stanford, he wrote several best-selling books. I admired not only Jim's ascents, but his ability to create balance in life beyond climbing.

For his fiftieth birthday, Jim wanted to climb the Nose in a day. He wasn't trying to free it, but just do it in twenty-four hours. One of the mantras he preaches in his books is that you must get the right people on the bus. Nick had convinced him that I would be the right person.

I couldn't help but be curious about Jim. But I was a climber to the core—a kind of antibusiness person. I'd always felt like a bit of a meathead, too, and was nervous about spending time with someone of such intellectual prowess.

Nick convinced me to at least consider the possibility. Jim and I talked on the phone, and we made plans to meet at a climbing gym during one of my trips back to Colorado.

The man I met, with the exception of his white hair, didn't look a day over thirty-five. He walked up to me, smiled warmly, and shook my hand aggressively. "It's a real pleasure," he said. We started climbing and I immediately wondered why he wanted my help to climb the Nose. He didn't seem to have lost a step.

We took a break and Jim pulled out a notebook. At that point, he was forty-eight years old—plenty of time to celebrate his fiftieth. He flipped through the pages and pointed: thirty-pitch training days in the climbing gym, several big climbs in Eldorado Canyon, a few Yosemite trial runs. At one point he opened to a page where he had analyzed a hundred years' worth of weather data and decided that September 26, 2008, had the highest probability of dry conditions, combined with good climbing temperatures and a full moon. To do the climb in under twenty-four hours, we'd be climbing plenty by headlamp and the moonlight would help. He thought this should be our target date for the climb.

I sat there dumbfounded. *This guy covers his bases.*

Jim was excitable, and clearly had an unabashed love of climbing. His data-driven approach fascinated me. He didn't want to just get his butt up the Nose, tick off another mark on his climbing résumé. He was devoted to the process. He wanted to do it in good style and to format the experience to maximize the potential for a positive outcome. We talked over the details of his plan, made a few minor tweaks, and locked in about fifteen days together leading to our target date for the Nose, which would have the side benefit of getting me out climbing while we were building.

As the autumn leaves changed color, the days grew short, the tourist traffic diminished. We cast long shadows as we worked, bulkier now in flannels and jeans.

The future Beth and I had envisioned started seeming a long way off, and our moods began to shift. Instead of imagining the kids playing on the deck, all we could see was what remained to be done and the shrinking digits in our bank account.

I wondered what my climbing friends were going to think of this place when it was completed. Our sport is so much about living through outdoor experiences, and rejecting the trappings of mainstream materialism. I was embarrassed to think that I'd sold out.

I wasn't alone in fretting. Beth worried constantly. "This is taking us too long. Eventually our sponsors are gonna drop us," she'd complain. Climbing isn't a mainstream sport. There isn't much money in it, and professional climbers are essentially freelancers.

I'd try to steer her in other directions by staying positive.

"Hey, we're making progress. Dreams take time."

I was stubborn and not about to succumb to any degree of outward depression. But the stress grew, and soon I experienced a persistent pain low in my gut. I couldn't see it then, but I was growing increasingly unsympathetic to Beth's struggles. I internalized my criticisms.

Why can't you be happy? Why can't you be like you used to be?

But what if her concerns were legitimate? Was I just burying the realities of our doubts and uncertainties beneath a front of blue-sky optimism?

Fall turned to winter. Snow fell. Regularly, daily, sometimes several feet of wet, heavy, Sierra cement at a time, slowing progress even more. Out of necessity and for therapy, I usually shoveled for two hours a day.

When was the last time we laughed together? When was the last time she told me I was handsome? It's Beth's fault. If she could just abandon the negative all would be well.

We figured relief would come when we finished the job. Our days turned to fifteen-hour marathons, a monotonous, repetitive routine of labor and sleep. Physically Beth was maniacal, always pushing forward. Back in our spider-infested apartment down the road, where we lived during construction, the blankets were too light to keep us warm, so we pulled out our sleeping bags.

"Why don't we zip them together?"

"Let's just get some sleep."

She doesn't even want to be next to me? Was I just a tool to help her build a house? Was I just going to be the seed for her children? Did she support my climbing just so I could make more money for her security?

I spiraled inside my head. Then I got sad. I missed my wife. I missed climbing. None of this felt right. We had gone months without any meaningful interaction with each other or with the outside world. Physically I felt rejected. It wasn't just about sex. It was about intimacy. I didn't want us to just be business partners.

The spring thaw began, but still I felt cold.

What would it be like to be married to someone who could embrace life with joy and love? Isn't that how she used to act? It's been so long I can hardly remember.

Climbing with Jim Collins felt like an escape. One of our first days was on the Nose itself. He wanted a sense of what he was getting himself into, so on an early spring day in 2007 we hiked to the top of El Capitan. A refreshing breeze blew off the snow-packed High Sierra, and the sun radiated warmth along the way.

Our conversation turned to our wives. Jim told me about Joanne, a former Ironman triathlon champion. He described how she went from being a world champion athlete to battling though cancer. When he talked about his wife his voice grew soft. He was filled with admiration and compassion, and I was struck by how his tenderness didn't seem to come despite the struggles in their lives, but because of them. Their relationship sounded vulnerable, challenging, and rewarding.

"You know, Tommy, at some point I realized that it can't be my job to make her happy," he said. "That has to be up to her."

I felt a sudden urge to run back to the house and tell Beth how sorry I was for putting so much pressure on her. All these years I had struggled to help her find happiness, but my expectations may have had the opposite effect. If she took charge of her well-being, maybe she would be more able to love me.

We were still talking when we reached the plateau atop El Capitan. I pulled two ropes out of my pack and set up a rappel. Jim paused, shot me a skeptical look, and changed the subject. "You mean we are going to just rappel right off the top here, and pull our ropes? That's pretty committing."

"Don't worry, Jim, I've done this zillions of times."

"You know, Joanne said that if I die, she is going to bring me back from the dead and kill me, then kill you."

We rappelled several times, until reaching the security of a prominent ledge about six hundred feet down. Jim breathed deeply to calm his nerves. I cracked a joke and tried to act extra relaxed, as we prepared to climb back out.

I could see Jim starting to loosen up, and during the climb we continued talking. Jim told me about American prisoners of war and how their attitude affected their ability to survive, how hopeful acceptance was better than blind optimism. He asked me about Kyrgyzstan, how I dealt with the ordeal at the time and later. He seemed curious about everything.

He then impressed me by naming each of the major El Cap free climbs I'd done in chronological order from the Saláthe Wall to Golden Gate. He spoke about the flywheel effect, how the first revolutions of it are hard, but once momentum is built the wheel turns more freely. I'd always thought of it in terms of a standard progression, not accounting for the effect one effort had on the other. When I applied Jim's ideas to my climbs on El Cap, routes that had originally felt nearly impossible to free, what I'd been doing made much more sense.

When we started, I was supposed to teach Jim. But by the end of that day—the first of many—he had become the mentor, and I the student. His clear thinking, his ability to articulate and make sense of ideas that I didn't even know I had, created order in a world that I viewed as chaotic. Foremost in my mind was the growing unease between Beth and me. But suddenly I realized that I could be loving without taking on her sadness. Talking with Jim made me feel that I could take the scattered pieces of my life and make them fit. It was as if he had held my hand as we pushed the first revolution of an extremely heavy flywheel that had been stuck, spinning in place, inside my mind.

Later that spring of 2007, as the weather warmed, Beth and I were still a long way from finishing the house. The excitement of building had worn off. We weren't cut out for this. Our parents offered to hire us more help. We gladly accepted.

We started climbing together again. First it was about getting back into climbing shape after nearly a year off. We started by going to the boulders. As summer shifted to early fall, we kept running into a dedicated crew of climbers who drove from San Francisco to Yosemite every weekend. Their energy toward climbing was something I missed. Soon, we were making plans to meet up and boulder together. At first Beth was standoffish, but as she got to know them she enjoyed their company. She hadn't made any new friends since Kyrgyzstan, and as I saw her opening up I felt proud of her.

As Beth regained her climbing prowess she wanted to find a challenging project. Rumor had it that a spectacular, nearly impossible single-pitch crack climb lay tucked in the forest, hidden in a gorge beside a waterfall. Although it remained a mystery, one of Yosemite's greats was said to have come across it in generations past, but had never been able to climb it.

While exploring one day, we crawled through a cave, wiggled under a huge boulder, and then popped out into a secluded amphitheater. A gentle waterfall flowed into a natural pool, flanked by an overhanging granite wall split by a laser-cut seam that disappeared over a bulge.

"That's got to be it!" Beth pointed, jumping up and down as if she had found the pot of gold at the end of a rainbow.

This is awesome. This is the Beth I know.

I scrambled around to drop a top rope on the line, so that Beth could spend the afternoon checking out the moves. The wall was a virtually blank swath of stone sixty feet tall. At some point in geological time, the piece of rock had split vertically in half, and the left side had shifted about one inch in front of the right. The wall itself canted forward about ten degrees. In places, the split had left a desperate crack, barely fingertips-width. In other areas the seam was closed, so to climb, Beth would pinch that one-inch offset with her hands while simultaneously pushing straight into the wall with her feet to create opposing forces. She looked as if she was trying to climb a palm tree—hips out, feet pressing in. Except she didn't have a tree trunk to wrap her hands around. Her fingers had to clamp on to that one-inch offset like vise grips, with simultaneously perfect foot precision and body position—the slightest imbalance meant an immediate fall.

As I watched her work out the moves I realized that the climb was a perfect fit for Beth, and harder than anything she had ever attempted. She was the best I had ever seen at this subtle style of climbing. If she was successful, it would be the hardest single-pitch crack climb in Yosemite. Maybe the world.

During the days we focused all our energies on her new project. I would set up the rope, clean any dirt or debris from the crack, and climb with her to help keep the motivation high. When Beth was resting I would go bouldering with our new friends from the Bay Area.

I told myself that we had gotten through the crux of our lives. In reality our relationship remained far from perfect. Beth and I lived together, but shared little beyond climbing. I felt as if I was hitting an emotional wall with her.

It's just that she's so focused on her project. Once she fulfills this obsession she'll accept me as a romantic partner again, not just a climbing partner.

Beth walked through the house rehearsing the moves in her head. She trained with a vengeance, as if her life depended on succeeding on the route. One moment she would be focused and positive, the next it was as if the specter of failure had descended on her. For the first time I felt undertones of hostility. My support seemed to only add to her stress.

By December, snow fell. After each storm I went to Beth's climb, scrambled up an ice-filled gully, and shoveled piles of snow from the top of the cliff so the route would stay dry. I remember sitting in the secluded grotto and thinking how, under any other circumstances, this would make a wonderfully romantic spot.

Maybe she needed a distraction from the stress?

One day I packed candles and snacks in my backpack as a surprise. On that day and each that followed, Beth was so focused on her efforts, and so devastated when she didn't succeed, that I never pulled them out. I tried to comfort her, but she would weep inconsolably. I thought again of my conversations with Jim Collins.

At some point I realized that it can't be my job to make her happy.

Logically, I understood his words. But I couldn't separate myself from Beth's pain.

She was exceedingly private about her obsession over the route, so I was surprised one day when she invited two of our new and recently engaged Bay Area bouldering friends to see the climb. Randy and Courtney's presence eased the tension and helped Beth relax. It was as if she didn't feel comfortable showing them her angst, therefore much of it evaporated. It freed her to try harder than ever. One day she almost did it—her best effort to date. Randy and Courtney seemed exceedingly impressed, almost starstruck. Especially Randy. Afterward, she even revealed to them her anxieties over the climb, and the "meltdowns" she was having. In a moment of levity, that became the name for the route: Meltdown.

This is good, this making friends. Winter's isolation is bad. Soon our stress will evaporate like the mist from the falls.

On Valentine's Day, 2008, the sun refracted off the spray from the surging waterfall like a million shooting stars. Beth tied into the rope and started climbing. The roar of rushing water drowned out her grunts and screams. She moved efficiently, placing just enough protection to keep her safe. Elation and anxiety welled in my chest as she went higher, climbing with absolute perfection, until finally she floated up the final moves as if they were nothing.

She lingered on top of the route for a few minutes before I lowered her to the ground. I wrapped my arms around her in the biggest and warmest hug I had. I held on to the moment, and spoke softly in her ear.

"I am proud of you, baby. You worked so hard for this one." I kept my arms around her, looked into her eyes, and moved in for a kiss. She wiggled uncomfortably and pecked me on the cheek.

She's wired. The rush of adrenaline from her success is coursing through her. She's just self-conscious after all that exertion. Whatever the reason, it's nothing personal.

Like my father, I have the ability to stuff away uncomfortable emotions. Sometimes it helps, sometimes not. But when things start to hurt, I force my brain to cover my heart. My heart was telling me that *nothing personal* was exactly the problem. I was back to being her climbing buddy again after all these years. I wanted us to be lovers, to be best friends, husband and wife, the most intimate of confidants. I wanted her to let me back into her life fully. Wasn't it obvious? Should I even have to ask?

Beth's foot injury had flared up again, and she'd torn a ligament in her finger during her herculean effort on Meltdown. With her on injured reserve, that spring I teamed up with my friend Justen Sjong to try another free route on El Cap called Magic Mushroom. While I was on the wall, Beth spent much of her time with Randy and Courtney. They bouldered together on weekends, with Beth mostly hanging out to let her finger heal. She even visited them in Berkeley one week. I was happy to see how content she seemed, when in the past my absences made her anxious.

I had a voracious appetite for challenging myself on progressively harder climbs. I started to know El Capitan much the way most people know the inside of their homes—all the dusty corners and places where things were tucked away in tiny drawers. Magic Mushroom went up one of the steepest parts of the wall via a series of flaring, holdless corners. It had been previously attempted as a free climb by a world-class pair of Germans, the Huber brothers. They had freed several routes on El Cap already, but declared it impossible to climb dihedrals that were so steep, smooth, and continuous. Following my success on the Dihedral Wall, however, I looked at routes like this with different eyes. Those flares and smooth corners hide secrets, utterly improbable sequences of nearly invisible face holds and minute shifts in the angles of the seams that allow glimpses of possibility. This could be, yet again, a logical next step. Justen and I spent a month working out the moves and then managed to free the route over five days. In a way it seemed anticlimactic, almost too easy. I knew I was capable of much more.

When we finished, Justen and I loaded our gear into massive haul bags and staggered down the trail to the valley floor. About to set off for home, I was surprised to see Beth standing in her road biking outfit, enthusiastically waving good-bye to a black Audi with an expensive-looking bike on top.

"Hey, baby, over here!" I yelled. She looked startled, then she smiled.

"How do you feel?"

"We sent!"

"I know, Justen sent me a text," she said (Beth had our shared cell phone while I was on the wall). "Oh, Tommy, I am so proud of you!"

I dropped my haul bag on the ground, slowly unslouched my shoulders like a ninety-year-old man getting out of bed, and stretched my arms. "Who was that?" I asked mid-hug.

"Randy. We just got back from a ride up to Tuolumne Meadows."

"Oh, nice, how was it?" I asked.

"Really beautiful, no cars, really peaceful."

I couldn't remember when I'd last seen Beth so sunny. I was acutely aware of my stench. As we stood there, a text pinged on the phone. She pulled it out of her pocket, giggled, and typed a quick response. Then we loaded up her bike and my haul bag and drove home.

That evening, while Beth was in the shower, I looked at our cell phone. The text was from Randy: "That was a truly magical day. Thanks."

It doesn't mean anything.

I was grateful that she was finding moments of happiness without me. This was the first time in eight years that I had returned home free of the guilt that came from leaving her by herself.

Then she said something that made me pause. "I feel so energetic these days. I don't even feel like I need much sleep." She stood smiling brightly, her eyes glowing.

That's how I looked and felt when I was falling in love with her.

I blocked the incident and the text from my mind. We went about our daily lives without further mention of it. I focused on climbing. I wanted to try to free Magic Mushroom in a day, and Beth said she wanted to support me.

The day before my planned attempt, we were driving through Yosemite Valley when our cell phone rang.

"Hey, baby, can you pull over for a minute," Beth asked. She jumped out of the car and ran into the woods, pacing back and forth as she talked. I was confused. After ten minutes I turned off the car and walked toward her, worried and frustrated.

What the hell?

She waved me off and mouthed, "Just five minutes."

I returned to the car, mind spinning, and waited.

"What's going on?" I asked when she got back.

"Randy and Courtney are having second thoughts, and Randy just needed to talk it out."

"That sucks," I said, "but I don't know if I'm okay with you being his shoulder to cry on."

She rolled her eyes and gave me a look. "Don't worry, baby, we're just friends."

I am worried. I don't care if you're just friends. You seem more concerned about his happiness than ours.

We started climbing at 5:00 p.m. the following day. I climbed fast and Beth jumared faster. My fears dissolved and I was happy to have her support. She seemed excited to be part of the action. We climbed the first 1,800 feet of Magic Mushroom through the night, before sunrise.

The style of climbing had become very comfortable, very familiar. Just a few years earlier this difficulty and type of climbing would have left me panting and screaming, just like so many other climbers who found it improbable, impossible; but now it warmed me like a campfire on a cold night. In a way I felt as though I had become part of the wall, like a spider effortlessly climbing its web. I pressed the palms of my hands and the soles of my feet into the steep, smooth, soaring corners with gentle precision, never second-guessing a move, finally feeling fluent in the language I had spent more than a decade perfecting. It seemed crazy to me that this climb was already being accounted for in the informal record books as the hardest big wall route ever free climbed. And now I was doing it in a day. I thought about what Jim had said about the flywheel, and was sure mine was about to spin off its axle. But as we got higher Beth began to inexplicably turn into another person, as if she didn't want to be there. Or to be there with me. She stopped encouraging me, didn't speak at the belays, wouldn't even look at me.

"What's wrong?" I asked.

"I'm just tired."

It was more than fatigue—her energy had completely dissipated. But this was the pinnacle of what we had worked so hard for. She was being hailed as the best female climber of her generation. I was about to achieve what I was sure would be the peak of my career. I shut off my thoughts, forced them away. I focused only on the moves for several more hours. When I was finished, twenty-two hours after starting, I sat calmly on the summit, looking across the valley to the spires and domes and the forest. I breathed deep with pride.

Beth arrived a few minutes later and quickly untied from the rope. She walked right past me without even looking up. She started running down the granite slabs toward the valley. I ran to catch up and asked what was wrong. She wouldn't look at me.

"Nothing, I need to be alone," and then she sprinted away.

For the first time I could remember, my heart overrode my brain. I crumpled to the earth, bawling.

The next morning I stepped out of the shower onto the cold tile of our newly finished bathroom, my sadness brimming my eyes with tears. Beth walked in.

"I need some space," she said. "I need to sort through some things in my head."

She sounded sad, as down as I'd ever heard her.

"I have to get back to being me, really me, feeling good about myself. I can't do that with us together. Maybe you should go spend some time in Colorado."

I need to trust her. Everyone goes through little internal crises at times. I just need to be supportive and let her get through it.

I loved her so much; I couldn't deny her that. I had felt the need for space myself at times.

"Okay. I'll pack some things. Be out of here soon."

I hate this. I don't want to go.

Had we become too close, too dependent on each other?

I drove for twenty-three hours straight and arrived in Estes with my mind still spinning and my guts spilling out of me. With some rest, I re-adjusted. I spent the next two months alone at the cabin, our first real time apart in eight years. I reconnected with old friends and went climbing on the familiar crags of my youth.

This is a necessary step in evolving together as a married couple. After some time apart, her eyes will once again sparkle with love and we will live the rest of our lives in marital bliss.

But when we talked on the phone, her voice was flat, emotionless. "What did you do today?"

I wanted to slice through the small talk and let my love burst through the telephone. But I didn't utter a word about any of this. I knew she would say that I was disrupting her need to find herself without me. She would cut our conversation short on each call. I had planned to be away for only a couple of weeks, but Beth insisted that she needed more time. Weeks became months. I did my best to remain focused on our plan of personal redis-covery.

We will reconnect soon.

Back in the spring, just before Magic Mushroom, we'd bought plane tickets for a late summer bouldering trip to South Africa.

A few days before our flight I drove back to Yosemite. I pulled up to our house, took a deep breath, and walked to the front door. Should I ring the doorbell?

No, that would be weird.

I hesitated for a full minute and opened the door.

"Hello?"

"I'll be down in a minute," she shouted from the upstairs bedroom.

As I sat at the kitchen table and waited, I stared at the wall of windows and remembered teaching Beth to use the nail gun as we put it together. I thought about the room we'd built as a nursery for our future baby. I looked out at the giant pines and contemplated how Yosemite had become such an important part of me.

As Beth walked down the stairs my entire being tingled with anxiety and desire and love. Before arriving in Yosemite I had pulled off the side of the road, run into the woods, and changed into some of my nicer casual clothes. I wanted her to remember how handsome I was. Suddenly I felt self-conscious.

As she approached she gave me a courteous smile. "How was your drive?" Her words came softly.

"Good. It was good." I tried to act natural. "The house looks nice. We did a pretty good job, didn't we?"

"Yeah." Her eyes turned toward the floor.

"Are you excited for our trip?" I smiled weakly.

"I guess." She looked out the window.

It was impossible to ignore the pain lurking inside, the way she folded her arms and wouldn't look me in the eye.

"Hey, would you mind sleeping in the guest room tonight. I still need some space to figure stuff out."

The blood rushed out of my head. I had to sit down. Beth turned and walked away.

We boarded the plane to South Africa. Upon our arrival at our rental, Beth pushed the twin beds to opposite corners.

There's the line in the sand.

I slept little, ate little, drank more than I should have with our ten young bouldering housemates.

Beth stopped climbing with us and started spending her days in the Internet café in town. I brought her flowers.

One evening about two weeks into our trip I found Beth weeping silently in our room. I walked over and sat down next to her. I asked her what was wrong. Then the words I had been both dreading and wishing for finally came.

"I miss Randy."

I sat there numb, not knowing what to say. As I let the anger and hopelessness seep in, tears filled my eyes.

"What's happening?" I asked.

"I don't know," she whimpered.

"Is this you finding your independence?" My head swirled. I couldn't look at her.

"I'm sorry."

I stood up. This time I walked away.

Back home, alone in our little cabin in Estes Park, every sense and emotion in my body was magnified. Only movement brought distraction. I ran until my body numbed and I could only feel the burning in my lungs. I spent sunrises scurrying across mountaintops, watching the dawn from above tree line. As the sun rose, moments of euphoria, pain, love, anger, and bliss would wash over me like waves.

Once or twice a week I would call Beth. Long periods of silence inevitably made our conversations too awkward. Eventually she told me that she and Randy had decided that they were not going to talk at all until she figured out what she wanted. I didn't know where to go from there, but I knew I couldn't handle this waiting game.

Beth had been seeing a counselor in Davis. She mentioned going there together, so I drove back to California.

The counselor was a suburban mom who reminded me of Beth's mother. Beth had been seeing her for a month, and I wondered what they had talked about.

We sat down and exchanged a few pleasantries. The therapist set the stage for the conversation by saying that we were going to have to open up some wounds. Then she asked Beth to say what was on her mind. Beth scooted over to me and put her trembling hand on my leg.

"I think it has something to do with the fact that our relationship really started in Kyrgyzstan." She paused to compose herself. "I loved you so much. It's just that I don't think I ever fell in love with you in the *same way* you fell in love with me."

"So what about the last eight years," I said. "We were so good to each other. I think everyone we know would agree that there's never been a couple that treated each other with so much compassion."

"You have to understand, I love you more than I ever knew was possible." She pressed her palms into her face as the tears started pouring, "It's just that I am not happy."

Of course she isn't happy. She has never been happy.

Maybe I was too hurt to feel any of the compassion I had talked about.

I turned to Beth. "Do you think we would be here today if it wasn't for Randy?"

I didn't know how to express the hopeless anger I felt. I wanted her to admit she was wrong. She stared into her hands. "I think I never would have been open to Randy if everything was good with us."

The rest of the hour faded in and out like static on a radio. I just sat and surrendered. We talked about my dad's overbearing nature, and how the way I loved Beth smothered her. Each new topic felt like another stab wound. One thing became clear: Beth wasn't going to therapy to repair our relationship. By the time we left in our separate vehicles to return to Yosemite, I felt like ramming my car into a cement wall.

I sought some sort of justification for my anguish. I believed I was the man she had fallen in love with. But maybe who she really wanted wasn't me, but an imagined human security blanket. I was still the person she'd broken up with in the weeks before Kyrgyzstan. While something like love may have grown after our ordeal, she never completely felt the bond of true love. What I never saw, what I couldn't see even then, was that a savior and a true love are not always the same.

Back at our house in Yosemite, Beth was a weepy mess. Between tears she kept saying, "I love you so much." At least she was talking to me now. Then she said she wanted to date Randy, but stay married to me.

Are you insane? Who does that?

My jaw clenched. I didn't have to say a thing. She knew exactly what I was thinking. I stormed out as her bawling echoed through the house.

I had always regarded free soloing as selfish, reckless, and stupid. I gagged when I heard self-righteous soloists talk about their "spiritual journey," or say, "It's not about cheating death, it's about living." "It's the time in my life when I feel most in control." That's crap, I would think. There's a difference between accepting life-affirming risks and being completely irresponsible. Those climbers just wanted to look like badasses, and were willing to risk hurting everyone who loved them.

But what if I allowed myself to be just as selfish? I love the heightened sense of awareness that comes when everything is on the line, when control and focus take over and all else fades into the background. Invincibility seems within reach. If I took away the rope, the experience would be that much stronger. That much more real.

Free soloing the Rostrum would be my warm-up. El Cap next. If I allowed myself to venture onto those walls unroped, I would enter a utopia, ultimate absorption in the thing I loved most, total commitment in a world devoid of heartbreak. And if I fell to my death, at least the pain would be gone, too.

I sat and gazed across the valley at the forests, the waterfalls rumbling below, the walls rising on the horizon. Climbing was my life. It had helped me through hard times. Besides Beth, climbing had been my closest companion. But there's a difference between using something as a tool and being a junkie. I thought about my mom's tenderness, how she always seemed to feel it when someone she loved was hurting. Did she sense my struggles now? And what would my dad have me do? He had lived his life by turning adversity into something positive, and from our earliest days he tried to instill the same ethos in me.

On the other side of the valley rose El Capitan, the wall that had so shaped my life.

This place and the climbing and the people were inextricably woven together within me. The last time I had climbed El Capitan had been less than two months earlier, when Jim Collins and I climbed the Nose in a day. His dream, yet I'd learned so much from him. What would Jim say to me now, what sort of advice would he offer me in my state of desperation and despair?

I thought back to that day on the Nose. We had gotten to a small perch a hundred feet from the top and Jim had turned to me. "Tommy, one of the finest blessings in my life has been the opportunity to spend time with great and inspiring people," he said. I knew he'd had direct interactions with some of the world's greatest leaders, from entrepreneurs and iconic Fortune 500 CEOs to four-star military generals. Even a former president.

I was only a climber, but Jim made me believe I was destined for more. He was the first person to ever make me feel smart. It took a second for what he said next to hit me. "I count you as one of the very top. Thank you for taking this journey with me. This has been one of the pinnacle experiences of my life."

I began to reframe my situation.

What might life be like without the weight of Beth's worries?

I knew it wouldn't be simple. The anguish in my heart wasn't going to magically vanish. I also knew that hard physical labor always seemed to be my best therapy. I could just climb my brains out—with a rope—as if I had nothing to lose.

I stared across the valley and remembered a time of unfettered optimism, when I had done reconnaissance missions onto a section of El Capitan that nobody had ever dreamed possible as a free climb. Its sheer improbability fascinated me. It was the biggest, steepest, blankest wall on El Capitan, infinitely harder than anything I had even contemplated climbing in the past. Even the name hinted at the route's potential; climbers have long called it the Dawn Wall for the way the light of each new day graces the face.

Something like a spark flickered inside me. I took a deep breath and stepped away from the edge of the cliff. Without bothering to put on my shoes, I turned and walked back up the trail, the tears on my face not yet dry.

PART
THREE

CHAPTER ELEVEN

I run my tongue along my teeth. *Ahhh, clean at last.* A mint taste replaces the fuzz of microwaved burrito and coffee that had taken up residence for the brushless past week.

As 2009 approaches, I've decided to end my month-long exile.

Rather than picking up a shirt from the piles on the floor, I flip through my mostly bare closet, skipping the pit-sniff test. I wonder if the red buffalo plaid is too bright against my fish-belly white complexion. My eyes look sunken, more underlined by dark bags than ever before. I try on a few more shirts before deciding on a subdued plaid, blue with white and green.

At the back of a closet shelf I find some partly congealed hair gel. I'm not a "product" guy but tonight is different. Gel and toothpaste, a private reminder that Tommy is changing.

I turn and tilt and eye my reflection from different angles, my eyebrows lifting as I assess.

There, not such a dork anymore.

Feeling a surge almost like confidence, for good measure I practice a few dance moves in front of the mirror. *Okay, best to stay off the dance floor.*

Feeling decidedly uncool, on the short drive I give myself a pep talk.

I'm going to walk in there and talk to people. That's right, talk to people.

At the Rock Inn, I step into a turbulent current of flannel and facial hair. The smell of craft beer and wood smoke mingles with the press of human bodies. Light shines from the vaulted log ceilings and people seem to bounce off the wooden support beams. A banjo player commands the stage, rocking out *while an impressively racked moose head stares from the wall behind him. The fireplace and wood stove duel for heating supremacy.*

I look around, hoping that maybe my buddy Shannon decided not to show. I can easily slip out, unnoticed and unmissed. A moment later, I see a figure across the room waving me over. I wade into the crowd, knowing that the test of my resolve is about to begin.

Beth and I wavered, fought, made up. Six times in seven months I made the twenty-three-hour drive between Colorado and California. I worked on being alone, and trying to learn that alone didn't mean lonely. I was confident when climbing, but my sense of worth and self-assurance always seemed to end there. Nevertheless, I inched toward an appreciation of my newfound freedom.

At one point Beth blamed my parents, my dad more than my mom, for our failed marriage. She had long felt that my dad was such a domineering presence that I lived my life trying to please him more than her. Sullen and angry, she insisted that we could never fully be happy until I was free of him. If it came down to it, did I want to be a husband or a son? As a last-ditch effort to show Beth I would do anything to keep our marriage together, I typed a painful letter to my parents, basically blaming my dad for everything. Half-believing, half-doubting, but fully dreading the words on the page, I slipped them into an envelope and a mailbox. I knew I could never say them out loud.

The letter didn't matter for Beth and me. In the end we couldn't reconcile our differences. Soon we were negotiating the logistics of our split. If I had an overly sunny view of marriage, Beth had an even sunnier view of divorce, suggesting we maintain our professional relationship as climbing partners. *Not interested.*

Miraculously, we kept the lawyers out of it. I'd keep the cabin in Estes, and she'd buy me out of the Yosemite house.

It was over.

The week after I'd sent that letter to my parents, I'd gotten a call from my mom. She'd said my dad was absolutely devastated. That he didn't see much point in going on living. He'd lost a son. Instantaneous regret pierced my heart; I wanted to drive across town to my parents' house to tell my dad how sorry I was for everything I had written. But I was too scared, too weak, too much of a coward. So instead I told myself that time would heal.

Rejected by the only woman I had ever loved, having dynamited my relationship with my dad, and unsure of everything, as 2009 moved on I holed up in the cabin and went on long runs by myself. I didn't know what else to do, so when the late autumn winds began to rip down off the Rockies I returned to El Capitan. Beating my head against the Dawn Wall became my beacon in the night.

I carried a huge pile of rope to the top of El Cap and started rappelling down in different spots, looking for a feasible passage through the upper Dawn Wall. If the route was even possible I would have to piece it together bit by bit. That's how you solve the puzzle of a big free route. You figure out a move, link a sequence of moves together, then connect these sequences until you come to a logical stopping point that marks the end of a pitch. The unwritten rule is that a pitch should end at a ledge or a stance (a very relative definition on a wall like this), or a break with a distinct change in the character of the climbing. After you have one pitch figured out, you work on another. Eventually you put together a complete series of pitches to make a collective, massive whole. And then you have to climb the entire route free, from bottom to top.

In a lot of ways, what I was doing was similar to what a gymnast and a coach or a choreographer might do. Each of the skills or moves was a thing unto itself—a double salto or an arabesque—that had to be linked to other moves and transitions. Unlike those activities, the rock itself dictated which of the many moves needed to come when.

I found a reasonable crack system in the upper thousand feet, what seemed to be mostly 5.11 and 5.12 climbing aside from two distinct blank sections. Hanging on the rope with my self-belay system, I bounced as far out from the wall as I could, trying to steal a glimpse of the nuances in the rock during the second or two that I was dangling in space. I saw a series of features far to the right and bounded sideways over to them. But the rock there was friable and flaky. The holds would break off, sending me sailing out of control for a forty-foot sideways pendulum. Ultimately those spots proved too frustrating so I moved on. I had plenty of other sections to try to figure out.

After a few weeks of this I made a portaledge camp in the middle of the wall. This allowed me to stay on El Cap for multiple days at a time before I'd come down to rest or resupply.

My camp hung amid an ocean of granite. Over time the portaledge became battered by the wind and bleached by the sun. After storms, shields of dense ice formed high on the wall and peeled off in the warmth of daylight, whizzing past and sometimes bombarding my camp. The ice made a high-pitched whirling sound as it fell, followed by explosions when it hit the wall. Each morning I'd zip up the fly and tuck my head inside my sleeping bag until the overhead offensive stopped. Dwelling there, subsisting on beef jerky, nuts, and rehydrated food, had the feeling of being stranded on a desert island.

In the past I'd always experienced an overarching sense of connection while on El Cap. But this time I felt estranged from the world. Worn thin, vulnerable, emotionally strung out, I found it difficult to shrug off the fear that comes with being alone in such a wild spot. The hard work, the pain, the danger, it all rang hollow. For the first time in my life, climbing felt self-glorifying, even pointless. I spent many nights weeping in my portaledge. Each day I'd wake, affix myself to the ropes, and try to piece together an elusive series of holds barely big enough to see with the naked eye. In between sections of possibility were vast stretches that seemed unclimbable. I would spend days swinging back and forth, searching the rock face with the palm of my hand, as if I were reading braille, unlocking sequences of moves that would inevitably lead to a dead end.

Several times I gave up and moved on. But then I'd return.

One day after a storm I rappelled eight hundred feet to inspect the middle section of the wall. It was even harder than what lay above, a giant blank maze with long stretches of smooth rock speckled with the tiniest features. I'd try over and over again to connect them by shifting my hips a few degrees this direction or that, figuring out the right way to press my toes onto the rock, contorting myself in this three-dimensional riddle until, for a moment, I'd stick to the rock before gravity peeled me off. The granite was freezing cold and my fingers went numb crimping the faint, rounded ripples.

I took a moment to rest and look around. Blood seeped through the tape on my fingertips. I dabbed them in chalk and climbed some more. My stomach groaned and I realized that I had been searching for more than nine hours without pause. My food, water, and warm clothes were hundreds of feet above in my portaledge. Clouds billowed below, and when they parted I saw the valley floor, over a thousand feet down, covered in white. Snowflakes drifted past me.

After a month on the wall, I started to see how the line might come together. In the hardest ten pitches, there were still long stretches where I wasn't even close to linking the sequences. I could barely do the individual moves in some places. But at the most basic level, the pieces were there. I needed them to be there. I willed them to be there. I spent day after day alone on a wall of rock looking for something to hold on to.

Eventually I realized that a free route up the Dawn Wall might be possible. But I also realized that I would never be good enough to climb it.

By the end of November, winter conditions had fully descended. With nowhere else to go, I returned to Colorado. I hadn't communicated with anyone in my family in four months. I wondered vaguely how they were doing, but didn't pursue the question.

One winter morning at a coffee shop in Estes Park, I ran into an old high school friend. Shannon Benton is small and built like a mini fridge. He was heavily into weight lifting, and veins ran up and down his forearms like earthworms. We'd casually kept in touch over the years, and he'd even met Beth a few times.

I must have had that far-off, insecure look of a beaten dog or a recently divorced human, because when Shannon saw me he smiled broadly. We shook hands and he nearly knocked the wind out of me with a big hug.

"Tommy Caldwell! Great to see you. Wow, it's been way too long!"

I was tempted to turn and run. But he didn't ask about Beth like everybody else did. I think he just sensed something was up by how skittish I looked.

"Hey, man, I gotta go, but do you want to come to the Rock Inn tomorrow night? There's a good band playing." On Friday nights, even during Estes Park's snowy, wind-blasted winters, the place was always packed with partying locals.

It wasn't really my scene, but before I could stop myself the words escaped my lips.

"Sure." My voice cracked from lack of recent use.

"Cool, man, I'll see you there at nine." Shannon fist bumped me and ran out the door.

A day and a half later, I walked into the Rock Inn and found it jammed with locals. Shannon immediately established a welcoming tone. He leaned in and shouted over the sound of music and laughter.

"Hey, remember that tenth-grade weight lifting class, when you showed me how do a one-finger one-arm pull-up from a sling?!"

"Yeah, I couldn't believe you could actually do it. If you had decided to get serious about climbing you could have been so good!"

"I'm not sure I really had the head for it. But remember in science class how you could pick the hot beakers right off the Bunsen burners with your bare fingers because of the calluses you had from climbing? I thought the girls would be so impressed by that!"

"It didn't really work out that way, did it?"

"I don't know, man, it might have worked if you were into it. You had that shy, I don't give a damn attitude, and you were always gone on climbing trips. It made you seem mysterious."

"Really?" I said, recalling discomfort more than anything remotely resembling confidence. "I remember being the kid with perpetual bed head, who everyone knew still wore tighty whitey underwear."

He walked me over to a table and introduced me to a bunch of his friends. "This is firefighter Rob, that over there is Nicole from Florida. And here's Dianne," he said, leaning and conspicuously whispering in my ear. "Be careful of her, she's quite the cougar, always on the hunt."

I was surprised at how easy it was to talk to these strangers. Maybe it was the sensory distraction of the loud music. Awkward silences went unnoticed. No one seemed to care about anything but laughter. All levity and fun, as if everyone had just checked their troubles at the door. That night I laughed more talking about absolutely nothing than I had in the past five years.

After about three beers I decided the Rock Inn was going to be the scene of my social rebirth. I was going to relax and be as fun, goofy, and carefree as Shannon. I'd risk making a fool of myself, and indeed try to make a fool of myself.

The next week, the bar threw a white-trash-themed birthday party for Shannon. I found the most magnificent mullet wig. The thrift store yielded a pair of heinously small cutoff shorts and a stained T-shirt with a picture of a bald eagle and a 'Merican flag. I cut the shirt into a midriff tank top. When I walked into the Rock Inn, somebody shouted across the room, "Hollywood!" Someone else slapped me on the back and shoved a beer in my hand. I headed for the dance floor. The rest of the night was a bit hazy, but I remember winning the costume contest. The prize was a half-rotten, bug-infested deer head. For the next month everyone at the Rock Inn called me Hollywood.

Nobody asked me about climbing, Beth, or Kyrgyzstan. I came by every Friday for the live music and visited on quieter nights to play chess with my new friends. Shannon and I became virtually inseparable. Soon we were hosting dinner parties with three to five women, which was saying something in a mountain town. I got much more comfortable in my own skin. It was as if I crawled out from the rock I'd been living under and discovered a whole new world. This bunch of goofballs welcomed me, showed me a lighthearted way, and inspired me to be more like them.

I had always believed that serious alpine climbing was too dangerous for a responsible husband. That didn't apply to me anymore, so I made plans to return to Patagonia with Josh "Safety Fifth" Wharton, so named because of his penchant for climbing huge, committing routes with no first-aid kit, no bivvy gear, and no margin for error. He'd made blisteringly fast first ascents all around the world. Wharton and another friend, "Sketchy Kelly," had gone two days without food and water at 20,000 feet on a climb in Pakistan's Karakoram mountains after accidentally dropping a good portion of their gear. They dubbed their approach Disaster Style. While that's a darkly humorous term for full-commitment climbing in big mountains, it also works in life. Just then, for me, that was the great thing about feeling empty: When you've got nothing to lose, it's no longer a disaster.

While alpine climbing might look like a crapshoot from the outside—and the nicknames we give our friends acknowledge the danger—the thing about Wharton is that he's also very talented and very strong. And yes, very bold.

Our plan was to go super light on a 4,000-foot big wall on the space-needle-shaped Cerro Torre. No sleeping bag, no satellite phone, no "just in case" safety gear. On climbs like this ounces become pounds and before long you're so weighted down that you can't climb well, or quickly. The danger actually increases. In a place like Patagonia, home to sudden, deadly storms, speed *is* safety. The concept is central to the paradox climbers face in balancing risk and the pursuit of meaningful experiences.

So Wharton and I and our overinflated ambitions entered the Torre Valley, walking through a corridor of blue glacial ice where spires shot skyward on either side like a scene from a fantasy world. The mountains in the Cerro Torre group are topped with bulging mushrooms of condensed moisture called rime ice—a snow-ice amalgam with the consistency of frozen cotton candy. Supercooled water molecules from the Pacific Ocean, just thirty miles to the west, race across the expanse of the ice cap, carried by those ferocious Patagonian winds, until they slam into the first thing they hit—the Torre group. The water molecules freeze and stick together, grow outward, sometimes to the size of office buildings, and overhang the walls below on all sides. The rime mushrooms tend to form biggest on the summits, making Cerro Torre look like a giant ice cream cone—the cone part being the rock wall, which is hard enough to climb on its own. When the weather warms, chunks of rime calve off and rumble down the face, scouring the wall clean.

As we walked toward the Torres, we could hear the thundering sounds of rime shedding in the midday heat.

"Do you think we need to worry about that?" I asked hesitantly. Standing with our backpacks of ultralight climbing gear, I felt like David standing beneath a roaring Goliath.

"Nah, people always exaggerate dangers." Reassuring words from a guy nicknamed Safety Fifth. "Rime is full of air. It'll just bounce right off you. Besides, if we go light enough we'll be able to get out from underneath the mushrooms pretty quickly." I knew of at least one person who had died at the base of this wall in an avalanche.

Couldn't we have a good adventure while bumping safety up to, I don't know, maybe third?

The route on Cerro Torre never came into condition (the rock remained wet and plastered with rime), so we practically ran up a nearby, technically challenging mountain called Cerro Standhardt. We scurried our way up a 2,000-foot lower-angled buttress of gray granite like a couple of ants climbing an elephant's hide, working our way from one crease to the next. Wharton was supremely comfortable amid the chaos of these wild, dangerous mountains, and I realized that I had the capability to feel the same. We placed one piece of gear every fifty feet, maximizing our speed. We topped out on the mountain by midday. I loved the kind of schizoid view—the Southern Patagonia Ice Cap stretching to the ocean to the west, the dry rolling pampas to the east—a place that time forgot.

Enraptured by our surroundings and with plenty of daylight, we decided to go for broke and continue traversing the chain of peaks. Since it hadn't been part of our plan, we hadn't brought extra food or bivvy gear. As we moved toward the next summit, the rime ice mushroom had become a sopping mess. We climbed around on wet rock, looking for a way, but we needed colder temperatures—like, first thing in the morning cold. At nightfall, Wharton started looking around. He cleared away rime and moved rocks, excavating a shelf about the width of a butt cheek. Home sweet home. We sat roped in, huddled together, occasionally standing up to do calisthenics for warmth, but mostly shivering uncontrollably. Come morning, bad weather was brewing and we bailed down a 4,000-foot wall with no established descent route. We rappelled off of slings placed around rocks and little metal wedges called nuts, some only the size of Tic Tacs, that we slotted into cracks.

I remember thinking, *Screw it, what do I care? If I ever want to climb Disaster Style this is the time.*

I liked the sexy appeal of it; I felt good, free, alive. So what if I made the same justifications the soloists made that I was always criticizing?

You would think that fear of death would play an upfront role in my views on risk. It doesn't. I can't fully explain why. Thoughts of my own death only induce fear when I consider what it would mean for the people who love me. My aversion to risk has always come from a sense of duty and honor, rather than some innate dread. When I am running it out far above my last piece of protection or ice chunks are whizzing past my head, my instinctual reaction is simply to respond to the situation at hand. I relish the joys of negotiating unknown outcomes.

Sometimes I view this as a gift, other times a curse. Only in retrospect, when I consider what it would have meant if I died, do I feel like an idiot for having been excited in the moment. The ramifications of a fall—just one slip, just one broken hold—make my stomach churn. I know from afar that I need to be cautious.

But for a time, nobody was counting on me anymore.

I went from one extreme to the other. After Patagonia I returned home to Estes for a few weeks, then went on my first-ever full-on vacation—no climbing involved—a surf trip to Costa Rica with Shannon and three female friends. A lot of time in swimsuits and a few too many cocktails. First it was fun, then a little complicated. I ended up dating one but ultimately had crushes on all three. Should have seen that coming.

Soon afterward, a good friend named Josh Lowell called. He and his brother own a film company called Big Up Productions. He wanted to gauge my interest in helping with a video segment.

Working on film and photo projects with talented and trusted friends has always energized me; I love the collaborative process, the creativity of coming up with new systems to capture and share the beauty of this incredible environment that so few get to experience firsthand. Josh and his team were working on a new film called *Progression*, about the stories behind climbing breakthroughs.

"Do you think the Dawn Wall will go?" he asked over the phone.

"I don't know, it seems kind of unlikely," I told him. "I've found a theoretical line of holds, but it's so hard. Might be something for a future generation."

"Any chance you want to go up there and make a film, just to put it out there?" Josh replied.

It may seem strange to someone outside the climbing bubble, but there is a stigma to hyping up a route you haven't yet climbed. I've seen plenty of climbers talk a big game and never follow through. It had always rubbed me wrong. I'd long stuck to the ethos of "Send first, spray later."

Our discussion soon shifted toward the future generation. This film could be different. I wouldn't claim that I could or ever would succeed on the Dawn Wall. However, I had developed the vision and put in the work to find the line, and Josh suggested that showing the climb to up-and-comers could be a gift to the future. Later, it would be amazing to watch some young crusher come along and show me what could be done.

I pondered the hypocrisy of doing such a film, given my "send first" philosophy—or is it just part of making a living? *Maybe I should do something to keep my name out there. I haven't successfully climbed anything in over a year.* I could hear echoes of my father's voice in those sentiments, but I didn't know how I felt.

The crew included some of my best friends, and the project would give us an excuse for a solid week together in Yosemite.

"C'mon," Josh said. "It'll be fun."

On a warm April day in 2009 I stood barefoot in El Cap meadow as the grass gently swayed in the breeze.

Beside me was a blue tarp stacked with food and climbing equipment. As I double-checked gear lists Corey Rich walked up and gave me a warm hug.

Corey is regarded as one of the great talents in adventure filmmaking, and Big Up had hired him for the project. He stands a solid five-foot-four, was a college champion vaulter in gymnastics, and talks with that Lake Tahoe drawl. Like me, he has a maniacal work ethic. On assignments, Corey's up at four every morning to get first light, and he doesn't stop until after dark. He's razor sharp, always seems to have an innate understanding of how life should work, and had been through a painful divorce himself. He'd often been my confidant. I was looking forward to some portaledge time with Corey.

"You excited for this?" I asked.

"Oh, man, it's been awhile, I can't wait to get back up on El Cap," he said. "So where does the route go?"

By then I had a macro-level concept of the line, even if plenty of question marks remained at the crucial level of actually putting it together. "See that faint dihedral, you climb up that. And the tiny speck of white way up there, that's my portaledge, where we'll make camp."

We talked and pointed at the wall, and then the other members of the film team arrived. Before long we shouldered our eighty-pound haul bags, and as the four of us began a four-hour trudge up the backside, I reveled at the goofy vibe. Lots of dirty jokes and laughter. My split with Beth wasn't public knowledge yet, and I'd been too embarrassed to tell anyone unless I had to. Unbeknownst to me, Corey had called the others before the trip and told them of my recent heartbreak, instructing the crew to try to keep the cheer.

As we hiked, I felt the perm-a-grin on my face and reflected on the contrast with my last trip on the Dawn Wall. Only a few months ago, my mind had spun with doubts, frustrations, and darkness. I thought about how perception affects experience. If you act serious and feel serious, the experience in fact becomes serious. If you decide this climb is going to be scary, it becomes a self-fulfilling prophecy. I started to wonder if in the last few months, it wasn't only my social tendencies that had undergone a renovation, but my overall outlook on life.

Up on the wall, even the route felt wholly different than it had before.

In the company of others, I tried harder and began to link big sections. The climbing felt easier. I even seemed to see better. One day I noticed an inconspicuous line of holds around one of the most troubling sections. More inspection revealed a miraculous sequence of edges, some only a millimeter thick, continuing for two hundred feet. The next day I came close to sticking a crazy eight-foot dyno—basically, an all-points-off jump from one hold to another—across a span of featureless rock. It's an incredibly rare technique on big routes, and one of the times when climbing actually does look like the stuff you see in *Cliffhanger*. I realized that I had finally found a passage through the maze. Or at least the possibility. In terms of scale and difficulty, the project still was bigger than I ever imagined. Dangling from the rope at the end of our third day, I screamed, laughed, and pounded my fists on the wall in a surge of giddiness.

That night a snowstorm rolled in. We hunkered down in the portaledge and ate burritos, drank whiskey, and told stories of past adventures. Soon we were talking about life. Corey thought that being a bachelor again presented me with an amazing opportunity. "Do you know how many women are going to be chasing you down?" he said.

I laughed it off. Still, I was enjoying the camaraderie. Normally I'd have kept this to myself, but I decided to open up a bit. I gave the guys a condensed version of the developments in my love life since my return to Estes post-Beth.

Her name was Becca and I had met her several months earlier at the Rock Inn, on New Year's Eve. I had first noticed her playful, confident smile as she danced with abandon to a bluegrass tune, as if she was born to it.

She had long legs, beautiful blue-gray eyes, sandy blond hair, and dressed like she was from the city. *What's a girl like that doing in Estes Park?*

To my delight, the song ended and she walked right up to me. "I just started climbing. Do you think you could help me learn to train? I heard you might know something about that."

"I don't know, we'll just have to see how we get along," I said, faking confidence. We spent the night swinging each other around on the dance floor. I'd always been too self-conscious to let loose, but Becca had a magnetic force that overpowered my internal hesitancy.

Watching her dance was like reading the back cover of a book and knowing you have to read the rest. One second she would be an Egyptian belly dancer, the next a seventies disco star, then she'd push the baby carriage and moonwalk like Michael Jackson. It was silly and ridiculous and fun, and unintentionally sexy. That she was dancing with me made me feel cooler than I had ever felt in my life.

Being so obviously out of my league made it easy for me to not care. I was sure that she would soon lose interest and move on to someone with style. But she didn't, and at the end of the night I had her phone number.

I waited the obligatory two days before calling, trying to play it cool but checking a hundred times to make sure I hadn't lost her number. We made plans to train together along with another friend. As we climbed, she couldn't handle the common sound of fingernails scraping the plywood walls. Each time it happened she shuddered. I thought it was cute. So I kept walking up to the climbing wall, placing my fingernails on it as if I was about to scratch, waiting for her reaction.

"You better not," she said, her eyes flashing through a feigned scowl.

"Try to stop me." I smiled defiantly.

She ran over and tackled me onto the chalky mattresses. I had never been so happy to be attacked.

A few days later we went to Eldorado Canyon and hiked for thirty minutes to a red-and-black-streaked wall, high on a sunny hillside. It was one of those warm Colorado winter days, T-shirt weather with snow on the ground.

I unloaded my pack and realized I had accidently brought two left climbing shoes. When I told Becca she just rolled her eyes. "You dork," she teased.

"No worries," I said. "I'll just climb in one tennie and one climbing shoe."

"Umm, that doesn't sound safe—maybe we should just go on a hike?"

"Nah, don't worry, I think it'll be okay."

"Have you ever tried climbing in your tennis shoes before? It sounds pretty hard."

I thought for a second. "How did you know I was a climber that night at the Rock Inn?"

"I was telling some friends about how I was taking up rock climbing, and how I wanted to get stronger. They said you were the person to talk to."

That's it? Not that I'm some Michael Jordan, but Estes is a small town. Especially at the Rock Inn. In winter.

I chalked my hands and pranced up the first pitch. When Becca tried to follow she struggled, falling on the rope several times. I worried that I'd picked a bad route. When she got to the belay she was flush with embarrassment. "All right, you're pretty good."

I had figured the only reason the most beautiful woman in the bar would ever talk to me was my small-time "fame." But she knew nothing about my climbing.

As we got higher, she began leaning into me at the belays. She'd never been that high on an exposed cliff before, and looked to me for confidence. I made sure to make jokes, to act relaxed.

We topped out, Becca's hair fluttering in the wind. I imagined myself kissing her right then and there. I'm like a thirteen-year-old girl when it comes to romance, and spending time with Becca felt like bingeing on an entire carton of Ben & Jerry's Half Baked. But this was supposed to be my time to figure out who I was on my own. Falling for her would be the most ridiculous thing I could do. Besides, I was eight years older than her and recently divorced. As far as I knew, she wasn't looking for a romantic partner anyway.

On the way home that night, she told me she was a Christian, and only wanted to date Christian men. Part of me was relieved. We had fun together, and I told myself I would be happy to simply maintain our friendship.

Soon after, I invited her to join me on a short trip to Indian Creek, a crack-climbing paradise in the high Utah desert, where spectacular red and orange sandstone cliffs rise from the Canyonlands. I picked her up after she got off from her restaurant job. She threw her bag in the trunk and then jumped in the passenger seat, balancing a large bag of homemade popcorn on her lap. As I drove we made small talk and grew increasingly comfortable, until she had the windows down and was singing at the top of her lungs. Then she looked at me and said, "You better start singing, too!" The more foolish I made myself, the more it was as if the car had been filled with laughing gas.

One moment we would be pumping our fists and singing along to some silly rap song, the next in deep conversations about life, love, and our pasts. She still had her youthful idealism intact despite a few painful bumps in the road. Yet she wasn't naïve; she was wise and insightful. She talked of her love of languages, and was empathetic to the core. Her confidence came across as nonjudgmental; she was beautiful but without a shred of self-centeredness.

She had grown up in a small midwestern farm town, and her family had traveled to Estes Park on summer vacations. After the obligatory teenage rebellion, she went on to nursing school. She then returned to Estes, figuring she could work in restaurants and live in the mountains while she looked for a nursing job. Her talk about languages intrigued me, but she'd made no mention of having spent time anywhere but in the United States.

"So have you traveled outside of the country?" I asked.

"A couple winters ago I took a two-week trip to Paris. It's kind of embarrassing, but I didn't even know what olive oil was before then."

Her lack of worldliness both fascinated and baffled me. Any knowledge that I had gained had come from living on the road and traveling. Becca had grown up in a rural area and had been almost nowhere. How could she be so interesting, so hip and articulate?

"How old are you?"

"Twenty-two," she replied. "How about you?"

"Thirty."

I could feel her weighing it out in her mind.

"What do you think went wrong between you and your ex?"

"Do you really want to go there?"

"Why not?" she said.

I hesitated to dive in. Being with her had been fun, and we'd been successful at keeping it light.

"Well, the easy answer is that she cheated on me," I said. "But you know it's complicated. People usually don't cheat if everything at home is perfect. The marriage counselor said it was codependency issues. Our relationship started in kind of extreme circumstances."

I told her how Beth had been my first real girlfriend, and about Kyrgyzstan and how tightly we had been wound around each other afterward, how I couldn't really leave her side for years. How I probably loved her too much and put pressure on her to be happy. In the process I tied my happiness too much to her happiness. Maybe I was smothering. Maybe we were codependent. We definitely were codependent. I hadn't realized that I can't truly make somebody else happy, and in trying to do so I probably made it worse for us both. Rather than two strands of rope working together, we became a single cord soon to fray.

Becca listened attentively and seemed fascinated, so I continued.

"The one thing I can't reconcile is that she said she never fell in love with me the way I fell in love with her. Maybe not right off the bat, but it sure seemed like she loved me. To me, that just seems like an excuse."

Part of me was still bitter and unable to admit that there are two sides to every relationship. Without intending to, I had slipped back into blaming Beth.

Becca seemed more excited about cracking open my heart than spilling hers. She speckled her comments with self-deprecating humor, not taking anything too seriously. Like she was a friend I could trust. Then we talked about her life.

"When I was younger, my relationships seemed like the most important thing in the world to me," she said. "I got my heart broken, broke some hearts myself, and got to the point where I decided I wasn't going to give a damn about anyone else. I was going to live for myself. Did what I wanted. I kept dating, but I was very self-centered. That didn't work."

Becca told me about some of her past relationships. The fact that we were "just friends" made the subject less taboo, and therefore more open. I may have seen more of the world, but socially I was like a fawn on ice. Becca was just the opposite.

We drove into those early morning hours where reality loses its sharp edges. The headlights shone into a raging snowstorm, creating a feeling that we were the starship *Enterprise* at warp speed. I shook my head, trying to avoid trancing out, and our conversation shifted.

"A couple years ago I was just coming off a breakup," she said. "I felt empty and was depressed. I knew I needed to find another way and I wanted to be a better person. But I just kept failing." She paused.

"What changed for you?"

"I started doing a lot of journaling and talking with some friends. One friend suggested I go to church." She paused again as if she was expecting me to protest.

"I had gotten to a point where I thought many Christians were so righteous and unloving, but I felt open to God, so I went. The pastor seemed cool, wise. He said, 'For those of you peeking over the fence at Christianity, you don't clean yourself up before you get in the shower. You just jump right in.' I started bawling. Something clicked. So I made the decision that this was the path I would follow. Over time the pieces started to fall into place, I started reading books, talking to people, and continued going to church. One book said that in relationships, being spouse-centered creates too much pressure. Being self-centered means you become your own God. That doesn't work either. You have to be God-centered."

The spouse-centered part hit me with a jolt of truth. The self-centered part made me think of climbing. I didn't know what to say.

"So you're pretty religious, huh."

"Well, I feel like I had an aha moment," she said.

I didn't know what to make of the turn in our conversation. To most climbers, believing in God is like believing in Santa Claus. I'd been through some moments powerful enough to make me feel there was some force out there that, at the very least, was beyond my comprehension. In moments of great pain or great inspiration, I had found myself talking to someone whom I called God. I couldn't say I felt as if I knew him, and he definitely never answered me, never gave me the proof of his existence I was looking for. But I believed that the universe was far too vast to be comprehended by our little minds. In many ways, the people who can truly believe create a simplicity that leads to strength. The other side is that it can create blind spots.

Suddenly, Becca rolled down all the windows. Snow came flying in, creating a micro-blizzard in the car and snapping me from my contemplations.

"Freeze out!" she yelled at the top of her lungs. Then she rolled the windows back up, popped a CD in the player, and turned up the volume.

Becca was such a crazy mix of paradoxes. Religious, but nonjudgmental. Liked to party, but didn't need to be drunk. Most of all she seemed genuinely life loving. And although I was skeptical about the whole religious aspect, I couldn't help but admire the strength of her belief. She told me that ever since she had that "aha" moment, she had been filled with love and compassion. To me, Becca seemed to be overflowing with joy.

Up on the side of El Capitan, I ended my abbreviated version of the Tommy and Becca story, "And yeah, the climbing was a blast, too. Indian Creek always is; she was psyched."

Everyone in the portaledge was smiling. I was clearly enamored, but she was too beautiful, too confident, too smart, too together for a climber guy like me.

"Damn, dude, she sounds awesome. You need a strategy," one of the guys blurted out. "You know what, I lucked into this house-sitting gig at a beautiful home north of San Francisco for a week. You two should stay a night and we can double-date and go to Napa. I know the owners of a winery. It's super dreamy."

I remembered that Becca had said she wanted to someday visit me in Yosemite—she'd never been and I was planning to stay awhile. The guys spent some time convincing me. After we finished the film project, we returned to the ground and I wrote Becca an e-mail. I spilled my feelings for her, and asked if she would come meet me in Yosemite. I spent a tortured couple of days waiting for her to respond. I didn't know it then, but she first consulted with her closest friends. Most of them were pretty skeptical, she later told me. But one, a climber, listened to her pour her heart out. "I think you should give him a chance," he said.

I met Becca in the Sacramento airport on her birthday, and we spent the next few days drinking wine in Napa Valley, walking deserted beaches up north, and wandering the streets of San Francisco. Then, under a full moon, we drove into Yosemite Valley. I brought her straight to the base of Bridalveil Falls, where we stood in the ankle-deep water that fanned out like a skirt in the spring runoff. She gazed up at the millions of gallons of water in free fall and the billions of stars overhead, laughing in amazement. In that moment I couldn't help but wonder if the feelings stirring inside me were God's way of speaking to me, letting me know that he moved in many ways that I couldn't comprehend, but could be enormously grateful for.

CHAPTER TWELVE

Pulling into the driveway, I see the damage the sun has done to the faux-log siding on my parents' house. My mom has been waging an ongoing battle with its drying, cracking, and fading. She's halfway through a sanding and re-staining project—the surface laid bare nearly as white as bone.

Six months have passed since the last time I saw the house or them. I'm not completely certain what I want from my dad—forgiveness, understanding, a second chance, a new way of dealing with each other. I am certain of this: If my mother hadn't called me to let me know how much the letter I'd sent had hurt them, I wouldn't be here now. She said that Dad no longer saw much point in going on living. Even when she'd first told me, months ago, that he wasn't doing well, I hadn't really understood the damage I'd done.

"He started to take down the climbing wall," she said, her voice catching. "It is too painful a reminder of you."

I knew I had to come talk with him. In the interim I wondered and worried, my sleep troubled by thoughts of what I could possibly say to make things better.

I stand at the door and raise my hand to the buzzer, for the first time in a long time aware of my absent finger.

I can't hear any sounds coming from inside the house. I flinch when the front door swings open and he's standing there.

He looks different, more tired than I remember. He nods and starts to open his cracked and sunburnt lips.

Without a word, he steps aside and ushers me in.

I settle on the sofa. He's in his blue recliner. He looks at his teepeed hands.

I scan the room. There's the framed article from the Estes Park Trail Gazette, *the story of him and me climbing the Diamond. Alongside his chair sit stacks of magazines, dog-eared and bookmarked to stories about me or articles I've written. Posters, photographs, videocassettes, and DVDs, a museum of images and words dedicated to me. At least they're still there, not something he wanted to dismantle or discard.*

"Dad, can we talk?" I say, hoping that more words will come to me, that I'll be able to help him understand.

"We should," he says, almost whispering.

My eyes drift to the funnel-shaped smoke stain that reaches to the ceiling of the moss rock fireplace next to him.

"I was in a bad place, Dad, and I'm sorry."

"I thought I'd lost you. Lost my son. I thought it was over—my life, us."

"I never meant to say that we were done."

When we finally allow our eyes to meet, his are pooled with tears, as are mine.

We go on using words to fill in the cracks and fissures of our fractured relationship. The awkwardness lingers, but we both need to push ourselves beyond our usual limit.

I lose track of time, catch my mother smiling as she stays briefly in the kitchen then moves on. The wind rattles a chime, the sunlight edges across the floor, our tears dry and return, the sun patches turn to shadow.

We sit and talk, two men entering unfamiliar territory with no maps to guide us through the landscape, each of us reshaped by time and wind, by rain and sun.

Back in the spring of 2001, I looked through a wall of windows facing the slopes of the Northstar ski area near Lake Tahoe, California. Around me a group of mountain guides and professional climbers sat on sofas and wooden chairs, notebooks balanced on their knees. Marmot outdoor gear, one of my sponsors at the time, had flown everyone in and rented a timber-framed house. For three days we discussed the direction and evolution of outdoor clothing. Each person had a wealth of knowledge in a specific niche of climbing or skiing, and was there to lend critical, expert-level feedback.

Sitting far to the side, alone, was a kid. Cargo pants, baggy T-shirt, smooth skin, and a skater-punk swoop of hair dropping to the top of his eyelids. I noticed him curling his fingers over the edge of his chair. *I used to do that in my high school classrooms, wishing I was out climbing.*

The athlete advisor for Marmot was sitting next to me. I leaned over and whispered, "Who's that kid?"

"Kevin Jorgeson. We just brought him onto the team. I met him at the climbing gym near headquarters," he said. "He's only sixteen—kind of a phenom. You should see what he was climbing, next level."

Then I remembered. When I had been staying with Beth and her family after Kyrgyzstan, I entered a little comp series an hour away for some motivation and to relieve my stir craziness. I remember thinking, *It's small-time, there won't be any real competition there.* Turns out, some little twerp with a bowl haircut beat me—Kevin.

He'd first visited a climbing gym at age ten, and it was a perfect venue for his prodigious talent. At the time of that Marmot meeting he was the top-ranked comp climber in his age group in the United States. The gyms are a controlled setting. You don't learn the old-school techniques my dad taught me, but you can add those later. Instead, you get damned good at climbing movement.

Soon after the comp in which Kevin whupped me, I was talking to Nick Sagar about a study he'd conducted for his newly developed coaching program. He tested an array of climbers on a series of sport-specific strength and endurance exercises. Nick had told me that Kevin tested off the charts. "His failure point was purely physical. Seemed to have no mental barrier." Those remarks left an impression on me.

After two days of meetings, we all took a break. Several feet of snow had fallen, so most everyone went skiing. But I had a different idea. Kevin was the only one who agreed to join me.

We drove to a roadside pullout and then wallowed, hip deep, until we found a granite corridor topped with freshly bleached pillows of snow. The walls rose to a hundred feet, and giant icicles dripped down most of the steeper faces. Almost everything looked wet. Just when we were about to give up, we spotted a semi-dry forty-foot-tall overhanging wall. We post-holed over to it and saw a series of flakes and a line of bolts. It looked hard. I glanced at Kevin—he was already studying the route, pantomiming the moves.

"What do you think, Kevin?"

"Looks scary. It's going be rad, though," he replied. As I pondered the density and depth of the snow against the height of the wall, Kevin threw down his bouldering pad. He sat on it and started wringing the water out of his socks.

I volunteered to go first. We figured the snow would probably be softer than falling on the pad, so we scooted the pad close to the wall and used it to shoe up. I started climbing. About fifteen feet up, as a test I pushed off the overhanging wall and sailed down, sticking into the snow like an arrow in a bale of hay. I smiled and swam back to the pad as Kevin started climbing. He went a few moves beyond, then jumped from about twenty feet.

We took turns climbing progressively higher. It became like a game of chicken. Soon we were nearing the top of the cliff. Both of us were giddy with adrenaline, like kids playing in the yard.

"I'm going for the top," Kevin asserted through wide eyes.

I encouraged him while secretly hoping he might back off.

He dried his shoes with the chalked palms of his hands, stepped onto the wall and started climbing. I noticed his precision and calm, mixed with a calculated and dynamic style. He sprinted through the harder moves, using controlled upward momentum to spring off the tiny holds as if he were a bouncy ball with hands. About thirty feet up, he paused at a big hold, alternately hanging on with one arm while gently shaking out the other. He breathed deeply. His focus only seemed to increase. Then, without further hesitation, he made the decision and executed flawlessly.

He mantled over the top of the cliff, turned, and looked down at me. "Oh, hell yeah, that was awesome!"

Well, shit, I thought. *Guess I have to do it now.*

Eight years passed before I saw Kevin again. He had gone on to make a name for himself, first in indoor climbing competitions, then in highball bouldering. Bouldering, of course, is climbing hard sequences close to the ground with spotters and crash pads. But "highball" bouldering is, well, way high off the ground, usually twenty feet or more. It's not deadly like free soloing, but it's certainly dangerous. You don't splat, but you might shatter. In the climbing video *Progression*—the same one in which my friends filmed me checking out the Dawn Wall—was a segment of Kevin doing the first ascent of a forty-five-foot-tall line on an egg-shaped boulder in California that blurred the boundaries between highball and free solo. It was being hailed as the hardest highball boulder problem in the world. Kevin's ascent required absolute mental mastery along with physical perfection.

In the closing lines of my part in *Progression*, I had made a call-out.

"This next generation of climbers are doing things on the boulders and sport climbs that I really can't conceive of. If they could apply that kind of talent to the big walls, that's what it would take to free climb this project. Even if I can't climb it, I want to plant the seed for someone in the future to come and inspire us all."

When Kevin and I crossed paths again in the summer of 2009, he commented on my Dawn Wall segment, saying he thought the route looked rad. He asked if I was going back up.

Although I'd sort of written off the Dawn Wall as too hard for me, I wanted to return. But my ambition was riddled with holes. For one thing, I didn't have a climbing partner. Many of my friends were great climbers, but the process of working on this climb would be different from the other routes I had done on El Cap. The quantity of hard climbing would require a mind-boggling amount of concentration and practice. This would take years. Even then, it still might not be possible. The Dawn Wall was infinitely harder than any of the other routes on the wall. Who could take that much time out of their lives? And, more important, who had the drive, the focus, and the ability?

Probably more out of politeness than anything, I told Kevin I was thinking of returning that fall. I don't remember explicitly inviting him along, but I must have said something that came across that way. Soon after, I got this e-mail:

Hi Tommy

It was good seeing you the other day. I would be honored and psyched to team up with you in October, November and December, learn all I can, work on the proj, and take it to the next level. I can commit to being in the Valley the whole time with very few exceptions.

I'm all in. Psyched as hell!!

KJ

I wrote off the idea at first. Kevin had never climbed El Cap. You don't just jump on the hardest big wall free route in the world; you work your way up. But was this logic talking, or ego?

I thought about it, and then I responded. I told Kevin to bring his gear and meet me in El Cap meadow on October 10.

The crisp breeze carried a hint of fall. Kevin sat in the swaying grass in a green fold-up chair, looking kind of bug-eyed, his head tilted back as he gawked at the wall the way tourists do. He was twenty-five. The cargo pants were gone and his jet-black hair was neatly trimmed. He's always smiling, very complimentary, and appears self-confident, with the demeanor of a friendly businessman.

We said our hellos. I recognized the funny mix of excitement and anxiety on his face.

"It's a beauty, huh," I said.

"Yeah, pretty crazy. Where does the route even go?"

I started pointing out the various features.

"You follow that diagonal crack system for the first six hundred feet to a small ledge. That's the only ledge in the initial 1,800 feet. Then you continue up and right to that big horizontal dike about halfway up. From here it looks to be short, but it's actually a two-hundred-foot traverse. I think it's going to be the hardest part. At the end of it is the big dyno you saw in the video.

That's where your bouldering skills and power are really going to come in handy." I spent fifteen minutes summarizing the line, and then delved into logistics.

"After all these years I've learned that it's easiest to work this climb from the top down. But today we'll do a few pitches at the bottom, just so you can get a feel for the climbing. Tomorrow, we'll hike all of our stuff to the top. I still haven't closely looked at the last three hundred feet. So the next morning we'll start with that. Then we will work our way down. I figure we'll establish a portaledge camp on Wino Tower—that pillarlike formation about two-thirds up—and sleep there that night."

"So we're gonna be sleeping on the wall two nights from now?" His eyes got wide.

I opened the back of my van and started throwing gear on the ground. Piles of ropes and cams, portaledges, boxes of food, haul bags. Kevin walked around snapping photos with his phone, a goofy grin on his face. Then he asked what he could do to help.

"Why don't you start cutting sixteen-inch sections of webbing, burn the ends with this lighter, and tie them through the eyelets of the beaks with an overhand follow-through. Leave about three inches of tail behind the knot, make sure to cinch it tight."

"Okay. . . . How do you tie an overhand follow-through? I don't really know my knots. Remember, I'm a pebble wrestler," he said, using a self-deprecating term for boulderers. I chuckled to myself. This was absurd. He had no big wall experience, but he had big ambition. I figured it was worth the shot; if nothing else, I'd get a belay for a week or two before he gave up.

We racked up for the day and walked to the bottom of the route. Kevin tripped several times on the short hike, distracted by the wall above. As you draw closer to El Capitan, features that blend together from afar begin to stand out. To a climber's trained eye, they begin to seem climbable. But with the Dawn Wall, even from ten feet away it still appears blank, with nothing to grasp onto. It isn't until your eyes are inches from the face that you notice the texture, the nuances, the possibilities.

"Jesus, that looks like porcelain," Kevin said.

"Yeah, man, that's why this route is so rad. It looks impossible."

I wanted to see how he'd handle the highly technical El Capitan climbing, so we cruised up the first three pitches. I was surprised that he looked comfortable right away. He methodically tested the friction of the slick granite with the rubber of his shoes. He played with the subtleties of balance. He climbed relaxed. When he got to a hard section he didn't waste energy needlessly flailing around. Instead he would stop, hang on the rope, and study the holds. He would temporarily mark the key bumps with bits of chalk and map out a sequence. Then he would massage his fingers into the rock, let each crystal settle into his skin, figuring out how much pressure he needed to apply. He examined each move as if it was a science experiment, gathering and dissecting the data, then building a theory and testing it. If it didn't work, he would try another approach. Once he found a solution, he performed it with incredible grace.

I had to admit, I was impressed. It can take months to adjust to a new kind of climbing. That's how it works for me. For Kevin, dealing with the slick granite seemed instinctual. He was like one of those savants who sits down at the piano for the first time, hits a few keys, then plays by ear. Almost immediately I found myself slowing down. Maybe in thinking about Kevin's lack of experience, I was seeing things from a different perspective, approaching the climbing more analytically. I wasn't just scoping out the holds themselves, I used my fingertips like sensors, transmitting data regarding the texture of the rock's grain. I was able to visualize how my fingers would interlock with the surface. It was as if my brain was constructing a 3-D model of the feature, one that I could turn to examine from different perspectives.

At the belays he would ask questions. I could see him observing and analyzing how I racked the gear, what technique I used to haul the bag. He seemed to instantly comprehend systems that take most climbers years to master. And he was humble. For such a talented climber, he seemed to have little need to make an impression.

We climbed until dark, and the next morning I heaved two eighty-pound haul bags out of my van. They hit the ground like dead pigs. Kevin tried to lift one onto his back. He got it halfway up before dropping it.

"Wow, that's heavy!" he said. "How far is it to the top?"

"I've done it in an hour and twenty minutes without a pack, but with bags like this, maybe four hours?" I wrestled one of the bags into my van's door well, crouched, and slipped the straps over my shoulders. Then, with a grunt, I stood up, my body tilting forward at a twenty-degree angle.

Kevin didn't know it at the time, but I was testing him. I knew he had the climbing skills and I knew he was bold. The part I wasn't sure about, however, was his toughness and his willingness to work.

Within ten minutes our legs were burning and our backs knotted. I was used to this, and knew that the initial half hour was always the worst. After a couple hours he quit talking. But he didn't stop moving. He kept up a slow and steady pace, and as his body adjusted to the stress he seemed to speed up, even as his face went red and his legs wobbled.

When we got to the top, he threw down his pack and stretched his arms. "That felt good," he said.

On our foray on the bottom of the route a few days earlier, Kevin had handled some exposure. But this would be different. It's not only being 3,000 feet off the deck, it's your boldness and talent and toughness and work ethic all rolled into one. Climbing hard on the boulders or at the crags is like showing perfect form in your Tae Bo class. We'd be stepping into the ring with Mike Tyson.

Kevin stood at the edge of the wall, looking down. I handed him a wire brush, gave him a brief description of where I envisioned the route going, and told him to scope it out while I organized our gear for the next day. He clipped his belay device into the rope, leaned back, and without hesitation dropped out of sight.

I waited about twenty minutes, then clipped into another rope and popped my head over the edge. Kevin was repeatedly pushing himself out from the wall, bouncing as far as his legs would propel him and trying to see around a bulge to his left. Then he started to run back and forth along the vertical wall to better enhance his view of the features, his arc increasing to forty-, fifty-, eighty-foot swings.

The kid was completely unfazed. I'd found my partner for the climb of the future.

———

Over time our personalities, along with our respective strengths and weaknesses, began to fit together like puzzle pieces. I was the dreamer and the optimist, with the founding vision and the big-picture view. Kevin was the scientist, the technician, memorizing every detail of each move.

If adventure is defined as embracing the unknown, then our cravings were covered. The exposure was intense, the weather sometimes inclement, but the climb was relatively safe. Although a lot of the protection was dodgy, the wall is sheer, meaning if you take a big fall you hit nothing. Scary, sure. But all of the anchors were bomber, and our modern ropes are strong—climbing ropes only break in the movies. Above all it was an exploration of ourselves, our potential, our ability to persevere.

We established camp at Wino Tower and Kevin spent his first-ever night in a portaledge, staring at the stars.

To allow us access to the various pitches we were working, we strung up a series of fixed ropes. We became efficient at commuting around, both by rappelling and then by using our mechanical ascenders. The ropes could get us from any spot on the wall to another within a few hours, like a human-powered shuttle system.

Days turned into weeks and we developed a routine: Hike to the top and rappel to our portaledge camp. Spend three to five days climbing, then rap to the ground for a few days of rest. Most of the time it felt as if we were cragging, only we were thousands of feet up, on the most breathtaking pitches we had ever seen. In the evenings the sun would reflect off the wall and surround us in a surreal incandescence.

We were learning, making progress, and I felt a growing sense of contentment. There was only one thing missing.

Over the previous months, Becca and I had grown closer. Our relationship progressed from initial infatuation, tinged with intermittent doubt, to something more like love and understanding. When we looked into our futures, neither of us could see anything but a life together. She started a nursing job at a clinic in Estes Park, and after hours she regularly visited a ninety-year-old, mostly blind woman who seemed to really enjoy her company. Coincidentally, this was Mike Donahue's mother. With the rest of her spare time, Becca exercised her remarkably social personality. My community of friends had always been small, composed of climbers, but it grew exponentially once I met Becca. I found that I enjoyed getting to know people, catching a glimpse into their lives, and showing them a bit of mine.

I was drawn to Becca's independence. She cherished her time alone and supported my desire to go on climbing trips. That absence of pressure led to a feeling of freedom. I could spend months in Yosemite and know that she would be fine without me.

None of this changed the fact that I craved her energy and company. I invited her to join me in Yosemite for a week. As soon as she arrived I taught her to jumar, so that she could join Kevin and me on the Dawn Wall.

We sat in a portaledge, feet dangling, the three of us side by side marveling at the view and passing around a bag of trail mix as if we were in a movie theater. An early snow had dusted the mountaintops of the High Sierra in the distance. The midday sun reflected off the granite; beads of sweat appeared on our foreheads even though the ambient temperature was only around sixty degrees. As usual, Kevin and I had stripped off our shirts to soak up some California rays.

Becca followed suit, stripping down to her sports bra.

"It's so amazing up here," she said, the wind blowing her hair, which inadvertently smacked Kevin in the face.

I looked over and caught Kevin blushing. Becca was simply being her natural self, which was unintentionally seductive.

"Yeah, definitely gorgeous," I said. "Aren't you even a little intimidated by the—" I caught myself and paused, but it was too late. "By the size of it?" I smirked.

"Nah, not really," Becca replied.

"Umm, should I go down?" Kevin interjected.

"No man, we gotta send the gnar," I replied, trying not to laugh.

We spent the rest of the day trading attempts on the pitch above the portaledge. All the while Becca cracked jokes, asked questions, and snapped photos. If Kevin was annoyed by my bringing Becca on the wall, he kept it to himself.

Soon after, I decided to take a week's break from the Dawn Wall so that I could spend time with Becca.

"You should go up without me, Kevin," I said. "You have some catching up to do in terms of time spent on the wall."

"Nah, it'd be nice for me to go home for a bit, you know, do some laundry."

I took Becca up some of the shorter classic climbs around Yosemite. We spent one particularly hairy evening getting caught by nightfall, without headlamps, a pitch from the end of our intended climb. Becca remained poised and positive. As the week continued I thought back over the five months since we had first met. It's not like I'd had a wealth of experience with women, but Becca seemed too good to be real.

If there were an instruction booklet to love, it would tell me that all of this was happening too soon. The scars of a failed marriage take time to heal. Yet my relationship with Becca was so different from anything I had known that I felt no opening of wounds, only a sense that part of me I hadn't even known I was missing had suddenly been restored. It's like finding a weathered coin on the ground, and then turning it over to see its other side, newly vibrant and open to the world.

There was one issue. Becca had been very clear that the man she was going to marry would have to be a Christian. She loved me, but she loved God more. When she had asked me if I was a Christian I didn't know what to say. I had gone to church as a child. Asked Jesus into my heart in Sunday school. I was baptized as a baby and prayed in moments of great grief or great inspiration.

Now I was recently divorced. I cursed. In my most godless years I had thought of Christians as dim-witted holdouts with a dangerously naïve view of the world. Never mind that I also viewed myself as dim-witted and naïve. I had never definitively felt God's presence, and I knew that loving God for Becca's sake was a long way from belief. I was genuinely curious but knew that blind faith can also be dangerous, as I had seen in Kyrgyzstan. But I loved how her belief challenged me to explore my own faith and ask myself questions. When I drove Becca to the airport at the end of the week I felt a deep craving to be with her forever.

When I kissed her good-bye, the fearful part of me wondered if she would still be there when I returned to Estes in a month. Although our love for each other was undeniable, I knew I could be happy without her. However, I didn't want to be the man who fell short of her expectations.

After Becca left, Kevin and I whittled away at the climbing. Thick calluses formed on our fingers. We had stopped noticing the exposure and could climb with the same confidence we had being just a few feet off the ground. The work was challenging and tedious, but neither Kevin nor I could imagine anything better than being in the middle of the best piece of stone on earth.

The climbing was so sustained that we had to commit thousands of moves to memory and execute each one perfectly. We would spend hours at night discussing every detail and rehearsing sequences in our minds. When a move gave us trouble we analyzed it—the angle at which to grab the hold, how to position our bodies. At what point is the rubber on our shoes peeling back, and how can we push differently on the rock to avoid this? La Sportiva let me design a new shoe specifically for the demands of this climb.

Just working out the pitches demanded all of our accumulated experience. To cope, we put on our own special "Dawn Wall belief blinders" and adopted an absurdly positive attitude. When pitches were wet we blasted out doubt and just climbed them that way. When the skin on our fingertips disintegrated, we taped them up and kept climbing. I felt a bubbling deep inside, a love for this place and its beauty that emerged with my desire to climb. The wall exists like a canvas, and it is your vision, ability, and creativity that turn it into a route. It's the sort of drive that's impossible to explain to those who haven't been engulfed by a singular, unbridled passion. The route and the wall entered my dreams; I'd go to sleep trying to work out a problem and awake with possible solutions spawned in my subconscious.

Sheer motivation had grown in me, not only due to the potential of this project and finding a solid, committed partner like Kevin, but also because of Becca. She was still there when I got home. My energy soared. I started some intensified training that went beyond climbing specifics. Even when the outdoor thermometer read ten degrees, I'd slip on my running shoes, walk out the front door, and turn face-first into fifty-mile-an-hour wind gusts. I'd just put my head down and start running. I knew that freeing the Dawn Wall was in my mind as much as—maybe more than—in my body. I had to expand my mental toughness, deepen my desire. To top off my training sessions, a force would pull me into the dusty storage room of my six-hundred-square-foot cabin, where I'd crank out a few sets of fingertip pull-ups on the hangboard, then do sit-ups and push-ups until my muscles shook with fatigue.

Becca and I started going to church together. I confessed that I wasn't confident about the whole belief thing, but I was searching. I wanted to try to open my heart fully to God and hope that he would grab hold of it. I started meeting with a pastor once a week to learn more.

The pastor was fine with my expressing my doubts and offered understanding in place of a demand for acceptance. The congregation was relatively small—two hundred or so—and I was warmly welcomed into the community. Their positive embrace of life was a refreshing tonic after all the sarcasm and snark that the rest of the culture was putting out there.

One frigid winter night, Becca and I were returning to Estes Park after a date in Boulder. It seemed as if the humidity had frozen and fallen out of the air; the sky was so clear that you felt as if you could touch the stars. The freshly dusted snowbanks on the side of the winding mountain road sparkled in the car's headlights. Partway up the canyon I purposely popped the clutch and killed the engine.

"Uh-oh," I said. "It won't start!" I released the hood and stepped into the squeaky snow and biting cold. "Baby, I'm gonna need your help. Can you get the flashlight out of the trunk?"

It's hard to get Becca to complain about much, and with a little grumbling she stepped into the snowbank in her high heels and dress. The flashlight was the type where you have to turn a handle to produce light. With a shiver, she shined it under the hood and started to wind. I had tied an engagement ring to the handle of the flashlight so that each revolution produced a loud clank.

"What is that?" She looked down, and then started to laugh uncontrollably. "You're crazy . . . you're crazy!"

CHAPTER THIRTEEN

I look over at Kevin. *The glow of his phone illuminates his face. He thumbs away at a text or an update. I wonder briefly how he's portraying this day's events on social media. Does he let his readers in on the frustration? He looks up, rubbing his chin, as if searching for a word.*

From his mini-speakers, a guitar riff rises through the night air. I can almost hear the pick making contact with the strings. A few seconds in, another guitar, a bass, and a faint drum thrash a power chord over the riff. Kevin looks over at me and begins to pump his fist. For a second I hesitate. Kevin's fist pumping intensifies, and I join in. For the next minute the beat carries us along.

With perfect timing, Kevin hits the opening lines, "Rising up, back on the street."

Images of Rocky flash through my mind. I start to laugh but join in the singing. By the time we hit the Eye of the Tiger's chorus, we're both belting it out at the top of our lungs.

By song's end, we've switched on our headlamps and laced up our climbing shoes.

The night is not over.

Praise be to Rocky Balboa.

Droplets of water the size of marbles fell from the top of the wall and paused in the updraft, as if pondering their position in space, floating and glimmering in the sunlight. Sometimes they hovered in front of our faces like swarms of giant fireflies, motionless for a few seconds before speeding away.

It became an early afternoon phenomenon, caused by the sun melting the snowpack atop El Capitan and sending water down the wall, while simultaneously, the solar-heated rock created an intense updraft that dispersed the streams into the atmosphere. The only problem came when the wind shifted, drenching both us and the rock.

By late March of 2010, the heavy Sierra Nevada winter was finally loosening its grip. The valley was quiet, sublime, holding the promise of spring. Weekly storms that dropped blankets of heavy wet snow interrupted sunny spells, as if the seasons were engaging in their own internal debate. The temperatures often plummeted at night, and the dripping water froze to the wall. The next morning, when the sun hit, the ice would peel away in huge plates. Sometimes they broke apart early and fell like bouncing ice cubes; at other times they whirled past like buzzing saw blades. The biggest chunks—we called them widowmakers—usually fell last, and we'd climb with mounting anxiety, awaiting the bombardment roaring down the wall.

On rest days I'd sit at the base of the wall, analyzing conditions and trying to draw conclusions. "Okay, I have it worked out. It's all a matter of the overnight low at the top of the wall, about seven thousand feet. When it's sunny and the temperature drops below thirty degrees, all the ice sheds by eight a.m., but the rock doesn't get wet until eleven. So that gives us a three-hour window to climb. And when the weather stays above thirty degrees, there is minimal ice buildup and only little cubes come down. So as long as we wear helmets, we should be okay to climb all morning on those days."

Kevin would look at me as if I was crazy. "Dude, you are so ridiculously optimistic."

"I know it seems scary, but the likelihood of our getting hit by one of the big chunks is extremely slim," I would say, shrugging my shoulders.

Kevin's brow would furrow. "Totally not worth it."

This from the guy who's established some of the world's hardest highball boulder problems, with insanely difficult climbing thirty or forty feet off the deck. But he figures that it's all up to him—if he climbs well, he won't fall. He controls the outcome.

Wet rock and falling ice aren't the greatest morale boosters, but there was an emerging element to our dynamic that I couldn't quite wrap my head around. While climbing, Kevin and I were like brothers. We laughed, encouraged each other, pushed each other. On those long nights in the portaledge, waiting out the dripping water, I'd try to get to know him. I'd ask questions, but he'd respond with brief answers, seemingly uninterested, all the while tapping away on his iPhone.

Off the wall, I'd invite him to hang out in my van so we could cook dinner together. Instead he would keep to himself in his truck. I'd long held this notion that the intensity and commitment of a climbing partnership creates a closeness that's rare in the everyday world. Each of my previous partners had gotten a piece of me, and I had taken a piece of them.

But all of my other big climbs had been with people with whom I was friends first. This relationship started differently: Kevin wanted to learn to free El Cap, and I wanted a partner. But we climbed well together, I liked him, so maybe our friendship just needed some time.

Whenever we did talk, there was one topic Kevin liked to discuss in depth: business. He was trying to start an organization called Professional Climbers International. The goal was to create more business opportunities and income for professional climbers. Climbing, after all, could hardly be considered a lucrative profession. It's been that way forever. Sponsors give you gear (which helps, as the stuff's expensive), maybe pay for some trips (with the caveat of returning with quality photos for them to use), and, for a fortunate handful out there (like me), some money. They're relatively small deals, nothing like the endorsements known to mainstream athletes.

In exchange, you provide value for the sponsor's brand. You appear in photos, ads, stories, and news clips reporting your (presumably significant) accomplishments. You try to be a positive face for the brand—that's why crusty climbers rarely have sponsors, no matter how hard they climb. In reality, for all the people who like to call themselves "professional climbers," in the United States you could probably count on both hands the number who make a real living, an income equivalent to, say, that of a janitor, based solely on getting paid to climb (versus income from climbing-related writing or photography, guiding, being a sales rep, and so on). There just isn't much money in climbing. But times are changing, and climbing is growing. Opportunities are on the rise, especially for talented, personable people like Kevin.

When we talked about it I felt as if he shifted modes, as if we were in a boardroom. He'd use terms like economically viable, and say things like, "In order to advance the business interests of professional climbers...." On an emotional level, it jolted me. Such thinking struck me as a violation of climbing's longstanding social contract. Money from sponsors is a mechanism to enable us to climb more—it has nothing to do with why we climb, and it should never compromise the purity of our pursuit.

"Climbing is a sport of nonconformists," I would tell him. "I'm not sure what climbers will think of its being turned into a business." I never aspired to be a professional climber; when I was young the occupation simply didn't exist. Over time, sponsors came to me, never asking me to sell my soul in return for their support. Which, of course, makes it easy for me to sit on my throne and act pious.

Throughout our conversations, I found myself thinking more deeply about my own motivations and intentions. I had now been working on the Dawn Wall for parts of three years. It had become my touchstone, my opportunity for self-expression. The way it started—alone—empowered me in my quest for independence. It felt creative, like taking a unique vision and seeing it through. I wasn't thinking of it as a business opportunity. Within that space, I saw Kevin as an apprentice. He was learning the ways of big wall climbing, while also helping me toward my goal.

Then one day Kevin made a comment that made me squirm. "Wouldn't it be badass if the first route I climbed on El Cap was the Dawn Wall?" Suddenly I wondered if Kevin was really interested in learning, or if the Dawn Wall was merely an avenue to gain recognition and up his value as a professional athlete.

When Beth and I divorced, I bitterly thought that her attraction to me might have had more to do with creating a desirable career path than actual love. Was Kevin using me the same way? Or was he just becoming collateral damage from the baggage of my failed marriage? After all, in a sense I was also using him.

While I only saw the businessman, and the guy who was psyched to figure out the moves, after two seasons of working together I knew there was more to Kevin. He was young, struggling to keep up, and exceedingly private. Despite his supreme talent, Kevin undoubtedly had his own insecurities. My intense drive toward this climb probably only made things worse. It reminded me, uncomfortably enough, of my relationship with my own sometimes overbearing father. I had never been able to go deep with Dad. I loved him and we had fun together, but in his powerful presence I withdrew emotionally. I always figured Dad wasn't burdened with an abundance of introspection. Maybe it's just how it is for men of that generation—they get the job done, drive forward without complaint. But what if there was more to it? What if Kevin viewed me as the overbearing father?

In one way, though, Kevin and my dad were alike. My dad was always acutely aware of what a rare opportunity I had—to make a living doing what I loved. At times, though, he seemed more willing (or able) to talk with me about my professional life than about how I was doing inside. After Kyrgyzstan, for example, I felt as if he was at least as concerned about my climbing as he was about my well-being.

Then again, these things overlap with me, and I probably needed the direction. Or the push. I wasn't driven by money, and I don't think he was either, but making money was the means by which I could continue to do what made me happiest for as long as possible. Certainly, if given the choice, my dad would have loved to have been a full-time climber.

My dad—like Kevin, probably—understood better than I did that idealism had to be grounded in the more mundane realities of rents and mortgages, utility bills, and car maintenance. Maybe, if I looked at things more from his and Kevin's point of view, I'd better appreciate the positive aspect to their more multidimensional approach: Climbing could also be a career.

Over time I convinced Kevin that if we timed it right we could manage the risks and make the climb safe. We began setting the alarm for 3:00 a.m. and climbing from sunrise until 11:00 a.m. Then we'd retreat into our portaledge to wait out the drip-drip-drip of water until midnight. We'd get some sleep, then rise at three and try again to solve the gymnastic puzzles of the crux pitches.

During those time-outs, bursts of wind regularly pummeled the portaledge. Occasionally we'd peek out and stare at the tourists in lawn chairs in the meadow, who were surely wondering what in hell we were doing. It felt like one of those cartoons where the rain cloud follows you around, always hovering just over your head. Boredom, more than physical exhaustion, was our primary challenge.

Before long, Kevin's motivation seemed to wane. I felt bad for always pushing him, making him do something beyond his comfort zone. After each stint on the wall, I'd spend rest days in the valley, scheming about our imminent return. Increasingly, Kevin would head home. Then he would get distracted and not make it to Yosemite for a few more days, leaving me without a climbing partner. When we left that May, I had my doubts about whether he would return.

I might have gotten discouraged after such a trying season, but life at home with Becca reinvigorated me. Our days were filled with loved ones and time outdoors. We savored the simplicity of our life in Estes, the countless treasures just outside the door of our cabin, as wildflowers bloomed and snow lingered in the mountains.

On a beautiful June day, under a perfect sky, Becca and I stood in an open meadow, joined by seventy of our closest friends and our families. The peaks of Rocky Mountain National Park rose in the distance. We held hands and I talked first, doing my best to not sound clumsy. Then Becca spoke, eloquently and lovingly, of our relationship as being like a climb, the way we would navigate challenges as they arose, both those expected and those unforeseen, through times easy and hard, remaining independent and connected as we strove together toward the highest expression of our selves. The pastor, who was also our friend, presided as we looked into each other's eyes and said, "I do."

I had never known love could be so joyful. Since meeting Becca my life had changed from feeling like a slow, painful, uphill slog to more of a skip across the clouds. Her lighthearted nature softened the rough edges of my past. Her love of people and endless curiosity about all things foreign and new filled me with happiness. Her touch made me tingle and her laugh made me spin. In those first months after marriage I kept shaking my head, expecting to snap back to reality.

For the past several years, climbing had kept me away from home an average of nine months a year. Becca and I wanted to retain our independence but didn't want to be apart that much. We made the decision that she would quit her nursing job and travel at least some of the time with me. Her talent for photography was emerging. We figured that if she devoted at least some time to taking photos, it would make up for the financial gap.

My parents understood and supported our decision—not that they would have meddled in our lives. Becca's mom and dad needed some time. Being from Minnesota, and professional climbers being rare birds even in the mountain West, they had difficulty grasping exactly what I did. They clearly loved their daughter and wanted her to be happy and secure. I could understand the risks they saw as inherent in a life like ours, but they trusted her and eventually came around.

Much of that was due to Becca; with her I felt that anything was possible, and soon my mind drifted back to the Dawn Wall. The route had started to morph in my mind. It was changing from a way to cope with the pain of rejection to a chance to test my limits and be an explorer.

This season, I would not only try harder, but be more analytical. I decided to examine what had gone wrong in the past and figure out what might work in the future.

The first step to prepare for the fall 2010 season would be to get stronger. The difficulties of the Dawn Wall were coming down to a handful of individual moves. I had spent decades developing endurance and specific El Cap climbing techniques. What I lacked was pure power. The best way to increase climbing-specific power is through hard bouldering, so I spent most of my training days in a glacier-carved valley in Rocky Mountain National Park called Chaos Canyon.

I'd begin by running up the trail for about an hour. The canyon sits between 10,000 and 11,000 feet in elevation. About a half-mile wide and two miles long, it is filled with house-sized boulders. My dad had first noticed the area's phenomenal potential a decade earlier when he was fishing in a nearby lake. It has since become a world-class destination for boulderers, with countless gorgeous, classic lines.

As you near the canyon you walk past babbling brooks and picturesque subalpine lakes full of lily pads and rainbow trout. In the lower canyon, the groves of stunted ponderosa pines look like green trolls standing beside the dark brown and gray colored boulders. The upper gorge is all rocks, some with intricate patches of bright yellow lichen, others marbled with swirling intrusions of black and tan. Each afternoon during the summer storms the skies would unleash, and I would retreat deep into a labyrinth of passageways and caves. I'd weave around, looking for that perfect combination of steep rock and adequate holds, while the rain hammered down and the thunder echoed.

I would boulder for four or five hours, then run back down, my upper body trembling, drive to my parents' garage, and do a couple more hours of exercises for climbing-specific strength and injury prevention. Some days, I would end the sessions with a half-hour CrossFit-style workout.

The volume and intensity of these efforts regularly exceeded my physical capacity. Each night I would be quivering with fatigue but deeply satisfied. The goal was greater than training the body; I was developing mental toughness and building a mind-set of invincibility.

I had control over my ability to work hard. I could draw on my past experiences of pushing past my body's point of perceived failure, to use my brain to remind my screaming muscles that they could keep holding on, or do another set. I wanted to close the gap between my performance and my true potential.

The second step for the season was to rethink the conditions on the wall. After the previous year's battles, I'd decided that spring's incessant seeping from snowmelt made the upper half of the route practically impossible to climb. The Dawn Wall had to become a one-season climb: autumn. Summer was too hot, winter too snowy. On cutting-edge routes such ambient conditions make all the difference in the world. Going forward, I'd spend the spring season training somewhere else.

The third step would be to reconsider the team. Although Kevin hadn't officially bailed on the project, I hadn't heard much from him through the summer. I needed to plan accordingly in case he wasn't into it anymore. Most of my past climbs had been done with a single dedicated partner. I wondered if a better approach for the Dawn Wall would be to crowdsource belayers.

Becca came to Yosemite that season, and although she was willing to belay me, I didn't want to add potential stress to our relationship. I wanted her to enjoy Yosemite. So I organized a network of friends to come up on the wall throughout the autumn. Surprisingly, people were eager to sleep on a portaledge in exchange for a little belay duty. The environment heightened the experience for everyone. Food tasted better, jokes were funnier. Pooping into a paper bag never got less hilarious. By the time the Dawn Wall season commenced in October 2010 the crew was almost too big.

And then, sure enough, Kevin arrived. He was psyched and ready to climb, and our crew of vertical-camping-belayer friends gave him an opportunity to share his newfound big wall knowledge, thereby increasing his confidence. The weather was great and we fell into a routine of going up on the wall for three days, usually accompanied by a third team member, then coming down for a few days of rest. Kevin still got sidetracked on his forays home to rest, but no big deal—I'd just go up the wall with others, figuring he could join us when he was ready.

One such friend was a teddy bear of a man named Cooper Blackhurst, a six-four, 230-pound former linebacker for Stanford. Cooper and I met at an American Alpine Club community climbing event. Before coming on the Dawn Wall he had never been more than a couple hundred feet off the ground.

"Dude, I could carry some big bags for you," he offered. When I handed him a massive haul bag to lug to the top of El Cap, he casually swung it onto his back as if it were a man purse.

Cooper reminded me exactly of the superhero cartoon character Mr. Incredible. He had blond curly hair, huge muscles, and a mischievous smirk. Within a single sentence his tone fluctuated from sounding like a twelve-year-old boy to sounding like Louis Armstrong. Fits of laughter burst from his stomach as if he was burping firecrackers.

Our hike to the top of El Cap was a mixture of dirty jokes and unadulterated overstoker energy. Every few minutes Cooper would stop, turn around, and look at the view behind us. "Oh, my God, dude, THIS IS SO RAD!" Then he'd softly add, "I can't believe we are actually here right now." Cooper regularly broke into monologues about the natural beauty that were so full of appreciation that I expected to turn around and find him weeping.

"Hey, Tommy, have you ever heard of the porch swing."

"Yeah, why?"

"Do you think we could do it while we are up there?"

"Aw, man, I don't know." The porch swing is a stunt that was first conceived by a wild-man climber named Scotty Burke. A decade earlier he had spent some three hundred days living on top of El Cap while working on freeing the Nose. Although he was a free climber, he was also kind of a throwback to the late seventies, when El Cap was a venue for hardcore drugs and death-defying stunts. Scotty was something of a cult legend, and the stories about him blurred the line between fact and fiction. In one telling, each day he would wake himself atop El Cap by snorting a line of coke and then tying into a rope and leaping off the top of the wall.

True story or not, calling it a "swing" didn't do the maneuver justice. It was more like a two-hundred-foot free fall, akin to a bungee jump but self-rigged with a climbing rope, and done 3,000 feet off the ground. Unlike most bungee jumps, on the porch swing you fall just a few feet away from the vertical rock face, creating an unnerving sensation of speed and a nearly paralyzing fear of hitting the wall. I'd contemplated setting it up on several occasions. But it never took me long to realize that I risk my life enough while trying to hold on. Falling is a by-product of climbing, not the objective. Jumping off for "fun"? No way.

"We have to do it, Tommy!" Cooper protested, slapping his giant hand on my shoulder and giving me a firm shake. Maybe taking a two-hundred-foot free fall from the top would be good mental training for the Dawn Wall, where we regularly took sixty-footers while climbing.

I rigged the jump, trying to quiet the voice of panic inside my head. When I clipped my belay device into the short strand of rope, my hand was shaking.

The way the porch swing works is you anchor one end of your two-hundred-foot dynamic rope to a protruding rock feature known as the Diving Board. The other end is tied to you, standing fifty horizontal feet away along the rim of El Cap. Just back from your position by the edge is a tree, to which you've tied a thirty-foot strand of rope. Then, you intentionally execute every climber's nightmare, the way in which many exhausted climbers have accidentally died: You rappel off the end of the rope (the thirty-foot rope).

Climbing is a game of control. The porch swing is all about letting go.

I slowly rappelled until the end of the short rope was inches below my brake hand, and the steepest part of El Capitan dropped 3,000 feet straight down. I stared at the rope leaving my harness, going a hundred feet down and then back up in a giant loop to the Diving Board. Cooper was at the anchor, filming.

"How does the anchor look, Cooper?" I asked, my voice cracking.

"I guess it looks good. I don't know. You're the one who set it up." He started giggling. "Oh, my God, dude, you're gonna fall a ways."

"I know," I said through deep breaths. "Just give me a second."

"Okay, do whatever you're comfortable with."

"I'm not sure I'm comfortable with any of it," I whimpered.

"Fuck it," I said, as I let the end of the rope slip through my fingers.

The rope pinged through my belay device, and my stomach vaporized as I went weightless. Down I zoomed, picking up speed in an instant to 9.8 meters per second squared. It felt even faster than that, as the roar of the wind rushed in my ears. The wall whipped past in a grayish-white blur just a few feet away, my mouth gaped open in a silent scream. After an eternity the rope stretched tight, forcing the last bit of air from my lungs. I arced across the wall in a giant pendulum and my terror transformed into adrenaline-induced ecstasy. For a full two minutes I swung at the end of the rope, praising God that I was still alive. Then I jumared back to the top.

"That was the raddest thing I have ever seen!" Cooper said, laughing hysterically. "I have to do it now."

We doubled-checked the system, Cooper tied in, rappelled down the short rope and hardly hesitated. I was amazed. He'd barely been off the ground before, and here he was, nonchalantly taking a two-hundred-foot free fall from the top of El Capitan.

That night Cooper and I descended to our portaledge base camp midway down the wall, and Kevin joined us the following morning. We spent the next three days climbing from our little nylon islands in the sky, while Cooper belayed and provided continual color commentary. Kevin seemed to come to life in Cooper's company, even cracking a joke when talking about two pieces of protection, each with names that double as anatomical slang. "Something suddenly felt wrong, the pecker was below the nut!" I began to see more of Kevin's goofy, fun-loving side, one that was often suppressed when it was just the two of us.

Afterward, when we descended, Cooper told me that he would have traded the best day of his football career for that trip on the Dawn Wall.

With that kind of energy, progress came fast. We free climbed all of the hardest individual moves, linking them into consecutive sequences of varying lengths, and then started to link entire pitches. While we hadn't successfully linked the hardest pitches start to finish, we were making steps toward sending the route. Our bodies seemed to be adjusting to life on the wall, and we were hitting our stride.

El Cap has the best cell reception in Yosemite, and each night I was on the wall I would check in with Becca on the ground, and come away from it feeling more energized and more eager for the next day. We had started talking about kids and the future. She told me how much she missed me when I was up on the wall, but also about all the fun she was having with her friends. She was getting into running, and going climbing with other people. She'd even started a blog titled *Life with the Caldwells*. It was a mix of adventure, cooking, and photography.

I don't know if it was something innate that I had to grow out of, or just the mysteries of interpersonal chemistry, or probably both, but in my previous marriage I often felt ruled by self-consciousness. It was nobody's fault but my own, or maybe nobody's fault at all, but when I was with Beth I was only a boy. Now everything felt different. I felt confident with Becca. Her energy and inner calm flowed into me. She held me to a higher standard. I could feel myself changing, rising, becoming a better man.

Early that November, after spending the previous five weeks working the route, Kevin and I decided to give the Dawn Wall our first ground-up free attempt. We would start at the bottom and climb to the top, all thirty-two pitches, without leaving the wall. I'd invested far more in this than any other climb in my life: three years, with over ninety days on the route and countless hours spent training off the wall. All of which was merely practice. The push is what matters. And for it to count as free, each of us had to free climb each pitch in its entirety (no midpitch weighting of the gear or the rope), whether on lead or while following. We could try each pitch as many times as needed, so long as we stayed on the wall.

We started on the morning of November 19. We had a camp and two weeks' worth of supplies stashed nine hundred feet up the wall. Josh Lowell and his brother Brett had flown out to film our attempt. Word had circulated among our friends and families, and I didn't want to let anybody down. I was nervous, and I could tell that Kevin was, too.

On only the second pitch, a 5.13a that was a warm-up compared to what was above, our feet skated and our bodies quaked. We made frantic stabs for the holds. We each fell a few times and had to reclimb pitches. By the end of the first day we were six pitches up and felt as if we had been through a war. Bloodied knuckles, taped fingertips, beaten spirits. I knew what the problem was, but that was little solace. Nerves had gotten the best of us. This attempt was like opening day of the season and game seven of the championship finals all rolled into one. We'd been practicing and planning for so long that the moment became bigger than us. It wasn't so much the pressure of everyone else's expectations, but a kind of distracted, is-this-really-happening disconnect that was troubling. The mental clutter translated into not trusting my feet, which meant using my hands more. I expended too much energy too soon and knew I couldn't sustain that level of output. Go that deep in your reserves too early, and you leave nothing in the tank.

Day two was blisteringly hot, and there was no way we could climb such desperate pitches in the sun. We waited for the cool of nightfall, which also allowed us some much-needed rest.

Although eerie, climbing at night is sometimes easier if you know where to go. Not only do the colder conditions minimize slippage, but on glassy-smooth rock the light cast by your headlamp angles straight across the wall, illuminating edges and crystals, creating shadows that make the footholds look bigger, and inspiring confidence.

At 10:30 p.m. on day two, we prepared for pitch 7, the first 5.14 pitch. We hadn't yet free climbed these pitches, so we estimated the ratings based on our experience and our previous attempts. It rose overhead as a hundred-foot-long offset seam, protected by a series of metal wedges, shaped like bird beaks, that we had hammered a few centimeters into a hairline crack during the previous month. We knew there was a chance that the protection wouldn't hold a big fall, but we reasoned that even if all the gear ripped out and one of us took a huge whipper, we'd be okay because the wall is so sheer that there is nothing to hit. Kind of like the porch swing.

I went first, and about three-quarters of the way up, the intense effort made my body start to shake. As it did, my technique and my nerve both abandoned me, and I grabbed the sling on one of the pieces of dicey protection. As gently as possible I shifted my body weight onto it and then Kevin lowered me back to the belay.

"My nerves are getting the better of me," I said. "You wanna give it a try?"

I watched as the yellow beam of Kevin's headlamp moved steadily upward, accompanied by the sounds of his labored breaths and carabiner gates clipping shut. He had climbed past my high point when his feet slipped. He let out an involuntary shriek and the light from his headlamp came racing down toward me. I listened for the pinging sounds that protection makes when it rips out of a crack, and braced for impact. Suddenly he stopped.

"Nice, Kevin!" I shouted through the dark stillness. "Good job going for it, man. Guess that piece of protection was good enough."

We began taking turns, each time gaining slightly more confidence and climbing higher than the last. On my third attempt I made it one move from the end of the pitch before pumping out and falling. As I lowered I blurted in excitement, "Oh yeah, this is what it's all about!"

"Seriously, this is really intense," Kevin replied.

Suddenly I saw a bluish, glowing light. He'd pulled his phone from his pack and then typed on it for a few seconds.

"What are you doing?" I asked.

"Updating Twitter."

"After every attempt?" *Why?* I thought to myself.

"Yeah," he said. "The ultra runners do it at races so that people can follow along in real time. I thought I'd give it a try with our climb."

Within an instant, my mind raced. *Come on, man, let's keep our heads in the game. Don't think about business right now.* You know, just the . . . four of us. Before I could say anything I clued in to the hypocrisy of my thoughts. Although the two other members of the team were my friends, they were primarily there as filmmakers. I already had a career; Kevin was still building his. If this is the modern way, best not to be a Luddite.

After Kevin finished he put the phone away, pulled on his climbing shoes, and sent the pitch. We both hooted as if he had scored a touchdown. The energy was contagious—the "send train," as climbers call it—and then I sent as well.

We climbed until 1:00 a.m., managing to finish off one more 5.13d pitch. Around noon we rose, spending the sweltering afternoon goofing off and preparing for the cooler evening. After a few days I forgot about the earth below. With Josh and Brett adding camaraderie, we were isolated from the worries of the world.

In previous seasons, some climbers had loosely followed our attempts through Josh's videos, various clips, and the few articles I had written for the climbing magazines. I wasn't truly aware of the way that Kevin's Twitter feed had boomed on the Internet, though. All of a sudden, the tension and excitement that we were feeling on the wall was being projected to the world outside of Yosemite, some of it in real time. During our midday rests, we'd get on our phones and read what people were saying about us. It was weird. I was extremely conflicted, but often couldn't resist the temptation. We were practically alone on the wall, but the virtual stadium of people rooting for us on the Internet seemed to fire Kevin up. He was climbing better than I had ever seen him climb before. More precise, less hesitation, stronger.

At 11:30 p.m. on day four, we faced pitch 10, which we rated 5.14a. It starts with a relentless, hairline-width seam. To send it we would have to layback eighty feet of tendon-straining piton scars, stem through a section of dripping slime oozing from the crack, attempt to dry our shoes and hands while standing on dime-width edges, and then burl through the hard part. The crux required pressing our fingers against a small roof overhead, then, with ironlike body tension, walking our feet up on miserable smears until they were six inches from our hands, then rocking our weight onto those foot smears and extending a hand far across to latch a sloping piton scar. It was so strenuous, involving every muscle from our toes to our fingers, that Kevin had named it the "lift the car off the baby" move.

We both made several unsuccessful attempts. Then, with a little added motivation from Rocky Balboa, we flicked on our headlamps, laced up our shoes, and lifted the car off the baby. Riding the momentum, we climbed the next pitch as well.

We took a day off, and then dark clouds rolled in. The top of El Capitan vanished. Without the sun's heat, I managed to climb pitch 12 in daylight. At 5.14b, it was the hardest yet of our push, and the entry to the heart of the route. Kevin had been watching the weather forecast and knew we were about to get pummeled. I remember looking up at the sky and saying, with my unrealistic optimism, "I think it's going to go around us."

When the rain fell, exactly as predicted, we packed up everything and bailed. Five days of high winds and heavy snow followed, dumping four feet atop the wall. It was an anticlimactic end to our first real attempt. We'd taken ten days to fail only one-third of the way up the wall. Strangely, we felt encouraged.

We'd put in a huge effort. But, simply put, overthinking had been our enemy. More time, more practice, more experience, and we'd climb more instinctually. We'd learn. With the pressure of the first real attempt off our shoulders, we hoped next time would be different.

I'd failed plenty before, and I knew that I would again. Experience and mentors had taught me that if you do it right, failure becomes growth.

CHAPTER FOURTEEN

Alone, I lie on my back staring at the fixed rope as it swings in the gentle breeze. Almost as if the rope has hypnotic powers.

I talk out loud to myself, meditate, visualize success.

"You can do this. You've done this before. You've put in the hours."

Then I prayed.

Dear God, please give me the strength and the power. Please help my skin to heal.

I shut my eyes and shake my head. I'm ridiculous. Do I really think that God cares about someone sending the Dawn Wall? How arrogant am I to think that he will hear me and grant my ridiculous requests?

But this means so much to me. Will these four years be a waste?

I stare at my fingertips. Layers of dried blood and skin flake and flap like tattered tissue paper. I gently press my thumb against each tip. Zings of pain shoot up my arms. I slather on hand salve and tape them up. I know the likelihood of their healing in two days is slim. But what am I to do? What would I do without this climb in my life? Where would I go, who would I be?

Hours later, I notice a tug on the rope running to camp from the ground. I ease my head over the edge and look down. I can make out my dad's familiar shape as he jumars. I'm eager to see him, and hope that his presence will breathe new life into me. I mark his stuttering progress. As he nears I notice how red-faced he is, how he slumps into his harness after every few feet of vertical gain. Even from here, I can hear his labored breathing.

Finally, he's within reach. He struggles to pull himself into the portaledge. A grunt escapes his lips.

"Thanks for being here, Dad. It's so good to see you!"

He settles in beside me and nods. His shoulders heave with his heavy breaths. He puts his hand on my shoulder and leaves it there. Some slack flesh hangs below his still-impressive biceps; wrinkles and sun spots mark his face. His aura of invincibility feels diminished. I realize for perhaps the first time how much Dad has aged. Suddenly, climbing the Dawn Wall seems insignificant. I want to give up. But Becca, my dad, so many other people have put in the effort. I owe it to them to keep going. I force a smile and lay my tender, painful hand on top of his. I want to thank him, tell him I'm sorry that I put him through my Dawn Wall obsession.

"It's so good to see you," I tell him again, wondering how much of him is in me.

We'd gotten the beat down. I drove the twenty hours home to Colorado without sleeping or even turning on the radio.

My head spun with every detail of what had gone wrong, what we had learned, and what we should do differently next time. When I was a teenager, failure was suffocating. Trying your hardest and coming up short can be psychologically and emotionally exhausting. But each time it happens and you begin anew you become better, inured to the feeling. In more recent years, failure has fostered in me a deep curiosity about the mysteries I have still to unlock.

I thought about how we had started too fast while climbing in the sun on our first day. That had rattled our nerves and eroded precious skin. Our decision to shift to climbing at night had come too late. For the next season, we would have to become nocturnal, like bats, hiding and resting under the shade of our strung-up sleeping bags during the days, and emerging to climb at night. But even the nights were sometimes too warm. Maybe we needed to push our timeline back to winter.

But with winter storms come falling ice. We could likely climb during lulls in the storms, when the rock was dry. But during certain hours on clear days, the freeze-thaw cycle would cause artillerylike icefall. As I drove, it hit me: Build an ice-deflecting shield. I had to pull the van over. I held my breath, closed my eyes, and started running calculations in my head. If we could build something robust that could sit at a forty-five-degree angle to the wall, it should effectively deflect the widowmakers. The idea solidified and I started shaking with excitement. I texted Kevin: "Three words: ICE DEFLECTING SHIELD!" I got so worked up about the idea that as I started driving again I drummed my palms on the steering wheel, shouting. "THAT'S IT, THAT'S IT!"

With the exception of falling in love, the Dawn Wall had become the most positive and engaging experience of my life. When I saw how my friends and family had rallied around to help, I realized that I wasn't the only one who saw its power. The Dawn Wall had become almost mythical in my mind, touching on elements beyond athleticism. Part of me felt crazy for thinking this way, but I didn't care. The support and interest had a way of validating my obsession, making me feel less crazy for wanting it so badly.

For the next eight months, life became all about preparing for the next season. This time, though, I would take breaks and strive for more balance. In the past, I would have tended toward overdoing things, drifting into obsessiveness.

Patagonia had always made me feel centered, and I wanted to show Becca a place I so loved. Just five weeks after returning from Yosemite we packed our bags and headed south. Storms racked the mountains for our entire four-week stay, so we spent our time enjoying the laid-back Argentine culture and bouldering around the town of El Chaltén.

I loved the remoteness of our Patagonian escape. The two places I'd lived most of my life—Estes Park and Yosemite West—aren't exactly big cities, but they're both gateways to major national parks. Tourism is the lifeblood of the towns, and Yosemite National Park, particularly the valley, is like a city unto itself with food stores, hotels, and restaurants. At high season it's a kind of mini-Manhattan, with congested roads and long lines and crowds.

Despite being located within Los Glaciares National Park, El Chaltén is an authentic frontier town that has only existed since 1985. The 130-mile trip from the nearest airport in El Calafate takes you across a desolate and sparsely populated region of southern Argentina. Though some amenities now exist, for a long time it lacked the infrastructure that so many people count on. I welcomed having neither Internet nor cell phone service.

On one particularly windy day, I went bouldering alone as sagebrush swirled in the gusts. I found a sheltered spot behind a boulder, sat down, and was rubbing windblown grime from my eyes when a little girl, no more than two years old, appeared on a nearby knoll. Her cheeks were round, snot had dried to her upper lip, and her long black hair twisted in the wind. She wore a purple down jacket that was covered in a layer of dirt. The wind blew so hard that she had to continually readjust her footing to stay upright. She was a startling contrast to the dramatic landscape, but she looked as though she knew it well. I was overcome with a rush of tenderness, and I smiled at her. She stood silently, trying to decide what to make of me. Then she darted away. For a moment, I wondered if I had seen a ghost.

I walked over to where she had been and saw her running down the hill below. There was a man striding along using a walking stick, whom I presumed to be her father.

That night, I told Becca about the encounter.

"Oh yeah, that was probably Tormentina," she said. "I met her and her dad, James, the other day. That family seems incredible. They sailed here from New Zealand, and last year they rode their bikes all over Patagonia when Tormentina was barely a year old. They even have a new baby now, too. I think they sold all their possessions and cashed in their savings to buy a sailboat. It's their home as they travel around the world."

What an amazing way to spend one's childhood. Over time, that image of Tormentina settled in my mind like a vision brought forth by a shaman. It was a flash of desire and a hope for the future, as I always knew that someday I'd want children.

After that, Becca and I would occasionally talk more seriously about starting a family. She had known that she wanted to have kids from the time she was a young girl. But she had just started traveling, there was so much she wanted to see, and I was worried about what raising children would do to my chances on the Dawn Wall. "Well then, you're just going to have to get it done before we have kids," Becca said. Although she supported me wholeheartedly, I think part of her felt like the Dawn Wall was my mistress.

Although the thought was unspoken, it was true; after all, we'd negotiated the entirety of our relationship around this climb. I didn't feel pressure from Becca, but I put pressure on myself to finish the climb. Every other El Cap project I had worked on had taken me one season to complete. I was already three years into this one. If I didn't do it soon, I figured I probably never would. Besides, we both wanted the option to go places other than Yosemite every fall. It was then, beneath the towering giants of Fitz Roy and the other Patagonian peaks, that I decided that 2011 would be my last season on the Dawn Wall. It was time to grow up and begin to think of things other than myself.

Back in Estes Park, as winter faded and springtime bloomed, Becca delivered a proposition. "I need a goal," she said. "What would you think of climbing the Salathé with me for my birthday?"

"Really," I asked, "you want to climb El Cap for your birthday?"

"Yeah, and I want to do it without jumars, actually climb the thing, even though I know I have no chance of freeing it. Maybe I can even lead a few pitches."

Part of me loved the fact that she wasn't much of a climber. One dedicated climber probably supplies enough neurosis for any relationship. But part of me took her idea as the ultimate compliment, so I concocted a plan to turn the climb into a lovely, almost leisurely experience. About halfway up the Salathé Wall is a pillar called El Cap Spire. Its top is perfectly flat and sits a few feet detached from the main wall, a hanging pedestal with dizzying exposure. It would be an incredible location for a private, romantic birthday party. In May 2011, we climbed to the pillar on our first day; it was Becca's biggest climbing day ever, and although she did splendidly, twenty pitches of climbing on El Cap—especially in wet spring conditions—will take its toll on anyone. I'd packed a real tent, envisioning setting it up atop the spectacular El Cap Spire, but instead we pitched it in an alcove a hundred feet lower to keep dry from dripping water. It's common to think that a particular bivvy spot is perfectly flat. You often don't realize that it isn't until you lie down and begin rolling downhill. Such was our romantic birthday bivvy, as our not-quite-flawless, harmonious blending of bodies and souls inside the tent clashed with the awareness of the 1,600-foot drop just inches away. Racking up the following afternoon, we joked about how we should have gone off birth control before the climb. What would we name the kid, Salathé, El Cap, the Captain?

Two days later we topped out the wall. While I was tearing up with pride, Becca was busy taking selfies and flashing the hang-loose shaka-brah hand sign. "Get over here and get in this photo with me!"

I did as asked and wondered if her success was a good omen.

Our ten-day push in November 2010 had left Kevin inspired by the exciting components of the climb, like the potential of stacking together a wall's worth of desperate pitches, filled with sequences as difficult as he'd ever done in isolation on boulders and crags. It seemed he was growing into an appreciation for what this climb demanded from him, and what it gave back.

All summer and early fall at home in Estes I would lie awake at night formulating logistical strategies, then train from dawn till dusk to toughen myself and prepare for the wall's severity. I lost hours of sleep on the zillions of little details that had to be memorized for optimum performance. The shape and size of each hold, how to place my fingers just so and dig them into the crystals in just the right way. The exact moment to push my weight an inch to the right so that the angle of my foot changes ever so slightly. Just a degree or two can make the difference, and it all had to be committed to memory.

First in the brain, then in the body. I sought out boulder problems in Chaos Canyon with sequences similar to the cruxes of the Dawn Wall, ingraining the connections in my nervous system. At random times, climbing movements would involuntarily play in my head. I couldn't turn them off, which would drive me batty. I was getting to the point where I could close my eyes and visualize every move of the first twenty pitches.

To climb well enough to meet the rock on its terms, your mind must be like a perfectly organized workshop. Free from clutter but with the right tools in their proper places. The most successful climbers find the ideal balance of Type A attention to detail along with an easygoing attitude that alleviates stress.

My mind became its own training ground, and in my visualizations my body would assume the form required to ascend the wall, working with, not against, the rock. The real battles are within ourselves; the mainstream accounting of man versus rock makes every authentic climber cringe. The surest way to show a climber that you don't get it, and are nowhere close to getting it, is to talk of "conquering" a rock or a mountain.

Kevin and I got back to Yosemite in October 2011. Our work started out well. We weren't yet good enough to free the hardest pitches in the middle section, so we decided to focus on the dyno move on pitch 16. Most of the climbing on the Dawn Wall is about subtle precision, like ballet or brain surgery. Every move had to be coordinated and monitored with disciplined precision and timing. The dyno is the exception. It's more like hucking an anvil over a roof. In an effort to get amped we had overdone the morning coffee and were fidgeting with energy. When Kevin threw himself at the move, his hands latched onto the finishing hold but his body's momentum violently sent his left foot into a small rock corner. He immediately dropped onto the rope.

"Oh, man," he said to me, flatly. "I just turned my ankle." I lowered him back to the portaledge. He tried the dyno a few more times, even sticking it on his final go. But his ankle was starting to swell and the pain was increasing. "I better get down fast before I can't move my ankle anymore." he said.

"Okay, yeah, just go. I'll pack everything up and bring it down."

He zipped 1,400 feet down the ropes, and before I'd even finished packing he sent me a text. "I think I should go back home and get my ankle looked at."

Just like that he was gone. Becca jumared up and belayed for a few days while we awaited the prognosis. Nothing was broken, but he'd bruised the bone and strained some ligaments. Kevin's season was over.

For all my desire to be friends, and the storied "bond of the rope," my decision to continue without Kevin seemed almost a given. Even though we'd now spent three seasons over two years climbing together—I'd been a year into the project when he joined on—part of me still didn't feel like he deserved the Dawn Wall. No doubt Kevin was super talented and tried hard in the moment, but he had put in about 5 percent as much time on El Cap as I had. His ability to pull it off when he showed up was impressive, and he seemed to have heightened motivation this season. But deep down I still felt like the Dawn Wall was mostly my project.

Kevin handled my decision to push on with incredible grace. He expressed regret and longing to be up there, and selflessly supported me. It made me realize that Kevin was not only the better climber, but also the bigger man. For the rest of the season, I would climb with an air of guilt.

As soon as word escaped that Kevin was out, a veritable mob of people volunteered to belay. There were the expected friends and family—people like Becca, my dad, Corey Rich, and Cooper—along with a multitude of complete strangers. Even Beth offered to come up. I was amazed, and my admiration for our community swelled.

But I wanted to make this journey with the people closest to me, especially when I was ready to free climb the route in a single push, bottom to top. Working on the pitches was one thing; that could be a party. This was now my fourth year on the Dawn Wall, and I had already decided it would be my last—it was time to finish it or be done. Going for the send would be hard and emotional, the accumulation of a lifetime's worth of work.

Whom did I want up there with me? The answer was easy: Becca and my dad.

We decided that Becca would support me for the first ten days. Then she would rappel down the fixed lines and Dad would come up. I started climbing on November 16, 2011.

I knew Becca could handle a lot. She wanted to be there. But I had no idea what I would be asking her to endure on this attempt. The battle started on pitch 3, where I took several big falls. Our difference in body weight meant that each time I fell she got launched upward. It was beating her up.

By day four, it had become bitterly cold. Becca was wearing two down jackets and belaying me from inside her sleeping bag. At 11:00 p.m. I was about to climb pitch 10. Moonlight shone off the walls, casting an eerie glow and revealing just how exposed we were. We were the only people on El Cap, and probably the only people climbing in all of Yosemite at that moment.

The wind blew hard, buffeting the portaledge. A creepy howl refracted off the features of the rock.

"How are you doing, baby?" I said through the wind. I wanted her to tell me she was scared, that we should head back to the comfort of our well-stocked portaledge base camp. I pointed my headlamp to the hood of her jacket, and just enough light shined on her face that I could see her expression: an unmistakable smile behind multiple layers of down.

"I'm good, go get it!" she said, and pinched me on the butt. Impressed and not wanting to let her down, I took a breath and started into a sequence of moves above.

Suddenly, I heard a shriek and looked down just as the wind flipped the portaledge and sent her flying to the end of her tether. Although she was tied in and backed up, my heart jumped. I threw in a micro cam, grabbed it, and shouted down, frightened. She righted the ledge and pulled herself back on. "I'm good!"

Soon after, at nearly midnight, I climbed by headlamp as the wind came in undulating howls. Water seeped down the crack. I kept slipping off. I'd sent the pitch the previous year with Kevin, but I wasn't playing tic-tac-toe. You can't skip around, you have to free the pitches consecutively, in sequence, on your push. One moment, hanging dejectedly at the end of the rope, I noticed car headlights passing slowly through El Cap meadow, and I wondered if they belonged to my parents. They'd taken a leave of absence from their jobs and come to Yosemite to support me. I thought about the work that got me here and the people rooting for me. But after years of effort, the Dawn Wall still seemed impossibly distant.

On our seventh morning, we awoke to an ice-encrusted portaledge. I unzipped the door and popped my head out.

"Wow, baby, you have to look outside." A foot of snow had fallen overnight, the wind had stopped, the air was completely still, and ice crystals slowly floated around us like tiny sparkling diamonds.

"It's just like Narnia," Becca said, giggling, "but better, because from up here we have the best view."

Within thirty minutes the sun hit, and the ice that had frozen to the wall overnight began to fall. First, little ice cubes bounced off the portaledge, ringing like wind chimes, then plates whirled past like buzzing saw blades. Then softball-sized chunks roared down the wall; we could hear them coming from hundreds of feet away.

"Get as close to the wall as possible!" I shouted, trying to sound more relaxed than I felt. For the next few hours we sat like ducks, with no place to run. When chunks of ice hit the metal frame, the entire portaledge shifted. I cursed myself for not getting my act together and building the ice-deflecting shield. Becca seemed shockingly at ease with the whole thing. Where did this comfort, this faith and acceptance of any outcome, come from?

Those ten days with Becca were surreal. As she dodged the daily icefall, rode out the high winds, and caught my big falls, Becca remained positive, supportive, and even fascinated. The storms and the wind were tough to deal with, but the cold weather made the rock feel crisp and sticky. Despite the improved climbing conditions and my elevated fitness, I was struggling. I fell more often than the previous year. My frustration grew; my struggles didn't make sense.

Eventually I made it back to my 2010 high point, sending through pitch 12, but I was a wreck. My fingers were throbbing, chapped, and cracking. Emotionally I was exhausted. I knew I needed to dig deep, try to summon belief. I had to figure out how to climb better than I ever had in my life. One night Becca asked me what I thought was different compared to last year's attempt. I pondered for a minute before answering.

"It's hard for me to admit this, but I think the difference is Kevin. Don't get me wrong, baby," I explained. "You have been the most incredible support I could ever ask for, but the collaboration and competitive energy I have with Kevin is really good."

Becca nodded but didn't reply.

"I don't worry about him as much. With Kevin I have to show optimism and toughness," I continued. "With you, I can be vulnerable. How much I love you weakens me up here. What do you think of giving me a few days alone, to see if I can get my skin to heal and pull it together mentally, then you can send up my dad?"

"Okay," she said softly. "If you think that is what you need."

Before she left she kissed me long and hard, and tears filled her eyes. "You can do this, baby, I believe in you." Then she clipped into the rope and rappelled out of sight.

My dad spent two days belaying me. It quickly became clear that life on the wall was hard for him. Dad was intimidated, no longer as fearless as I remembered. I didn't sleep well. I fell over and over in the same place on pitch 14. My fingers deteriorated even more. Blood smeared my clothes. The conditions were perfect for hard climbing, but I made no progress.

I had seen how my dad had aged, and I had to acknowledge that Father Time was edging ahead of me as well. As so many other athletes have said, no man can beat time. I knew that I was past my physical peak, but I also knew that I was far more experienced than I was in my early to mid-twenties. Maybe I couldn't build as much power in my body through my intense workout regimen as I once had, but I could climb smarter, train smarter, and pay even more obsessive attention to detail to overcome that inevitable decline.

It was hard for Dad to watch me struggle so hard, to fail. He tried to be positive, but I could see the pain in his eyes. In between attempts and on the portaledge at night, he talked lovingly about my mom. It had been only two days since he had last seen her, but I understood how deeply he missed her. Knowing that it was best for him and for me, I suggested that he send up Kelly, my closest friend from back in Estes Park, who happened to be in Yosemite. I thanked my dad for his efforts and he wished me luck before he headed down. Both relieved and saddened at his departure, I tried not to focus on what had just happened and focus instead on what was next.

Kelly had been my main shoulder to cry on during the divorce. He was self-deprecating, a true skeptic, and a hard-core alpine climber. He wouldn't let me take myself too seriously. Before he was a climber he was a competitive boxer, and I knew he understood the internal battle—that if I could succeed, it would come from the mind.

Over the next two days I failed again and again. Despite Kelly's best attempts to cheer me up, the fire was gone. I hadn't taken a step on flat ground in sixteen days. I had nothing in the tank physically and mentally. With no flat ground to walk on I was spending most of my time sleeping, fourteen to fifteen hours a night. Spending that much time lying around made me even more lethargic and made it more difficult to get into gear for the climb.

Worse, my fingertips would not heal. I added that to my list of fixes to find.

People were supporting me from afar, sending me positive messages. I'd even followed Kevin's lead and started doing Facebook updates from the wall. But toward the end, even those words of encouragement came to seem more like expressions of pity.

And now I regretted my decision to be so publicly vulnerable. Four years of training, of relentlessly beating my head against the wall, and I'd come up short. Not even halfway. Failure can lead to growth, but you also need to know when to stop. *I'm not good enough, will never be good enough.* A hollowness ran from my chest through my gut. I had wasted four of the best years of my life. It was time to move on.

CHAPTER FIFTEEN

I'm in a blissful daze. I lift my shirt and let the little body rest on my bare stomach. As his heart beats next to mine, my own doubles in size.

I rock back in the chair with Fitz cradled in my arms. Fear, lack of sleep, and a primal instinct to protect well up inside me.

Time pauses and I stare at his tiny fingernails and toes. I caress his head. His eyes are crystal clear, and in them I see infinite potential.

What does it mean to be a good father?

The cruxes in my life have been problems born of want and need.

I needed my dad to love me for who I was, not what I did.

I needed Beth to love me for who I was, not to use me for her own security.

I needed the Dawn Wall as my own way to heal.

But what did I really want?

Desire and need. The first encompasses passion and energy, is unencumbered by the weight of pressure and expectation. The second too often saps that passion and energy, makes the easiest tasks more difficult, burdens you.

I look at Becca. She smiles and the questions dissolve and resolve themselves into another kind of desire. A desire to be more like her, to be free of judgment, to find such joy in bringing smiles to other people's faces, to embrace an unending love of life and of people. To go to the lengths she does to show kindness to others while expecting nothing in return. To accept our flawed nature, as she has always done, to forgive others and forgive myself. Only God is perfect, she believes. Only he can be the source of all our strength, she's told me.

I want my son to have a strength of belief like Becca's, to believe in us, in love, and in himself.

For all of my familiarity with failure, I wasn't any good at it. At home I kept talking about the climb.

"If only I could have found a way to make my skin last a bit longer."

"If only I had rested more."

My overwhelming preoccupation with the Dawn Wall unsettled me. Having a project on which to intensely focus had energized me, but it had begun to take over too many other parts of my life. At times, I wished that I could be less maniacal about my pursuits. I didn't want to *need* anything. I would tell myself, *It's just a silly rock climb, let it go.* But in those words, I could feel a piece of me die.

In many ways Becca and I had put our lives on hold for this climb. We wanted to move on, travel to other parts of the world, start a family. Even my dad had suggested that I should let it go; at this point, he worried about what other opportunities in life I might be missing. After all, complete reliance on any one thing is dangerous. I needed to create some space, to know that I could live without the Dawn Wall.

The biggest holdup was this: Even thinking about giving up made me feel like a failure. For most of that winter I vacillated. Logic told me I should quit. Emotion told me to go back. Becca was patient. She understood the dilemma but left it to me to decide.

In spring 2012 I was in Italy for a slide show tour. A week into the trip I called home to check in. "I'm really nervous about telling you this," Becca said. "I went to the doctor today for my annual appointment, and on a whim decided to get my IUD taken out. It wasn't even the plan when I went in. But the doctor was quizzing me about when I wanted to have kids and I just kind of decided. What do you think?"

I didn't quite know what to say. Sure, we had discussed having a child and we talked about starting seriously in a year. *Had it already been that long? Was I ready to swear off the Dawn Wall?* Sweat beaded on my forehead.

"Ha, ha," I replied. "You totally got me, so funny."

"No, I'm totally serious."

Long silence.

"Yeah, right."

"I'm telling you, I'm not kidding."

I sat down.

"What do you think?" she said. "Are you excited?"

"I think so. You kind of dropped a bomb here."

"I figured they can always put it back in if you wanted. But then I got to thinking, they say that on average it takes people a year to get pregnant. And why would it have to change our lifestyle anyway? I think traveling and climbing would be an amazing way to raise kids."

"Whoa, kids, as in plural? Baby, let's not get ahead of ourselves. What about the Dawn Wall?" I said, disregarding all I'd previously thought about kids and travel, how the birth of one thing needn't be the death of another, and so on.

"I'd be psyched to hang out in the valley with a kid. We're only there for like two months a year anyway."

Bringing our kids to Yosemite, traveling the world with them? My thoughts quickly shifted to the idea that the Dawn Wall didn't have to be a ruling force over our lives. We had talked about that notion after meeting Tormentina, the little girl in Patagonia, but it was all talk until something happened. Now something had happened. Unless I declared otherwise, once I got home we would officially be trying. I flashed back to my childhood, floating down the Merced River, staring in awe at the raging waterfalls. How magical it would be to share that place with our children.

Without even realizing it, I downgraded the Dawn Wall to just one of many great things happening in my life. Almost as quickly, I decided to return to Yosemite in the fall, not with the goal of sending the Dawn Wall, but just to enjoy my time up there and see if I could work out the crux sections. I was now pushing thirty-three. I'd let go a little and allow any progress to happen organically.

In the meantime, I started to consider plans for other climbs. Maybe the Dawn Wall was just too much for me. Numerous pitches were near the upper limits of climbing's current standards, and they were stacked one atop the other for the whole route. It was more like a series of sprints than an ultramarathon.

Perhaps the answer lay in focusing more on ultra-endurance climbs. I'd

My first major alpine climbing trip,
the first free ascent of a 5,000-foot route
on Cerro Fitz Roy in Patagonia.

On El Capitan's Dihedral Wall.

The line of the Dawn Wall.

With Becca on the Dawn Wall.
We married in 2012.

With Alex Honnold on the iconic
Fitz Traverse in Patagonia.

Right: The Dawn Wall is the steepest,
blankest big wall in the world.

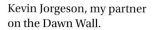

Kevin Jorgeson, my partner
on the Dawn Wall.

Twelve hundred feet off the deck in our portaledge on
the nineteenth day of our final push on the Dawn Wall.

The middle of the Dawn Wall, the hardest section of the climb.

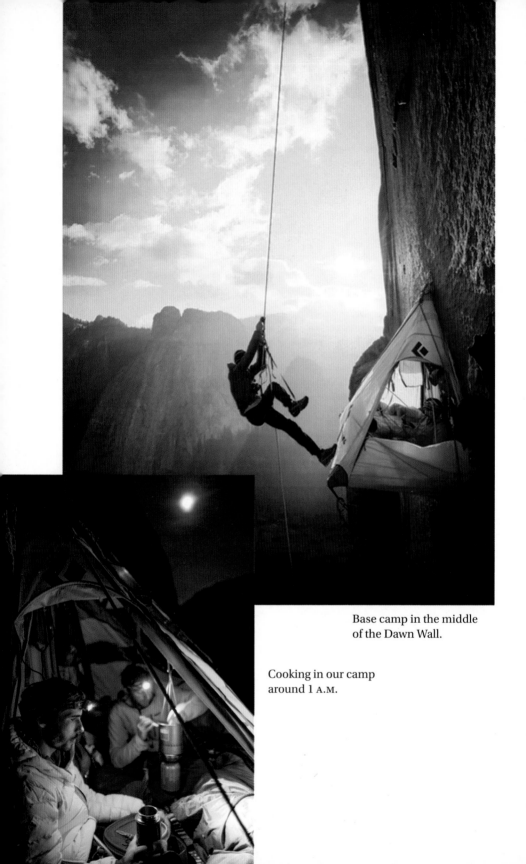

Base camp in the middle
of the Dawn Wall.

Cooking in our camp
around 1 A.M.

The most spectacular pitch of the route.

Above: Finally on top of the Dawn Wall. A surreal moment.

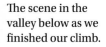

The scene in the valley below as we finished our climb.

Becca and me with our children, Fitz and Ingrid.

always loved those challenges—things like my first trip to Patagonia, my linkup of two free routes on El Cap in a day, and even Kyrgyzstan—and it's a style that seemed the most natural to me.

In 2008, a lanky kid named Alex Honnold came seemingly out of nowhere and blew the lid off the climbing world with two big wall free solos that were taller, harder, and more committing than anything done before: the Moonlight Buttress in Zion, Utah, and the Northwest Face of Half Dome in Yosemite. These two climbs, and many others in the years since, represented a paradigm shift in the high-stakes game of free soloing.

Alex grew up in a suburb of Sacramento, California, and learned to climb in the gym. His mom was a French teacher; his father died when Alex was nineteen. When he started climbing outside, he often climbed alone because he couldn't get partners—he was shy and awkward. Then one day Alex jumped straight from the suburbs to being the most badass and bold climber the world had ever seen. CBS's *60 Minutes* ran a segment of him calmly climbing 5.12 terrain 1,000 feet off the ground in Yosemite, unroped. It's impossible to watch the footage without breaking out in a cold sweat. Alex, on the other hand, seemed unconcerned as he climbed, making small talk with the videographer. If free soloing is about being unencumbered, then Alex certainly was. His lack of reliance on anything but the force of his own abilities made him untouchable. By the age of twenty-six he'd amassed some of the most significant ascents of our times.

I saw Alex as one of the true greats. Although we hadn't climbed together, he always expressed admiration for my climbs. When I reciprocated, he would respond, "Why don't you free solo big walls? It would be so easy for you."

For Alex, it seemed like the obvious thing to do. Climbers nicknamed him "No Big Deal Alex" because that's what he always said about his climbs. And how they were "casual." He saw me as one of the few people with the mental coolness, experience, and climbing ability to make big wall free soloing reasonably safe. To Alex, the fact that I didn't go for it was like owning a really nice sports car but only driving the speed limit. I wasn't so much concerned about going faster than the legal limit, I was worried about the possibility of crashing and burning.

In 2011, when he first mentioned the idea of getting together to try to free climb, in a day, the three biggest features in Yosemite—Mount Watkins, El Capitan, and Half Dome—I told him it might be a bit much for my aging body. But I was also worried about what appeared to be his cavalier attitude toward risk. Seven thousand feet of difficult free climbing, up to 5.13, in a single day would certainly be a climbing ultramarathon. In order to do it, we would have to use a relatively risky technique called simul-climbing—it's safer than free soloing because you're tied in, climbing together (simultaneously) at either end of the rope, with the leader only occasionally placing protection. But it's done without a proper belay; the idea is to match each other's pace, so that no excessive slack accumulates in the system. If someone pitches off, it won't be pretty but the rope and protection will still catch you. It's fast, but by definition you only simul-climb on terrain where you don't think you'll fall.

All my life I'd constantly refined my own sense of risk by considering not just the obvious factors—exposure, weather, rock quality, runouts—but also ego, motivation, mental health, and the inevitable peer pressure (which exists, even if everyone tries to deny it). I seemed naturally able to metabolize fear; I loved to suffer (elective suffering, that is), and I had excellent stamina. But I saw risking my neck on dangerous climbs as selfish, disrespectful of how my getting hurt or killed would affect my family and friends. I worried about doing something I didn't feel was morally right in order to cash in on fame and notoriety.

When we saw each other again in May 2012, in the Upper Pines Campground of Yosemite Valley, Alex once more mentioned the linkup. He argued that it really wasn't that dangerous for the two of us. "The climbing on those routes is so far below our limit, dude, you know you're not going to fall," he said. "I don't think it's that big of a deal." He shrugged his shoulders and leaned against a giant cedar tree. Most of us are ruled by emotions. When something attracts us, we gravitate toward it; when we experience fear, we run. Alex seemed to treat his emotions like the volume dial on his car stereo. If the music got too loud, he just turned it down and kept driving.

"I bet I've fallen completely unexpectedly at least ten times in my life," I replied. I looked toward Half Dome and I tried to imagine myself unroped high on the Northwest Face, as he'd been, an ocean of granite disappearing beneath my feet. I threw open the door of my van and sat down. Photos of my family were pinned to the bare plywood wall. In one picture, I knelt behind Becca, my arms wrapped tightly around her torso, my face nestled in the crook of her neck.

What if Alex was right? In the past few years, speed climbing technique and technology had evolved. Lightweight devices allow the rope to move forward through a piece of protection, but stop it from moving backward, thereby eliminating the catastrophic risk of the second climber's falling and pulling off the leader. Strategic use of these devices, along with a strong understanding of systems, had made simul-climbing considerably safer.

In an age of technology Alex's drive reminded me of a lost instinct, like a laid-back version of those mythical ancient warriors who fearlessly charged ahead. I was curious about how he did it. I had a lifetime of experience assessing risk, and Alex drew the line in a very different place than I did.

At 4:45 p.m. on May 18, we roped-up below the south face of Mount Watkins. Alex's fingers slid in and out of the cracks with perfect precision. He rarely stopped to place gear, only a few pieces per rope length. Somehow that boldness, the confidence that he wouldn't fall, was contagious. Pitch after pitch flowed by effortlessly. When we got to the free climbing cruxes, we stopped and belayed; otherwise we simul-climbed. The continuous movement felt much like free soloing, but with far less risk.

Mount Watkins took us only a few hours. We ran to the nearest road, where Becca picked us up, drove to the valley floor, and shuttled us to El Cap. Darkness fell by the time we started climbing Free Rider.

By 3:00 a.m., high on the wall, we stopped to belay below a corner. I was beginning to feel nauseated from exertion, while Alex was still motoring along. One of the harder sections of the climb, a steep and smooth corner, rose above. We discussed the moves. Alex remembered previously treating it like a round in a boxing match, grunting through a series of powerful liebacks. I knew I didn't have enough power left for that kind of effort. I took a different approach, born of a decade of El Cap free climbing experience, and started inching my way upward by stemming on invisible footholds—pressing a foot and a palm into each of the opposing walls. Alex isn't generally effusive with compliments, but his voice rang through the night with astonishment: "Wow, I had no idea it was even possible to climb it that way."

A few pitches higher I jammed one hand into an overhanging crack. With my other hand, I clicked my headlamp on high. Nearly 3,000 feet of granite sparkled in the moonlight. All was silent, aside from the faint rumble of Bridalveil Falls across the valley. On the upper end of the rope, Alex was simul-climbing out of sight and earshot. The rope arched above me past a dark offwidth—and was clipped to nothing. My arms quivered with fatigue; my head pounded with dehydration. I hoped to God that he had some gear in above. I took a deep breath, liebacked for ten feet over a bulge, and threw my leg deep in the crack.

Twenty minutes later, we topped out as first light touched the horizon. We ran down to the van, where Becca and a friend were waiting for us with breakfast. We devoured burritos and hopped in for the shuttle to Half Dome. On the mattress in back, I was out by the time my head hit the pillow. While I snored, Alex just lay there staring at the van's ceiling, twitching with excitement like a little kid, a huge grin on his face, whispering to himself, "This is so cool! This is so cool!" We boogied to the base of Half Dome, and started simul-climbing once again. Later that afternoon, we reached the summit by the Regular Northwest Face route. We'd free climbed almost eighty pitches in about twenty-one hours.

I'd expected the trifecta to be a supreme test of human will and endurance. I'd wanted to visit that place again, where we're reminded that human capabilities are nearly limitless and that our world still contains mysteries. But Alex was too good. The big walls seemed to shrink to only half their size. It ended up being merely an especially tiring day of climbing. A scenic vertical hike. It occurred to me that this was the first time in ages that I had drafted off someone else. Alex was inspiring and fun to climb with. Our respective strengths and styles jibed like a perfectly humming engine. With Alex I was suddenly in a Lamborghini—and of course I went over the speed limit.

———

Becca held her breath as she waited for my reaction. She was pregnant. All I could think about was something a climber dad had told me a few months earlier: "The first year I had a kid, I only climbed twenty days. The second year, five days." I had to check myself. My immediate reaction was about what this would mean for me, for my climbing. I knew I was being selfish and hypocritical, but if I couldn't climb I wouldn't be me.

Instead of a loud scream, all that escaped my lips was "What?" The feeling was not unlike starting up a big, daunting mountain. You want to do it, that's why you're there, but you're scared. So you just have to start climbing and see what happens. Becca ran around, fidgeting like a caffeinated toddler. She wanted to stay up all night every night talking about baby names, gadgets we needed, and parenting theory. We kept our news quiet early, as you do. The second the pregnancy reached the twelfth week she called all of her friends, and sirenlike squeals, in octaves I hadn't imagined possible from the human voice, rang out from the telephone. Half of me wished it had actually taken a year to get pregnant.

"Promise me that we will not stop traveling," I said to Becca. She agreed.

Over the next months we traveled to Europe and extensively in the United States, mixing professional obligations and play. At home, I maximized my time running around in the mountains. Along the way, as the realization of raising a family settled in, I felt unexpectedly calm and content.

I still wanted the Dawn Wall, but no longer felt as if I needed it. Our plan still held to return in fall of 2012, with a more relaxed agenda. But initially I didn't have a partner—Kevin had decided to float the Grand Canyon instead. A lot of people have asked why I didn't invite Alex on the Dawn Wall that year. The answer is pretty simple: If I'd thought he would be into it, I'd have loved for him to come up there. But Alex likes to move too much—he's wonderfully impatient with his climbing. He prefers to get on things he is relatively certain he can do, and try to do them exceptionally well. When soloing, absolute confidence in success is essential. On the Dawn Wall, success was never going to be assured. I'd heard him say, in his classic Alex way, things like, "No way, dude, that sounds heinous. Too much work."

Instead I called my friend Jonathan Siegrist, an occasional training partner back in Colorado and the hardest-working and most talented sport climber I knew. He was up for giving it a go. We spent October on the wall together. He has the energy of a wind-up toy. Up on the wall we talked about life and had a hell of a good time. Down in the valley we hung out together drinking beer, bouldering, and even doing calisthenics. We made big improvements on the wall, linking significant sequences on the hardest pitches, 14 and 15. I loved Jonathan's maniacal work ethic. We chatted incessantly about things like nutrition, training, neuromuscular synchronization, and muscle fiber growth. He would have made an ideal partner, but he lacked one critical ingredient: belief. He was a few inches shorter than Kevin and me, and not an extremely explosive climber. He couldn't imagine doing the pitch 16 dyno. He stuck it out for a month, but eventually opted out.

A week before Jonathan left, Kevin finished his float trip and drove straight to Yosemite. Although he hadn't climbed in a month, he jumped right on the hardest moves of the climb and bone-crushed them. He moved over the rock powerfully, gracefully, with the exacting precision of a CNC machine. He looked as if he was born to do this. Jonathan and I just stared, mouths agape. Kevin was a much better climber than I was, even without training. But the lack of training had taken a toll on his endurance. He could only manage about four or five hard moves in a row before melting off the wall.

The three of us climbed together for a week. On our last day we were working on the section of pitch 14 where I had stalled out on my two previous ground-up attempts. I decided for the hundredth time to look for an alternative sequence. I rappelled down a few feet and stuck my face up against the rock, hoping to see something different. There it was: a dome-shaped nubbin similar in shape and color to Madonna's mole. I marked it with a little chalk and then started to rebuild the sequence. My foot, pasted on this little bump, supported only a few pounds of body weight, but it held me in place so that I could reach a decent sideways hold. Beside that handhold was a tiny hairline seam, not much bigger than one of the lines on a weathered basketball. Typically, on a wall this steep it would be unusable— but combined with the mole and the sidepull, it might be enough. I began to play with a new solution.

Kevin and Jonathan watched with rapt attention. To anyone else it would be like watching paint dry. Twenty minutes more of fiddling as I dangled on the end of the rope, and I had worked out a sequence. I asked for some slack, pulled myself onto the wall and reached my foot down to the mole. I grabbed the sidepull and reached my other hand to the fracture. Then, with all the power I could muster, I pulled as hard as I could on the handholds, held my upper body stiff, as if it were a kite momentarily suspended in the sky, shuffled my right foot in and smeared it straight into the wall on absolutely nothing. Holding my breath and every possible bit of core tension, I matched hands on the sidepull, shot my left hand out to another sidepull, and barely, strenuously, maintained enough composure to shift myself over onto the next semi-resting position. I had solved the puzzle.

"Oh, hell yeah!" came a shout, as Kevin and Jonathan both cheered. "How was that?"

Not wanting to celebrate just yet, I yelled back, "It worked, let me try it again."

I used the rope to swing back, then I did it again. Then a third time.

I lowered back to the portaledge and rested a few minutes while excitedly describing every aspect of the new moves to Jonathan and Kevin. Then I tried it from the beginning. For the first time in five years, I reached a new high point on pitch 14, linking most of the way through the pitch.

A few days later, as we stripped the wall and called it quits for the season, I couldn't help but chuckle at the absurdity of it all. The discovery of a mole-sized nubbin of rock and a barely visible hairline fracture had filled me with so much energy that I knew I had seen a path forward for the next year. If the secret to happiness was the ability to find joy in the little things that had been in front of you the entire time, then the Dawn Wall was truly a Zen-master teacher. I left Yosemite on a high, figuring that, at the very least, training was something I could do during the rapidly approaching days of fatherhood.

"Come on, baby, push!" I shouted the following spring. Becca grunted and screamed, her hair plastered against her forehead, as tears streamed down her cheeks. Like most of us, Fitz Caldwell entered the world through struggle. We named him for Fitz Roy, in Patagonia. It towered over the town when Becca and I were there, on that trip when we first thought about having children. I reached out and this beautiful creature, crying and covered in slime, slid into my arms.

The greatest thing I learned from my dad is that if you can summon joy in the pursuit, then the things that tend to affect us negatively—pain, fear, suffering—fade into the background. Becca had done the hard work, and now I was left to think about what I wanted to teach our son.

I wanted to show Fitz how to love and respect others. I believe human relationships can and should follow the mind-set of adventure, defined not by climbing but by its greater meaning: embracing the unknown. In remaining open to others, you gain knowledge, and your perspective of life and of the world expands.

To foster these qualities in myself, and thus in Fitz, I have to be true to who I am. Otherwise, what credibility would I have? So who am I? I'm not the smartest, most handsome, or most talented. I believe my gift in life is that of desire. My greatest expression of desire, and of embracing the unknown, is in my climbing.

Becca and I readied for our autumn return to Yosemite. It would be our first big trip with Fitz. Over the summer we had taken him on hikes, showing him the wonder of nature in the mountains around Estes Park. We were determined to fold him into our world. Friends had told me that life after children was impossible to balance, that I would have to give up on time-intensive pursuits. That was like hearing the doctor who walked into my hospital room after I chopped off my finger and told me that I was done climbing.

In the fall of 2013, we arrived in Yosemite's Upper Pines campground a week before I planned to go up on the wall. Becca and Fitz would live in the van during the warmer early autumn. I'd split my time between them and the wall, and they would head home when the temperatures fell. For the first few days we introduced Fitz to the ancient redwoods, the waterfalls, the forests, the boulders, and the base of El Cap. We set a picnic blanket in El

Cap meadow and acted like tourists, picking out the climbers on the wall. We pointed to where Daddy would be for many days during the next month (I'd come down to sleep with the family most nights). I noticed that when I was with Fitz I became fascinated by little things I'd normally overlook. The camouflage of the praying mantis on the reed of grass. The way the clouds took on the shapes of zoo animals. We rigged a harness to bungee cords and hung it from a branch; Fitz would bounce around like a jolly little elf while we bouldered and climbed. We would set him in our piles of ropes and climbing gear and he would use the carabiners as teething rings. Sometimes in the evening, when the campfire smoke hung low in the campground, we would bathe Fitz in a little pink dishwashing basin. His wide green eyes seemed full of wonder and innocence. Becca and I marveled at what it must be like to see this world for the first time, with a sense of newness and possibility.

I invited another of the world's best climbers to join us that season. It was the same person who'd blown my socks off in sport climbing as a teenager, Chris Sharma. I hoped that he would bring fresh perspective and energy to our efforts on the Dawn Wall.

As it turns out, Kevin's success the previous fall had reinvigorated him. He was all in. But before we could get started, bureaucratic bickering in the government shut down all of the national parks. By the time we were allowed back into Yosemite, it was mid-October and cold, so Becca and Fitz flew home.

I was eager to introduce Chris to El Cap free climbing. Since we had climbed together as teenagers, Chris had matured into a full-on climbing icon. His warm smile, chiseled physique, and wolverinelike determination made every male climber want to be him and every female want to date him. He has a phenomenal dynamic style on rock and is widely considered the most accomplished sport climber in history, but he had never been on a big wall. I couldn't wait to see his world light up the way Kevin's had during our first year together on the Dawn Wall.

I soon learned that both Chris and Kevin had recently been dumped by their girlfriends. You could see the heartbreak on Kevin's face. "I would have married that girl," he said, but not much else. Chris was open about how he hurt, and while we were packing he got a call from his ex and wandered into the woods for a thirty-minute talk. When he returned, tears streaked his face. He sniffled them back and stood up straight.

"That was heavy, man. A big wall adventure will do me good right now."

I flashed back to when I had been in the same place. My friends had come to the rescue, and I wanted to do the same for these guys. We stopped at the store to pick up some whiskey and headed up the trail. Soon after starting, Chris asked, "How are you doing, Kevin?"

"I'm in the depths of it, man," Kevin said. "I just have to work it out in my head."

I knew how he felt. Maybe, I thought, if I can be a good friend in this moment of need, it would break down some barriers. "The good news is that you are both super rad and good looking. Do you know how many girls are going to be chasing you down?" I told them. "Bachelor life is going to be amazing!"

"Yeah, I am psyched for that," Chris said. Kevin just looked sad.

As we hiked I told Chris all about the route, and what we would be doing for the next few days. "I can't wait to try that dyno," he said. "It was so amazing to see Kevin do it." A video of the crazy upward-horizontal leap over an eight-foot stretch of a vertical wall, fifteen hundred feet off the deck, had become well known in climbing circles. Kevin finally loosened up and started talking.

Up on the wall, the exposure was like a shot of epinephrine straight to Chris's nervous system. Trembling and giddy, he yanked so hard on the tiny holds that I worried he might pull them off. He yelled like an Olympic power lifter as he lunged from one hold to the next. His was the polar opposite of Kevin's calm, scientific approach. Right off the bat Chris made huge links on some of the 5.13+ pitches. Then we went to the dyno, which I was certain he would dispatch in one or two tries. Turns out he was just a bit too intimidated to do such an insanely wild move without first becoming more accustomed to the daunting exposure. He agreed it was one of the most extraordinary single moves he'd ever seen.

Because of the way we'd rigged the ropes, we were able to work the individual pitches out of sequence. I figured out that the best time to try the

5.14d traverse pitches—the two pitches leading up to the dyno—was on cloudy, windy days, just before the storms unleashed their fury. One day, the gusts were bucking the portaledge and blowing snowflakes straight up the wall. Kevin and I were trading burns, making good links and super excited to have these rare daylight hours with good sending temps. Chris sat in the portaledge, hood cinched, hands buried deep in his pockets, looking at us as if we were totally insane. This was a far cry from his typical scene of shirtless climbing on the sunbathed cliffs of Catalunya.

After a week, Chris headed home. Once again it was just Kevin and me. For all of my questioning his devotion he was clearly the only person willing to stick it out. Kevin and I narrowed our attention to just the crux traverse pitches, 14 and 15. Pitch 16, the dyno, was slightly easier but intimidating and highly dependent on explosive power. Dialing-in these three, as Kevin put it, were "the last boxes that we need to check before another push." He wasn't talking much, but maybe he was adopting the now-proven approach of handling heartbreak through self-imposed Dawn Wall abuse. He had the focus of a panther on the hunt. Every step of progress was being chronicled on Kevin's (and now my) Instagram feeds. Kevin's new sponsor, Adidas Outdoor, was releasing regular Dawn Wall updates and publicizing them as broadly as possible.

In any good Hollywood-worthy saga, this is the point where disaster strikes. On cue, we headed up, hoping to finally send pitch 15. I was jumaring the lines seven pitches up, and had a twenty-five-pound bag, filled with our day supplies, hooked beside me. A two-hundred-foot haul line was tied to the bag, with the other end clipped to me. All of the slack dangled in a big loop below. Unexpectedly, the haul bag came unhooked. I watched the bag begin its fall as if in slow motion. I considered trying to unclip it from my harness, but worried that I would rip more fingers off if I wasn't fast enough. I grabbed my jumars, stood up hard in my foot slings and braced for the impact.

The bag plummeted two hundred feet and the rope snapped tight against the back of my harness. I exploded downward a few feet until the stretch in the rope I was hanging on ran out. A crunch rippled through my torso. Shock and adrenaline masked the pain. I felt lucky to be alive but knew something was wrong. I rappelled to the valley as fast as I could, but by the time I got to my van I could barely move. On the drive to the clinic I cursed myself for being so careless. An X-ray revealed displaced ribs. I would be forced to take several weeks off. It was the exact reverse of the 2011 scenario when Kevin had sprained his ankle. Kevin had encouraged me then; I would do the same for him now.

For two weeks he rallied his own partners and worked on the pitches. "It required me to take ownership of the project," Kevin later told me. He went on to explain that he had felt for the longest time that he was the stepfather of the Dawn Wall effort. He had been living in my shadow. We had our differences—mostly about exploiting commercial opportunities and what the climb meant for our lives and careers—and that grated on our relationship. But with me no longer on the wall, some of the anxieties and pressures he was feeling diminished. Climbing without me, he could make his own schedule; he could descend and rest whenever he needed, without my giving him a hard time.

I went home to recover and returned in late December. The rest had been good for me. Winter had set in, and Yosemite was covered in snow. A stiff, fresh wind blew straight up the wall. I first noticed how light I felt as I climbed. Most of the hard calluses had shed from my fingers while I was out of commission, and the supple new skin underneath molded itself onto the rock. The holds felt bigger. My confidence soared. I tried the crux sequence on pitch 15 and floated through it with little difficulty. Next I tried the entire pitch from the beginning. Before I even knew what had happened I sent pitch 15, ticking one of the three remaining boxes. Kevin was shocked, and congratulated me wholeheartedly, but there was also an underlying air of jealousy like what I had so often felt toward him. His two weeks of hard work without me had amounted to this?

We had become so damned competitive, like two teammates pushing each other to a point that neither could reach alone. We came to two realizations. For one, rest was good. In the past we—or I—had perhaps pushed too hard for too long. Maybe a better strategy for the future would be to take a midseason break. The second was the reinforcement of the idea that cold conditions were essential. If we were ever going to climb the Dawn Wall it would have to be done during a clear, sunny spell in a dry winter. That would require extraordinary luck. Just before Christmas, as winter in Yosemite ramped up and the snow began to fall, we pulled everything off the wall and headed home.

CHAPTER SIXTEEN

I sit and stare out the window. Distracted and hesitant, I notice the thinning skin on my hands, the brown spots freckling my forearms. Decades of sun and wind and cold, spells of intense exertion have taken their toll.

Becca opens the metal door of our wood-burning stove and tosses in another log. The smell of roasted pine and smoke recalls fires doused long ago. Sparks tumble to the hearth, flare up, smolder, and fade to black. Fitz sits in his chair, scooping blueberries with his tiny fingers, his brow furrowed in concentration.

What if it had been me who died in Patagonia?

We had been climbing on the same mountain, just hours apart from each other.

Would family and friends try to justify my passing by telling themselves and others that "he went out doing the thing he loved"?

I fight against the thought that it could have been me, try to hold the image of the three of us here together as a shield.

I have to change my thinking. I can no longer wonder what if. I have to do all I can to make certain that it won't be me, that I won't leave the two of them alone to grapple with the why.

Becca takes my rough, scabbed hand and squeezes it. My face flushes. I wonder if she would love me the way she does if I were a different man, someone whose mind didn't burn with the desire to travel through barren landscapes.

After Alex Honnold and I did our big free climbing linkup in Yosemite, I started to wonder what it would be like to take those speed-climbing tactics to Patagonia. Generations of climbers had talked about—and some had even tried—a futuristic project: enchaining the major spires of the Fitz Roy skyline in a continuous, multiday push. The three-mile-long traverse begins at Aguja Guillaumet and finishes with Aguja de l'S, crossing seven major summits and involving 12,000 vertical feet of technical climbing, with Fitz Roy as its apex.

In Spanish, *aguja* means spire or steeple. It's also the name given to the garfish—a long, thin, needle-nose predatory species. The same can be said of the range. Like rows of sharpened teeth the mountains sit in a menacing fashion, jutting high into the supercooled atmosphere. The moisture blowing off the ice cap to the west condenses when it hits the tops of the mountains and casts a plume of fog that can extend for miles, like the ash of an erupting volcano.

To climbers it's one of the most iconic and beautiful mountain vistas in the world, and traversing the Fitz Roy chain would require the full arsenal: hard rock climbing, easy scrambling, complicated route finding, snow and ice climbing, and the skills to pull it off with minimal equipment. Otherwise, you'd be so weighted down you wouldn't stand a chance before the storms—and your own fatigue—caught you.

But is climbing in Patagonia something I should do as a father? Becca and I incessantly debated the dream versus the risk. She had read the climbers' obituaries, heard the discussions. Closer to home, a friend's first love had died in a car crash. Recently, another friend's husband had died in an avalanche. Becca saw and felt the depth of their grief. Both of these friends seemed forever haunted by what could have been. Yet Becca also knew that I wouldn't be me, the person she loves, the father of her child, without the core elements of who I am. What do you do if your one God-given gift, the thing you seem preordained to do, the thing without which you might become a hollow shell, is something that could kill you?

"You can't tell me that you know for sure that you will come back alive," she would say. I would mumble shallow justifications. *We never know, we could die in a car crash tomorrow, life is dangerous.* I couldn't deny that alpine climbing was dangerous, much more so than regular rock climbing.

"We're picking the safest objectives and staying out of avalanche traps,"

I explained. "The route is a ridge traverse and the rock is good, so there's nothing above to fall down on us. We might not even get to try it. You know how bad the weather is there. And, baby, we are really good climbers. Most of the deaths happen to people who either don't know what they are doing or are being reckless. We will be careful, I promise." Even as I listened to these words escape my mouth I knew I wasn't being completely honest with myself or with Becca. I think that what rattled her the most was that my partner was going to be Alex Honnold. He was famous for his cavalier view of risk, and Becca knew he wasn't going to tighten up his program just because he was climbing with a father.

She was right about everything. I didn't know what to think, what to do. But God, how I love places like Patagonia. Climbing is about personal discovery, fulfilling your own wants. Child-rearing is about giving yourself to someone else.

How much of being a good parent is the ability to recognize when you need to feed yourself? We all see examples of helicopter parents, families where the kids are the nucleus, and everything becomes about providing for them, even micromanaging them. Parents can lose themselves, lose each other. Most of the families I know have a line item in their budget for a psychiatrist. It's so hard to get the balance right.

Becca was skeptical, but she also saw my burning desire, how climbing nourishes me and provides me something to give. Eventually I had her blessing to book the trip to Patagonia. I promised her that everything would be okay. That night, as I scrolled through flight options on my computer, I felt a twinge of dread. What if I was blinded by my own aspirations?

We arrived in El Chaltén bleary-eyed and hungry. High, dark clouds loomed behind the towers of the massif, and the sun shone through below, making their undersides glow against the inky backdrop. The parched, sweet smell of the place induced immediate nostalgia. I'd envisioned having my family join me on my globe-trotting expeditions and now it was coming true. With gratitude and excitement racing inside me, I exited the bus. Once out, I hoisted Fitz on my shoulders. "That's the mountain we named you after!" He smiled and giggled in a way that made me believe he understood.

We dragged our bags past newly constructed restaurants and bakeries, the remnants of the frontier town still visible in the random ramshackle buildings. We rounded a corner onto a dusty road and Carsten, our jovial Swiss landlord, greeted us with hugs that made our eyes bulge. When I had e-mailed him months earlier, asking if he had room, he had said, "Only if you bring your family. Then you can have my personal house." So we arranged for our arrival to coincide with his departure; we would house-sit his airy, timber-framed chalet. It was a far cry from the damp tent I had festered in for five weeks on my first trip to Patagonia eight years before. Also on the property were several little A-frame shacks, occupied by an international crew of climbers. There was a patch of grass, a slackline, and an asado pit. The bench in front of our house soon became a social hub. No one had cars and the Internet was so slow that it was surely run by a hamster wheel—we spent our days actually talking to each other. Everyone was there to live idealistic dreams of distant summits and a simple life. This was my South American Eden.

One night early in our trip we went out for dinner, meeting a group of climbers at a rustic old restaurant called La Senyera, where photos of mountains adorned the walls. A young woman in an apron, with a bandanna wrapped around her head, greeted us.

"¡Aww, que bebé más hermoso!" she said. Then she snatched Fitz right out of our arms and carried him to the back of the restaurant. I looked at Becca, she shrugged, and we walked over to a large table of climbers, most of whom we knew from our various travels. The community of core climbers is small but global, and certain areas become the center of focus during their respective best seasons. Each meeting is a little like how I imagine an Italian family reunion must be, filled with hugs and laughter, and reminiscing about the last time you shared a rope with this or that person.

I had no idea what bringing a baby into this scene would be like. Over the next few weeks, the climber formally known as Badass Alex Honnold became Uncle Alex. He carried Fitz on his shoulders, making goofy faces and delighting in his little laughs. "Dude, you're going to be so jealous when I'm the one who gets him to take his first steps," Alex said. He was living in the house with us and we felt like one big, well-adjusted, happy family.

My goal was to never spend more than two weeks away from the family, but I also knew that I needed time to completely focus on my own climbing, especially in such serious mountains. We had planned for Becca and Fitz to return home early, leaving Alex and me thirteen days for the Fitz Traverse. You never know how conditions will pan out, but it just so happened that the weather raged in the mountains while Becca and Fitz were there. We spent two blissful weeks hiking around the lower elevations, skipping stones in the serene lagunas, sampling empanadas, enjoying asados, and sipping Malbec. Groups of climbers would gather around midday to stay fit on the boulders. The whole thing had the feel of a beach vacation—but with a backdrop of hulking mountains, cloud caps streaming from their summits.

Our ambitions for the Fitz Traverse began to look like a pipe dream. Some of the best alpine climbers in the world had been attempting the traverse for over a decade, and the rime-coated giants towering above town served as a stark reminder that Alex and I were pretty much only rock climbers. Sure, I had climbed Fitz Roy, and Alex had climbed a big alpine rock face in Alaska. But both of us had been with highly experienced alpinists, who could essentially escort us across all of the snow and ice, and give us the confidence that we were doing things right. Overall, I was far more experienced in the alpine, but even that amounted to only about ten days in crampons. Which was about five times more than Alex.

In theory, having the fastest and boldest rock climber in the world as your partner would be an advantage. But here, Alex was looking to me for direction. Even in that he was pretty laissez-faire. Before the trip I had sent him a detailed equipment list. He had brought about half of it. "I figured we could just make do," he said. I worried that he had no idea what we were getting ourselves into.

The weather cleared the very day that Becca and Fitz flew home. In the early morning twilight I kissed and held them both in my arms. Becca's eyes were rimmed with tears, and I fought back my own.

"Be careful, I'll miss you," she said, sniffling.

Then she gave Alex a look: *You better not kill your older brother.* But all she said was, "It's a good day for sending." Alex's expression was a reassuring: *Don't be such a sap, I won't let anything happen to him.*

"Take lots of pictures." It was her simple way of giving us her final blessing, as if we were going out for a leisurely stroll in the hills. In our brief time living together, Becca had learned part of the secret to Alex's success: The belief that everything is no big deal can be a self-fulfilling prophecy. Or so we hope. It's worked for him thus far.

I pulled Becca into my arms again and held her for a few extra moments, kissed Fitz hard on the forehead and told him, "I'm going to go climb your mountain." Then we turned and walked away. It took all of my willpower to not look back. But I knew if I did, I would see Becca crying and lose my strength.

After a few hours of hiking across a huge lowland floodplain, past eroding riverbanks and rickety bridges into a goblins' forest, we reached a vantage point where we could see the entire range. We stopped to study our hoped-for route. Plumes of snow blew from each of the summits. Ice plastered all of the shaded south faces (in South America, the north faces are the sunny ones). Small spindrift avalanches washed down gullies. I tried to comprehend what it would be like to navigate that mammoth labyrinth. I hoped that the mountains would clean themselves of the remnants from the storms as the weather cleared. That's what's supposed to happen, anyway. I sighed loudly and looked at Alex.

"Those mountains look pretty intense."

He looked back at me and shrugged. "I don't know. They don't look that big to me." *No big deal.* If I weren't so intimidated, I would have laughed. Problem was, Alex was serious.

Ahead rose a series of irregular saw-toothed summits. Climb one face and then rappel down the opposite to begin the next ascent. Up and over and repeat for days on end. Imagine a kind of roller-coaster ride with near vertical rises, pointed crests, and precipitous descents. Adding to the challenge was a virtual absence of horizontal terrain, making bivvy spots scarce.

In some ways, I envied Alex. He didn't know what lay ahead.

We hiked four more hours, and as the mountains grew closer Alex's perspective seemed to shift. "Oh, my God, I can't believe how gnarly those mountains look." But instead of appearing intimidated, Alex seemed giddy. His eyes widened with excitement.

Another hour later, after a big scree-covered hill, we reached the foot of the glacier. Its bottom margin was steep and icy, so we pulled crampons from our packs. When Alex tried to strap his on, I noticed something was off. "What the hell," I said to him, "those are not aluminum strap-on crampons. Those are made to go on a mountain boot. All we have are tennis shoes." In the equipment list I'd given him before we left, I included specifics about crampons—important, since to shave weight we were going to navigate the ice with lightweight sneakers rather than sturdy boots, a sketchy maneuver to begin with. "How am I supposed to know that," Alex said with an irritated shrug. "You're the alpine climber."

I stared up at the ice-encrusted mountains. When I climbed Fitz Roy in 2006 we'd brought only one pair of crampons for three people (the first guy uses them, then can either pass them down the rope or make the others just deal without them on a tight top rope). Maybe we would be okay. But the mountains had been much less icy then.

We shrugged off the crampon mix-up and Alex climbed the bottom of the glacier by leaping between rocks that had half melted into the ice. We roped up for protection against hidden crevasses—snow can obscure them with shallow cover, like booby traps—and started wallowing through knee-deep snow.

"I sure am glad you're the alpine climber, so you have to do all the work," Alex cracked, as I led the way up the glacier and he followed along in my footsteps.

An hour later, I felt a sudden jolt in the rope and turned around. Alex had disappeared completely into a crevasse. Luckily he had landed on a snow bench just a few feet down, and as he pulled himself out he started laughing, "Did you see that? Whoa. That was crazy." Then he resumed merrily plodding along.

It crossed my mind that Alex's amygdala (the part of the brain that processes fear) might be malfunctioning. But I also understood that one of the things that sets him apart is his ability to look at situations logically, while others respond emotionally. After all, we were roped up, so if he fell deep into a crevasse I could just haul him out. Alex never seems rash when he is climbing. Quite the opposite—all of his partners notice this, and you can see it in the videos—he's methodical and calculated.

Alex simply doesn't waste any energy worrying about things he can't control. Some might call this delusion, or false optimism. Some might go so far as to call it reckless. Alex is the only person I have climbed with who just calls it reality. We analyzed the situations as we encountered them. Start at the beginning; see what happens. And, while we are at it, we might as well have some fun.

We bivvied at the base of the first spire, Aguja Guillaumet. Its rocky, twisted peak reminded me of Lady Liberty's torch.

As we were about to start climbing in the morning, Rolando "Rolo" Garibotti and Colin Haley passed us. They are two of the most renowned and accomplished Patagonian climbers ever, and were gunning for the same overall objective—the Fitz Traverse. There's a weird phenomenon in which certain climbs fall into the collective consciousness all at once, and multiple parties end up vying for the same first ascent. A massively difficult, un-climbed line suddenly becomes low-hanging fruit.

Rolo and Colin are our friends, and they are true Patagonia gurus—the knowledge they've gained through their many ascents in the range, and their willingness to share that knowledge, has helped revolutionize Patagonian alpinism. As they passed, we asked what they thought about Alex's trying to make the wrong crampons fit.

"I don't know, sounds pretty dicey to me." Colin said. Rolo just gave us a concerned look. "Well, we don't need crampons to climb this first mountain," Alex said, shrugging. "We know we can rappel without crampons, so we'll just start rapping if it gets too dicey."

Rolo and Colin raced ahead. We romped up the first wall, chopping ice from nearly all of the cracks as we went. When the ice was too thick, we ran it out and face-climbed around the cracks.

"Dude, this is pretty snowy," Alex shouted down, a rare hint of hesitation in his voice.

"Yeah, but the weather's only supposed to get better!" I yelled back. "I'm sure the cracks will dry out as we get farther along." It was almost as if we were trying to out-optimist each other.

Halfway up Guillaumet, we found Rolo and Colin sitting on a ledge, looking a bit forlorn. "Rolo's feeling pretty under the weather," Colin said. "We've decided we should go down." Then it became clear why they had been waiting. "You should take these," Rolo said, handing Alex his crampons. "I don't think yours are going to work."

The Fitz Traverse had been a goal of Rolo and Colin's for many years. They had made two previous attempts and were potentially giving up their dream of becoming the first to do it. Now they were handing us the tools we needed. In this land of giants, I felt humbled once again. Colin nodded his encouragement and sent us on our way.

That evening, as we were setting up our bivvy, Alex grabbed the camera and started playing interviewer. "What are you doing, Tommy?"

"Building our anchor for the night."

"Is that because our tent is pitched on a forty-five-degree angle on the side of a giant cliff?"

Before I could respond, he blurted out: "Dude, this is so rad. This is the kind of stuff I see in *Alpinist* magazine. But we're actually doing it!"

A day and a half later we had climbed up and over Agujas Guillaumet and Mermoz, and had reached the top of the North Pillar of Fitz Roy, a prominent subformation of the peak. In a few hours, Alex had led an epic 1,000-foot block up some of the harder rock climbing of the entire route. Here, in the snow atop the pillar, we reorganized our small quiver of gear. Trying to move fast, we'd brought very little to sustain us—only what could fit in one thirty-five-liter and one twenty-five-liter pack. One sleeping bag and one down jacket. A stove and some food. A light tent. We'd pared our climbing rack to the bare minimum.

To the west, the evening sky washed in pale purple. Far below, the shadow of Fitz Roy, which tops out at just over 11,000 feet, stretched across the eastern plains. The steep, sharp lines of the massif shot up and down the jumbled glacier and beyond to rolling brown grasslands. It was February 13, 2014.

I looked up at the next section of the route. A waterfall, part stream and part precarious icicles, spilled from a giant hole, the result of the extraordinarily wet season. Bits of rime and ice shattered and fell down the wall. The next thousand feet, to the top of Fitz Roy, would be my lead. I was gripped.

"I guess the rime will stop falling when the sun goes down in a few minutes," I mumbled. Again Alex picked up the camera and began to narrate, sticking his finger in front of the lens.

"Check out the freaking shadow. Here we are on top of the North Pillar," he said, pointing to the prominent shadow cast by the massive formation onto the plains, so many miles below. Then he moved his finger two inches. "And here's the actual summit. *That* is cool."

That's how it is with Alex—I was gripped, as the headwall looked horribly out of condition—but suddenly he brought amusement, if not outright levity.

I knew that once I entered the waterfall we would have to keep going to avoid hypothermia. In the daytime, it wasn't terribly cold. Soaked in ice water at night would be a different story. I considered bivvying where we were and waiting until morning, but once the sun hit that bright northern aspect, the rime would start to tumble. I took a deep breath and racked up.

Alex started to babble. "This is no problem for you, you got this. You're a total boss."

The sun set and sure enough the rime stopped falling. I walked up to the waterfall and hesitated. I let the pick of my ax pierce the sheet of flowing water and strike the newly formed ice beneath. The point glided around for a moment and then stuck in a small slot. Water splashed off the ice tool, spraying me in the face. I realized I had to move. The cascade would soon freeze and coat everything in verglas. Our cams would skitter, useless, out of the cracks, and the aluminum crampons strapped to our tennis shoes would be more like skates. My hand trembled. Fitz's giggle echoed in my ears. I could see his hands pattering across the dusty tile of the house as he crawled up to wrap his arms around my calf, just before we had left. I'd looked into Becca's blue-gray eyes. "Don't worry, baby, we'll be careful," I had said, sliding my callused fingers under her streaked blond hair and behind her neck. "It's just a rock climb."

Above Fitz Roy, the twilight deepened to a darker violet. I climbed through the waterfall, gasping as the cold flow seeped into every conceivable opening in my clothing. Fighting to keep my hands steady, I placed a nut, stepped in a sling, and used my ax to chip ice out of the crack—this route wasn't about free climbing, not for us, not in these conditions. We yarded on gear when we had to—yes, the games climbers play.

I looked down. Sixty feet below me, a large, dry ledge extended like an island. A growing chill and the heavy pull of my sodden clothing reminded me that it was already too late to retreat. The only option was to keep moving. I had wanted an adventure but this was almost too much.

For thirty minutes, I flailed upward like a hooked fish in a vertical rapid. I noticed a dry crack to the right. Leaning hard off my ice tool, shivering with cold and fear, I swung myself onto dry rock. Fingertips alternately burning and numb, I watched the final light flicker to the west. The immensity of the ice cap sent an unneeded reminder of how far we were from home. I switched on my headlamp, and my world became contained within its beam. Beyond that light was the remainder of the 4,000-foot-tall rock needle on which we clung. A perfect hand crack traced a dark line up red-gold stone before it faded, once more, to black.

I continued to aid climb until my hands and shoes dried, then pulled off my crampons and started free climbing. Coarse rock grated my skin. Blood splattered on stone. With each move, ice crackled from my frozen jacket and chimed down the wall. The rope became as stiff as a steel cable. I climbed faster, trying to create more body heat, knowing that I had to get my internal furnace burning hotter. We had to dry our saturated clothing somehow; if we didn't we would surely be overcome by hypothermia in minutes.

Miraculously, cracks weaved around most of the ice. Every sixty feet, I short-fixed the rope—a speed-climbing trick—so Alex could ascend and bring up our small rack. Occasionally, my only option was to chop through the rime that blocked our passage. Large chunks hit Alex's back and shoulders with a guttural thud.

"You okay?" I shouted down.

"Yeah, man, you're doing great," Alex yelled back, but his words sounded forced.

Each time I reached a small ledge, I paused for a moment and let the exertion, the darkness, and the starlight buzz through me. Skirting the edge of a 3,000-foot sheer drop, I looked toward the glacier to our west. I kicked a chunk of loose rock and watched it fall beyond the beam of my headlamp, listening for the sound of impact. What seemed like an eternity later I heard a faint crack, like a distant gunshot. I knew we had passed the point of no return; the fastest way down was to go over the top of the mountain. And if in the process something were to go wrong, rescue would be days off. No radio, no way of communicating with anyone but each other.

Above, the angle eased. Snow-filled gullies flowed like rivers between shadows of stone buttresses. The most difficult part was behind us. I kicked my feet in hard, knowing that Alex would have to balance in my footsteps.

Around 2:00 a.m., just below the top of Fitz Roy, we found a place where the wind had shaped the snow into a cornice, creating a nook large enough for us to lie down. The expanse below was bathed in moonlight. The snow mushroom atop Cerro Torre, the stunning needlelike spire to our west, shone like a lighthouse. Alex looked at me and nodded. "This is freaking cool." We set up our tent and stuffed two worn-out bodies into a single sleeping bag.

I woke up shivering. When I moved my hands, pain shot through my fingers like electric shocks. The intensity of the previous night's climbing had gone. My body just hurt. I checked my wristwatch. Six o'clock. We'd slept for three hours. We packed up and climbed easier terrain to the summit. We paused long enough to take a few pictures, and continued. Twenty rappels led to an icy saddle on the south side. We were carrying twenty pages of the guidebook, information that Rolo had acquired over a lifetime of climbing in Patagonia. Yet the next part of our traverse was uncharted. The sun shone directly overhead. We stripped to short sleeves, climbed across a sharp ridge toward an unnamed summit, and onward toward Aguja Poincenot, another of the jagged incisors.

In silence, we let our instincts guide us. Whenever we thought we'd come to an impasse, we'd find a hidden crack or secret passage. I watched Alex tiptoe up rock around snow patches, always solid and controlled. *How comfortable he seems in this new environment.* Once in a while, in my exhaustion, I felt as though I'd slipped back through time to my first Patagonian trip. Now I was the older one, and my partner was experiencing everything for the first time. Gradually, this strange situation started to feel normal.

Sometimes we'd stop to sip water out of horizontal depressions in the rock and from small cascades; mostly we kept moving. When I looked at Alex, I could see that his cheeks were growing sunken. It's impossible to consume enough food, and it was too heavy to bring much of it anyway. You don't eat nearly enough; instead, you draw your fuel from someplace else. But Alex's usual bored slouch was gone, and his eyes glowed.

I felt content here, where the wind stripped away all evidence of our man-made world. The way forward was very complex, and yet very simple. All we had to do was climb. From atop Aguja Poincenot, we caught a glimpse of the remainder of the enchainment. We knew exactly where we were headed. The end was literally in sight—at least for a few moments. Three more peaks to go.

On our third night I flaked out our rope as a sleeping pad: All the threads of the sheath had been cut by now, and they stuck out like some kid's plush toy. Come morning we dragged our aching bodies from the tent, fired up our little camp stove, melted snow for water, and dumped in some powdered electrolyte mix. I downed a double caffeinated Clif Shot and a couple of Advil. Only then, and bathed in the divinity of the morning light, did I feel myself coming back to life.

Before we could climb to the next summit, we had to rappel down a 2,000-foot wall. The core shot in the rope had ballooned into a fuzzy mess, so we cut it. Three more mountains to climb, and we now had only 120 feet of tattered rope left. I dropped one of my climbing shoes. The seams on my approach shoes blew out. We had already burned a hole in the sleeping bag, and the tent floor was riddled with holes from the jagged rocks. Our packs were torn from being dragged through chimneys.

Plenty of labyrinthine climbing still remained. Maneuvering around, over, and between the immense broken bits of mountain took enormous, shoe-shredding and muscle-burning effort. My world had become a fog, my limbs seeming to move of their own free will.

More and more, we thought as one. A sixth sense seemed to warn us of each loose block or hidden patch of black ice. Lines focused and became crisp. Each footstep was sure and precise. The absurdity of our situation made us giddy.

We climbed over Agujas Rafael Juárez and Saint-Exúpery, and on the last night, as we made camp, we laughed hard, intoxicated by the absurdity of our odyssey.

"This has been a crazy four days," Alex said.

"I can't believe you just admitted that," I replied. I shoveled polenta into my mouth with a pair of broken sunglasses—I'd lost my spoon—as Alex flashed a familiar, mischievous smirk. We both knew we were nearing the end of one of the grandest journeys of our lives.

In the morning, we climbed to the summit of Aguja de l'S, the final peak. All I could think about was Fitz's giggle and his shining eyes, filled with infinite possibility. Numb to the exposure while navigating the descents with our shortened rope, we intermittently down-climbed in between the rappels. Swirling clouds obscured the summits. Our timing was perfect, almost to the hour.

At the bottom, we jumped across the bergschrund and post-holed through knee-deep slush. On a dry rock we packed up for the long march to El Chaltén, laughing and talking as the wind roared.

Five hours later, we found our friend Jesse standing in a patch of weeds near the door of our home-away-from-home. Dust devils blew in the street. He walked up to us and wrapped his big arms around my shoulders. "Man, we were starting to worry about you guys. Pretty much everyone else is back."

His eyes were glassy.

"What's wrong?"

Jesse dropped his head. "There's bad news. Chad Kellogg is dead." He breathed deep and looked me in the eyes. "He pulled a block on his head rappelling. Died instantly. Jens was hanging shoulder to shoulder with him. He's taking it pretty hard."

My hands and feet tingled. I couldn't speak.

"When, where?" Alex asked.

"A couple days ago, near the top of the Supercanaleta." The wind reverberated off the tin siding of the chalet. For a moment we said nothing. "You guys need to get some sleep," Jesse said. "Glad you're back safe." He gave us both a gentle fist bump and walked away.

Alex and I had been doing the same thing Chad and Jens Holsten had. We had also rappelled down Fitz Roy, not far from the Supercanaleta route. Chad had died. We hadn't. Unlike what I'd said to Becca, he wasn't being reckless, he was simply unlucky.

I remembered that night before the climb when my family was still with me. We had sat at the restaurant around a huge table with Chad, Jens, and a bunch of other climbers. Fitz was in the safe hands of the restaurant owners, being paraded around so the other patrons could see him and greet him. I kept looking over my shoulder to make sure that he was okay. That same sense of independence and protectiveness applied to my climbing brothers. I just wish I could keep all of them safe.

At moments like this, feeling completely gutted after the terrible news about Chad, I had to wonder what it all meant. We can tell ourselves that we minimize the dangers. Pick objectives we're relatively certain we'll live through. Alex can calculate every ropeless move with precision. I can choose to use a rope. We can approach our climbing as a series of athletic goals or as a quest for enlightenment. But the truth is, this kind of accident could have happened to any of us. Chad knew what he was doing. He was one of America's most experienced alpinists, and he wasn't any more reckless than the rest of us.

For the next few mornings in El Chaltén, a hush weighed on our little community. People wandered the streets, unsure what to say or do. Each night, we congregated under the dim lights and wooden tables of La Senyera and drank red wine. Gradually, the laughter returned. But when we talked about our climbs, it was with our heads down, our voices low. The nights seemed to press against the windows; the hollow and eerie wind howled. The internal battle raged about risk and justification, but we didn't talk about it. Our answers would always feel empty.

Days later, miles above it all, I look out my window to where I've just been. The familiar landscape holds my attention, even after the aircraft rises into a bank of clouds and the summits vanish. I close my eyes.

I've been to places of incomprehensible beauty. I've been in driving snow when flashes of lightning shuddered the atmosphere around me, spent quiet nights perched below the immaculate stars of distant skies, laughed as the wind blurs sunlight and erases all sound. At such times, wonder saturates every cell in my body, provides me with a deep well of energy and an infinite capacity to love. It changes who I am.

For as much as I have transformed I am still a kid, full of curiosity about the world, chasing dreams of faraway summits. But I'm also a father. I think about where I draw my lines, and I promise myself to be safer. I promise Fitz. And Becca. In Patagonia I pushed too far.

CHAPTER SEVENTEEN

The familiar smell of sweat and climbing chalk fills the air. I strip off my fleece top and lay it on a pile of handmade dumbbells my father had fabricated, remnants from the old days.

Bodybuilding equipment has given way to a homemade climbing training center. Still my parents' garage, still infused with the same spirit. A place where hard work is king.

My rest period ends. I rise.

High tempo electronica music pulses like the beat of my quaking muscles. Repeaters.

I eye the Beastmaker hangboard and exhale. For the next forty-five minutes, I'll be doing muscle- and tendon-searing timed hangs—half pad edges, slopers, one- and two-finger pockets.

I step forward. The stopwatch counts down.

Every synapse in my brain fires, focusing my concentration on the first hold.

Hang for seven. Release for three. Hang for seven. Release for three. Repeat, repeat, repeat.

Weakness comes from the mind. Don't let that be the limiting factor.

I go until my muscles fail and I can't do another rep. I rest.

Then I clip ten-pound weights to a waist belt.

I start again.

I'm forcing every possible motor unit to fire, forging utmost neuromuscular recruitment. For years I resisted my dad's efforts to take a scientific approach to this part of my climbing life. Now, I embrace it.

278

Some talk about "tricking" your muscles into various adaptations, but maybe I'm only tricking myself.

Of course I am. We're built to seek pleasure and avoid pain.

And there's no trick to hard work. You just have to do it.

Our life at home in Colorado was full and active and engaging, but Becca and I still craved seeing new places, meeting new people, and experiencing different cultures. We booked a three-month trip to Europe shortly after I returned from Patagonia. I was able to once again blend work and play, primarily due to the building interest in the Dawn Wall (our success on the Fitz Traverse certainly didn't hurt). A slideshow tour and work with sponsors covered our expenses, and we had plenty of time in between for climbing and travel.

Our first stop was Céüse in Southern France. We rented a small house on a farm. We'd invited friends from back home to join us. Each morning after we woke, Becca and I led Fitz into the rolling pastures and vineyards. We walked on our bare feet, his little fingers wrapped around my pinky for balance. We'd feed the chickens and pet the horses, then load Fitz into a backpack and walk for an hour up to a wave-shaped, mile-long cliff that contained some of the most flawless limestone on the planet. For three weeks we spent our days sport climbing on the blue-and-gray-streaked rock. With friends, we alternated between belaying and climbing and watching Fitz explore his little world.

We climbed until the sun dropped, and then stood in silence as the light shifted the hues of the waterfall that fell from the top of the cliff from pink to orange to fire red. Sometimes my mind flashed back to scenes from Patagonia, to the many images that played like a dream in my mind. Sometimes I thought about Chad's death, but I kept it mostly at a distance, compartmentalized. Captivated by the day-to-day experience of being in such a wondrous place with my family, I felt the joy of that Patagonia trip continually surface. And as I watched Fitz scurry around the base of the cliff studying rocks and bugs and blades of grass, I quietly renewed the promise I'd made in the wake of our Fitz Roy traverse.

We left Céüse and rode trains through the Swiss countryside, walked the cobbled streets of Prague, swung on ropes overlooking the turbulent seas by Kalymnos, and ate gelato in oceanside cafés in Sicily. Fitz provided a link to tender moments with people we otherwise never would have met. An old man in a flat cap playing bocce ball in the park crouched and gently poked him in the belly, hoping to get a giggle. A young lady selling candy on the street passed him a free sample with a smile and a wink. When traveling with Fitz we could easily view the world as full of compassion and love.

Our final stop was Chamonix. Fittingly, Fitz took his first steps on the flanks of Mont Blanc, the highest mountain in the Alps. His chubby little legs wobbled under his own weight, and he beamed with joy, the peaks rising behind him. Nine of his first eighteen months were spent traveling—Fitz visited nine countries, and could count to ten in English, French, Spanish, Japanese, and German.

While in Chamonix, I trained and climbed with Alex Megos, a twenty-one-year-old German sensation. He has shaggy blond hair cut in a bowl, lucid blue eyes, and typical climber's build—from the abs up he's muscled like a thoroughbred; below the waist, he resembles a bird. A bird with a baby's face—I was always taken aback by how young he looked. Alex has spent nearly half of his life under the tutelage of a coach, raised like a future Olympian. It's the sort of thing that just doesn't happen in the United States, where climbing is still emerging from an awkward adolescence.

Alex is stronger than anyone I had ever met and confirmed my recent observations about the importance of training specifically for hard, technical rock climbing. Alex climbs outside very little, at least compared to me and everyone I know. He spends tons of time in the climbing gym, and loves doing sets and reps and all sorts of exercises with gymnastic rings and yoga balls. His coaches take a very scientific approach, directing Alex's training in a way that can be carefully analyzed and quantified. In working on the hangboard, he'd do precise numbers of repetitions and sets with specific time intervals and rests in between. Those numbers were computed based on the latest research into muscle development and the proper balance of stressing and resting tissue. He climbs or trains six days a week and does almost zero cardio exercise. When he does climb outside, he absolutely crushes.

Although the difficulties on the Dawn Wall involve far more than just strength, if I couldn't reliably do the crux moves and sequences, I wouldn't be able to send the route. My experience and technique on El Cap were as good as they could possibly be, but greater specific strength would certainly help. When I was younger, I would have dismissed Alex's approach entirely. It was almost the antithesis of what we believed in. Quantifying anything was anathema to most of us. We'd stick to old-school training methods. Meeting and climbing with people like Alex made me wonder if my thinking was outdated. These kids were getting very strong very fast. I decided that summer I would train like him.

I got into a routine back in Estes Park. Not doing the same exercises as Alex, exactly, but adopting a similar mind-set, intensity, and strategy. If I really wanted to step up my game, I would have to clear my plate of everything but family and training. I started purposely dropping the ball on many of life's little details, like answering my phone and e-mail. I talked to Becca about how I would have to treat my training like a full-time job, clocking in for eight to ten hours a day. She gave me her blessing.

I changed my diet, cut out bread and processed sugar, alcohol, and caffeine. I split the summer into training cycles. The first was to build my power through heavy and explosive fingertip hangs, weights, and bouldering. I spent half of each day on the overhanging blocks of Chaos Canyon. For an older athlete like me, overuse injury was a serious concern, so I also started a strict routine of injury prevention work, including foam roller massage and opposing muscle workouts. At first, the increased activity beat me up. I was constantly achy, sore, and lethargic. For a while, my quantifiable strength (like how many seconds I could hang from my fingertips on the rounded half of a two-inch wooden dowel) actually decreased. But gradually my body adjusted.

Midsummer I started an endurance phase, swapping out a few afternoons a week of bouldering for long days of sport climbing. I wanted to climb the four hardest routes at the Monastery, a local crag, in a single session. I had bolted and climbed these routes as a teenager and had used them as a measuring stick post–finger loss. As a result, they could serve as a benchmark for my progress. The rock at the Monastery is overhanging and blank with lots of widely spaced holds. The climbs themselves consist of super-hard boulder problems interspersed with the occasional resting stance, much like interval training. Individually these are still some of the most difficult sport climbs in Colorado. No one had considered doing all four in a day. If I could pull it off, it would be solid evidence that my training was working. On my third trip to the Monastery that summer, I was successful.

Also, I could feel my body changing. When I looked in the mirror, I could see more upper-body muscle and less leg mass, as if a giant hand had been squeezing me from the bottom up. The new diet and increased exercise, however, naturally sent my weight down. I lost nearly ten pounds, down to 143 on my five-foot-nine frame. My strength-to-weight ratio skyrocketed. By the end of the training season, I could hang forever on tiny crimps, and I'd finish my sessions with two sets of fifty pull-ups.

My confidence for the Dawn Wall steadily rose, except for one thing: the dyno. The previous fall I had brought a tape measure on the wall and downloaded an inclinometer on my iPhone. I took pictures of the holds, measured the distances and the angles between them, measured the angle of the wall, and mapped out the move as precisely as I could. Then I replicated it on the side of my storage shed at home.

One hundred and one inches between holds at a fourteen-degree upward angle. (To put this into a context, I'm sixty-nine inches tall and my wingspan is exactly that same number.) I would try the move for an hour or two every day. First I reduced the distance between the holds to ninety-one inches. I practiced until I could reliably stick the move. Then I increased the distance in small increments. I got to where I was reliable at ninety-nine inches, but I couldn't do it at the full distance—only two inches more.

I tried hundreds of times. I videoed myself. I analyzed every component and played with every detail, from the angle of launch to my body position during flight to my body's distance from the wall. I played with my mental state. Blind conviction, cool composure, laser focus, all-out ballistic aggression. Sometimes it felt so close that I would truly believe I would get there. Other times it felt impossibly far. I brutalized myself until I could no longer sit up straight due to the soreness in my stomach. I developed a nagging pain at the top of my left shoulder. The frustration would build and I'd explode in little fits of rage. I would yank off my shoes and throw them across the yard. *Am I really going to be stopped by this one move?* I'd flail my hands in the air and scream "WHY?!"

Becca would see me stomping around the yard and come out with a glass of water to calm me down. She must have thought I needed to join Fitz for a juice box and a nap. Instead, she just offered gentle encouragement. "Don't worry, baby, you'll get there." She would have been justified in concluding that I was going batshit crazy.

I wondered how Kevin was doing. By now, I'd become accustomed to minimal response from him. When I called, he would reply with a one-sentence text. I didn't want to be a nag, so for most of the year it had been radio silence. I kept tabs on him through his Facebook page. He was posting a lot of throwback images of the Dawn Wall, and based on his online persona, he seemed highly motivated. In fact, he used those exact words in his tweets. I was confused by the contrast. In most of my direct communications with him, his responses were far more blasé.

Midsummer I tried to check in directly, calling and leaving a message. A few days later, I received an e-mail.

"The Dawn Wall is the first thing on my mind when I wake up and the last thing before I fall asleep," he wrote. "Unfortunately not with burning psyche, but rather with a heavy weight. When I send the probe down to find my fire, my psyche, my passion, it's just not there. As a result, I haven't been training nearly as hard as I should, which only makes the weight heavier." He didn't want to let me or anybody else down, but said that his confidence was low, and offered to just come up on the wall that season to support me.

When I first read his words, I felt queasy. The Dawn Wall had become such an improbable yet maybe-just-possible goal in my mind that I couldn't imagine how he could see it differently. After a bit, guilt set in. Despite our differences in approach and temperament, the two of us had invested serious time and effort in the project together. We'd developed a brotherlike bond—not a best friends kind of relationship, but one with some elements of sibling relationships—competitiveness, resentment, care.

I thought about what it must be like for him. We'd had so much success in our last effort and now he seemed to question his desire and commitment. What was going on in his life that made him feel this way? I hoped it wasn't too bad.

I decided to wait before I replied, let my thoughts settle more comfortably in place. When I finally wrote back to Kevin I struck an empathetic note, explaining how I'd struggled with motivation at times. I usually just pushed through such doubts, beating my head against the wall until sufficient inspiration arrived. I invoked the notion of genuine motivation fueled by curiosity and obsessive drive, about how we were explorers on the verge of something big, how not many people would ever get a chance like this, and how every great journey entails great hardship. I hoped that my words might deliver a useful push. "If your heart isn't in this anymore, and you decide not to continue, I will be forever grateful for the time we spent up there together," I concluded. "If you decide you want to continue, we will give it hell. I hope these thoughts help in some way."

I've always loved the idea that passion breeds success. I now realize, much to my chagrin, that telling someone who doesn't feel the fire to simply follow his passion is a little like telling someone who doesn't have any legs to run to the fridge and get you a sandwich.

Kevin had been continuing mostly out of a sense of obligation to me and his sponsors. But it was also clear that he did not want to give up. That last part—not wanting to quit—might have been the key. Doggedness can be the match that ignites the fire. Perhaps the inverse is also true: Success breeds passion. Maybe Kevin just had to get going and reconnect with his own talent.

"I just wanna say thank you for that last e-mail," he wrote back. "It was really kind, helpful, and nonjudgmental. I'm getting more and more stoked. In short, I'm in."

In late October 2014 Kevin showed up with a conviction and ownership of the Dawn Wall project that I hadn't seen in the past. We met in Yosemite and spent three hard days hiking loads and rigging the wall, followed by a month of working on the hardest pitches. For the first time we had both cleared our schedules for the winter. Our plan was to spend a couple months in the fall working on the climb. We would take a midseason break over Christmas. If the California drought cycle held strong we would head back midwinter for a ground-up push.

When we started climbing it was immediately apparent that my training had paid off. I breezed through pitches that had previously felt nearly impossible. Kevin was as precise and as strong as ever. But his lack of specific fitness for the Dawn Wall—by any normal standard, of course, he was exceedingly strong—caused him to fall behind. While he was able to link sequences, he was having trouble holding on for entire pitches. His frustration grew. There were still six or seven pitches he had yet to completely free. I started to worry that I was going to be ready to send, but he wasn't. What would that mean?

For me, it felt as if it would be only a short time until I could put it all together. Now, in my seventh year on the project, I had freed everything at some point except for one move, eight measly feet—the dyno. Actually, I'd sort of stuck it once, the year before with Chris and Kevin, but I think it was a fluke. I was counting on some sort of supernatural moment for those eight measly feet.

Over and over I would visualize myself launching off the starting flake, upward and left, pushing off my legs to maximal extension and flying through the air like a monkey. I saw my fingers latch the finishing flake—it's huge by this route's standards, about an inch and a half wide and incut—and my left foot skidding along the rock to help control my swing, keeping my body on the wall.

Once a week we'd shift from the other pitches and return to the dyno, and I would try again. And again, and again. I would climb to the starting hold, which was big enough to get all of the tips of my fingers behind. In the split second before launch, however, doubt would seep in like water through a crack. As soon as my fingers grabbed the finishing flake, my legs would swing far to the left and I would explode off the wall into space. I knew the move so well. I had tried it over a thousand times. I had to find a way. Kevin made it look so easy. I was stressed out.

By early December, Kevin's fitness was beginning to catch up and he was linking all the moves on the hardest pitches. I continued to climb the best I ever have. The cold temperatures made for ideal conditions. The Dawn Wall was looking possible for us both, but winter was coming. We would need a stroke of divine drought-cycle luck with the weather. Then a big storm rolled in and dropped a foot of snow in Yosemite. In mid-December, we headed home early for the holidays.

I spent much of the holiday break pacing my living room in Estes. Just before Christmas, a midwinter high-pressure system hit the Sierra Nevada. The forecast showed ten days of perfect weather. Crisp, clear, cold. My obsessiveness kicked into high gear.

I e-mailed Kevin, hoping he'd move his Christmas celebration with his family up a few days so we could get to the valley and send. While I was awaiting Kevin's response, I called Josh Lowell of Big Up Productions. For the past few seasons his motivation to film the Dawn Wall had been waning. I knew he only wanted a call if we thought we might actually send. "I don't know about Kevin, but I feel ready," I told him.

Josh jumped on board and his brother, Brett, made plans to skip Christmas with his wife and two small kids to help with the filming. In a best-case scenario, we would finish the route in two weeks. I was charged with figuring out both a rigging plan for the film crew and how to keep everyone alive on the wall for so many days. I did the math. Three liters of water per person per day, for climbers and film crew. Fifty-six gallons of water. Four-hundred-and-sixty-seven pounds of water. Plus food, sleeping bags, portaledges, ropes, gear. Deargodman. My mind spun.

I called my friend Eric Sloan. Eric is an accomplished aid climber, and I'd learned valuable aid techniques and systems from him. The first time we climbed together, we rocketed up a thirty-two-pitch route on El Cap called the Shield in fourteen hours, narrowly missing the route's speed record. He'd fallen on some hard times and was now living out of his car. I figured he could use some work, so we started talking logistics. We came up with the idea of Eric not only helping with the filming, but resupplying our food and water on the wall every five days.

Phone calls and e-mails bounced back and forth. Josh, Eric, and I were in frantic planning mode, with everyone more than willing to miss

Christmas for the chance to see the Dawn Wall go down. There was one piece missing: I hadn't heard back from Kevin.

Finally, I got a message. "I would prefer to go after Christmas, like the twenty-seventh (since Jacqui and I celebrate our anniversary on the twenty-sixth)." *Anniversary? You're not even married yet. What is this?* "How are you feeling?" Kevin continued. "Are you happy with what we've gotten done so far? I can go either way. I still feel fit but it's hard to maintain 'project focus.'" *Seriously, are you insane?! Am I happy with our progress?! We're ready to send!*

I could not fathom how we could be on such different planets, but I sensed that dragging him up on El Cap against his will would be pushing it. So I crossed my fingers about the weather and made the call to push our climb back. Part of me was relieved, as I felt slightly guilty thinking about the sobbing children on Christmas morning, including my own, wondering where their dads were. I called Josh, Brett, and Eric and told them that their holidays had been saved by Kevin's second anniversary of the first date with his girlfriend.

Then I texted Kevin back. "All right, man, I'll get there right after Christmas and prepare everything. After your date drive straight to Yosemite. We will start up when the shade hits at 2:00 p.m. on the twenty-seventh. All you got to do is show up and climb."

I spent Christmas Eve dinner fidgeting in my chair, and Christmas morning scribbling lists of gear on the back of wrapping paper. Becca cast wary looks my way, reminding me of what a dick I was being, a there-but-not-there husband and father. I mentally added guilt to the list of things to pack away.

I boarded the first plane out the next day. When I was waiting on the runway, sitting still for the first time in days, my heart felt heavy with doubt and guilt. In an ironic turn, just before leaving I'd chosen social media as a venue to spill my manic, half-distracted, half-justifying, half-heartfelt feelings:

I am always thinking about the kind of dad I want to be. I know that the best way to teach is to show by example. For me the Dawn Wall is the perfect venue for some of the most important values I want to show Fitz. Optimism,

*perseverance, dedication, and the power of dreaming big. But leaving Becca
and Fitz at home is never easy. I love you guys.*

I got to Yosemite and spent the rest of the day shopping for food, packing
and double-checking everything, and making a game plan with Eric and
the film crew. Late on the twenty-sixth, Kevin texted me again. "Can we just
start on the twenty-eighth? I don't know if I can drive the five hours from
Santa Rosa and start climbing the same day. We need to be in a relaxed state
of mind to climb at our best. You can tell me to suck it up if you want,
though."

With Beth I was a doe-eyed pushover. For much of my life I lacked confidence. Climbing was one area where those things didn't apply, and as I'd
come out of my shell post-divorce, maybe I'd grown a spine or maybe I'd become too critical of other people's desire for balance. To any rational person,
Kevin was being perfectly reasonable. With the Dawn Wall, here and now, I
definitely was being a judgmental hardass. But there it was. I wrote back:

"I just ducked out on my family right after Christmas, flew from Colorado, shopped for all the food, packed everything. Organized the film crew.
Found a porter to help haul loads up. I stayed up for twenty hours straight
yesterday to get all of our stuff ready. If you start driving at 6:00 a.m. we can
still be chill and start up tomorrow. Yeah, suck it up."

PART
FOUR

CHAPTER EIGHTEEN

Moonlight filters through the trees and into the windows of my van, illuminating the steam of my breath. The winter cold has driven all but a handful of people from Upper Pines Campground, leaving it eerily quiet. Climbing moves and logistics swirl through my mind and I thrash beneath the covers. I reach over and tap my phone. The light of the screen makes me flinch. It's 2:00 a.m., December 27. I need to get some rest.

My eyes blink open. Daylight filters in. *When did I fall asleep?* I hop in the front and drive toward the meadow. A thick layer of fog blankets the valley floor. A coyote trots alongside my van before veering off and disappearing into the whiteness. Otherwise, I see no one.

At El Cap meadow I step out of the van and let the cold sting my lungs. I throw back the sliding door and toss a few bags of equipment onto the grass. Frost shatters off the weeds with an audible crunch. I scurry about, packing supplies and going through checklists. El Cap's hulking silhouette outlined in the soft light of dawn.

I pause, look up, and close my eyes.

The silence is broken by the screech of a timing belt. Eric Sloan's car pulls up. He hops out and walks over. He wears a faded fleece hat, tattered trousers, and a greasy down jacket patched with duct tape. He looks exactly the same as he did fifteen years ago when we first climbed together. The way I used to look.

"Where are you sleeping these days?" I ask. He tells me about his secret spot, secluded and with a good view of the stars and El Capitan. It sounds nice, but I shudder to think of being homeless in Yosemite in the middle of winter.

I start packing last-minute items in a haul bag. Precooked salmon and a big Tupperware of fresh veggies, a large bag of kale. Ziplocs full of almonds and cashews. I glance over my checklist one more time. Eight pairs of brand-new climbing shoes. Various files and creams. A skin care kit rivaling that of a beauty queen. Band-Aids and multiple kinds of tape. A big bottle of Advil.

Another car pulls up. Two guys jump out dressed in thrift store cargo pants and well-worn harnesses. "I rallied some local climbers to help us get everything up there," Eric tells me. "They work housekeeping in Camp Curry and are psyched to help out. You know, not a whole lot going on around here this time of year."

They walk up looking overcaffeinated and, uncomfortably for me, starstruck. One of them asks for a selfie. I put my arms over their shoulders and smile awkwardly. I am glad they are eager, but hate being held up on a pedestal. It feels like only yesterday that I was the nerdy kid wishing I fit in with the Yosemite dirtbags.

I hand each of them a sixty-pound haul bag and we hike up the trail. I talk through the logistics. Our fixed ropes are still in place from working the route, and our "ground-up" attempt will use our already established portaledge "base camp" 1,200 feet up. Each night after climbing we'll ascend our fixed ropes to that base camp to sleep (or rappel down to it after climbing the pitches above). We'll then return to our previous ground-up high point in order for both Kevin and me to continue free climbing all of the pitches in sequence. In the case of a fall we can hang on the rope to rework moves. But before moving on we must free the pitch bottom to top, with no weighting of the rope or gear. Only when we've freed through pitch 28 will we haul a portaledge and lightweight supplies to make another camp for a night, and then blast the remaining four pitches to the top.

As we walk I talk in pleasantries, a little uneasy with the fact that others are doing my blue-collar work. I always thought it arrogant to have someone else do the heavy lifting for you. If you don't own your grunt work, can you really say you've done the climb?

Kevin doesn't seem to worry much about such things. "What would the Tour de France look like if the riders had to carry all their equipment with them?" he has argued. I try to be open-minded; no two ways about it, the climbing on the Dawn Wall is so difficult that we're making big compromises in style.

After ten minutes the trail steepens. Although the base of the route is only five hundred feet higher than the valley floor, the natural architecture of this place creates crazy temperature inversions. By the time we reach the rock, it's easily twenty degrees warmer than down below. We all stop for a second and strip to T-shirts before continuing. The trail intersects the wall and skirts the base for a quarter mile. It passes an exquisite granite slab, polished smooth as glass. After all these years the view of the wall above still leaves me breathless. I lay my hand on the cool stone and run my fingers along its surface. Then I lay my cheek on the wall and turn my eyes skyward, a ritual I have performed hundreds of times, paying homage to creation. I close my eyes and thank El Capitan for being here. Then I ask her to keep me safe through this journey.

We walk to the start of the climb. I uncoil the rope and lie down on the slabs, my hands folded behind my head, looking up at the route. I know this will be my last quiet moment. I linger for an hour as Eric and his friends start hauling.

When I return to my van I see another six cars, three more than I have ever seen in El Cap meadow this time of year. A short, stout man smoking a cigar spots me and walks over. It's Tom Evans, a Yosemite cult figure. He knows and loves climbing, lives in his van during the climbing season, and thinks Yosemite is the center of the universe. Tom watches from the meadow, tracking El Cap climbers with his telescope, taking photos, and blogging about their progress. Oftentimes in the summer twenty or more tourists gather around his lens, taking turns looking through the eyepiece and gawking at the "crazy people who sleep on the side of the wall."

"Hey, Tom, what are you doing here this time of year?" I ask.

"You won't believe it, but I got a sponsor."

I stare at him blankly. *Huh?* It turns out that Kevin's sponsor, Adidas, has hired Tom to send them images from the meadow for their promotional dispatches while we climb.

I had no idea.

I start to fill in the blanks. Kevin had recorded short video clips on his phone during our last season. Adidas edited them into a series, *The Dawn Wall Project*, calling it "The Hardest Route Never Climbed," complete with a dramatic voiceover. It made me think of a WWF promo.

As I chat with Tom, a handful of people form a semicircle around us, some snapping photos. This kind of thing never happens in our insular little climbing world. I smile bashfully. Out of politeness I shake a few hands, and then, like a skittish deer, I jog to my van and reorganize our equipment for the fifth time.

My hands tremble with anticipation and anxiety as I fiddle with climbing gear. I had hoped that climbing midwinter would allow some anonymity beyond our immediate friends and family. Now I realize that as soon as we start up and the first dispatches go out, a lot of eyes will be on us. It underscores what I have long known: Everyone has pressed pause for me—my family, friends, sponsors. Even people I don't know, fans of the project, seem truly inspired by someone going all-in on their dream. I don't want to fail for any of them. I am afraid to fail for them.

Around 11:00 a.m. Kevin's black Toyota truck pulls up. Climbing paparazzi swarm him as he steps out. I'm comforted by the fact that he, too, looks a little uncomfortable. He exchanges pleasantries with them and walks toward me. I'm nervous. Is he going to be angry? For years now I have pushed him hard, but I'd always stopped short of telling him what to do. Maybe I stepped over the line when I told him to suck it up and get to Yosemite. I'm not sure how he will react. There's always been so much unsaid between us.

Kevin walks around the side of my van and throws a small haul bag on the ground. "Here is my contribution to the packing," he says as he pulls out two items: a bottle of whiskey and a bag of coffee. "You can't put a price on morale." I laugh and he gives me a big hug.

Just like that the tension evaporates.

We hoist our bags on our backs and leave the small crowd in the meadow. For the second time today, I walk the winding trail through the dark forest. This time it's different. This time it's for real. I notice that I'm slightly nauseated, adrenalized, jittery. My feet seem to float across the dirt. The trees look as if they're sliding along the ground. Kevin and I barely speak. I try to quiet my racing mind. I'm ready, I know I'm ready. Still I doubt myself.

We reach a break in the trees and gaze up at the now blindingly white, sunbaked rock. We continue up talus to where the trail meets the wall. Kevin splays his arms out, presses his chest against the wall, and gives it a big hug. Then he pats it as if it's a big hairy dog. I give him a moment.

I feel as if I'm in a dream, brightness obscuring detail. I tilt my head back. A tiny white square sits 1,200 feet above us—our portaledge base camp. Home for the next two weeks. I wrestle with the feeling, the knowledge, that this will be my final attempt.

It's 3:30 p.m., December 27, 2014. The sun slips around the side of the wall, casting a shadow across the bottom of the climb. We lace up our climbing shoes, scramble along a ramp, and clip ourselves to a couple of bolts that mark the start of the route.

"One pitch at a time," I say, nodding to Kevin.

He ties in and exhales slowly. "The low-pressure push," he replies. We are both thinking of the last time we went for it free, ground-up. In 2010, we had been too nervous and the climb punished us handily. Kevin's strategy is to try to fool himself into thinking this is no big deal. Just another practice round. He knows the first moments will set the tone.

"Go get 'em, dude."

Kevin starts up. His fingers press gently into the crystals. His feet dance along the micro-ripples. The pitch is a warm-up, mostly slab climbing with bolts and some old fixed aid gear. It takes him less than fifteen minutes.

My vision is oddly blotchy, and I can't stop blinking. It's this weird thing I do when I'm exceptionally nervous. I can't help it. Strangely, though, my body feels strong and light, as if I could deadlift a car or walk on water. I follow, imitating his every move. At the anchor, I clip and rerack the gear.

On pitch 2 the angle kicks up to near vertical as the sun dips low on the horizon. The holds feel sharp, like grabbing the ends of nails. A foot slip can mean torn skin, so I climb carefully, distributing my weight evenly among all appendages. The pitch goes flawlessly, and my confidence builds.

Pitch 3 is the first truly difficult one. Kevin has the lead. He launches into a delicately powerful layback, fingertips pulling outward against the edges of a thin vertical crack, his feet pressing against the rock in opposition. If his feet slip he'll fall directly onto my head. I extend my tether and ready myself to swing out of the way. Kevin doesn't fall, though, and at the first rest position twenty feet higher he flashes me a thumbs-up. He climbs smoothly to within a few feet of the anchor, but then, without warning, slips off.

"Damn it!" he yells, dangling on the rope ten feet down.

I lower him, he clips in next to me and unties, and we pull the rope.

"I'm just gonna go again right now, I'm not even that tired."

It's a risky move. One slip we can deal with, but if it keeps happening we will surely lose energy and momentum. Normally, he'd take more time between attempts. I trust Kevin, though, and he starts up again. I can tell he's still a little fatigued, and the rope between us quivers ever so slightly. He manages to climb through to the anchor. As I follow the pitch a nervous tingle pulses in my limbs. I grip the holds too tightly and my forearms get pumped, but I manage without falling.

On pitch 4 the cracks widen to the point where we can slip our hands in to the wrists. The hand jams give us momentary respite from the difficulties. Still, I have the disorienting sensation that I am dwelling in someone else's body—a feeling that stays with me the entire day. I lead as the sun sets and I switch on my headlamp when I reach the anchor. As Kevin climbs the temperature drops, crossing the dew point. Steam rises through the beam of my light.

Pitch 5 overhangs slightly. Mud and water seep from the cracks. Kevin climbs slowly, methodically. Between moves he wipes moisture from his shoes onto his pants. I think back to the first time I watched him climb this pitch five years ago. Despite being perfectly dry then, he couldn't climb more than a body length without hanging on the rope. Now it's dark, wet, and there's pressure pushing down on us. But Kevin looks calm, controlled. I'm proud of him.

By 9:00 p.m. we're done for the day. We've sent the opening five pitches with relative ease. We ascend three hundred feet of fixed lines to base camp, set up a second portaledge, and get situated. It would seem logical for Kevin and me to share a portaledge, but over the years I've learned that he needs his alone time. So I bunk with Brett, who's up on the wall filming. We huck piles of food, camera gear, and sleeping bags into our portaledge, and strap solar panels to the outside. Climbing gear dangles from slings at the entrance. Our hanging home looks like the Beverly Hillbillies' car. I push myself through the chandelier of equipment and stuff myself into my sleeping bag. Brett crawls over my legs to his own spot. I look around and laugh. It's cluttered, but cozy and warm, like a bear's den. Or a junk show.

I look across at Kevin's ledge. A single sleeping bag and pad. His climbing shoes hanging neatly by the door. Like an Apple store. Plenty of room to stretch out and think. *It must feel lonely and cold*, I think.

That night I spend thirty minutes attending to the skin on my fingertips. I trim the burs on my fingernails and carefully sand my roughed-up calluses. Then I heat water in our single cook pot, wash my hands thoroughly with soap, and apply a cream called Ridiculous to my fingertips. Specifically formulated for this climb by a skin care expert, it contains a plant steroid that increases blood flow. Last I apply a moisturizing ointment and wrap tape around each finger. I set my alarm for 4:00 a.m., at which time I will remove the tape so that my fingertips can dry and harden before climbing. This will become a daily routine.

We sleep until 7:20 a.m. Some bees have trapped themselves in the cone-shaped cylinder atop our portaledge fly, and their buzzing and bouncing serves as our morning alarm. When the sun hits it's blindingly bright. I make coffee in our press, then hand a steaming-hot bottle to Brett and toss another to Kevin. Sandwiches, with bell pepper, cucumber, avocado, cream cheese, and smoked salmon, are next.

"Damn, you really stepped up the food game," Kevin says with a smile.

"Wait till you see what I have in store for tonight."

Brett and I while away the morning talking about our kids. He has two boys, five and seven. Brett is big and strong, built like a brick house, but he's totally chill. The kind of guy you want on your side in a bar fight. When he talks about his kids he oozes tenderness.

"Just wait until Fitz turns two," he tells me. "That's when the personality really starts to emerge. Having kids is so rad."

While Brett's job takes him to the most beautiful mountains in the world, it also takes him away from his family for long stretches, sometimes months at a time.

"What's it like being gone so much?" I ask.

"It kind of sucks. But then I look at my brother, and while he's around running the business, he always has to be on the phone and computer. At least when I'm home I am totally there for them."

I feel a twinge of guilt for having been so distracted at Christmas.

We spend the first part of the day lounging and chatting, waiting for the wall to cool down during this crazy winter warm spell. Kevin makes occasional visits to our ledge but mostly stays zipped inside his.

Necessary alone time, I guess.

This year there's a new dynamic on the Dawn Wall. AT&T installed a 4G tower practically within eyesight of the climb. We had been able to use our phones for years, making calls and sending e-mails, but getting online was unreliable. The addition of the tower makes my Internet connection almost faster than it is at my house.

It's a glorious day and I'm sitting with my shirt off in the open door of the portaledge, admiring the view. I should be holding a rum cocktail with a little umbrella.

From inside Kevin's ledge I hear a low murmuring. I figure he must be talking on the phone. It's impossible not to eavesdrop. As I listen closer, I realize that he's making a recording, like a news-style summary of what has happened so far. When the sound stops, I shout.

"Hey, Kevin, what's going on over there?"

He replies without unzipping the door. "Adidas asked me to send them a two-minute video update each day. I'm just making a recording."

Ah yes, *The Dawn Wall Project*. Probably merged with Tom's shots from the meadow.

"How are you gonna get them the video each day?"

"I downloaded a Dropbox app on my phone. It actually works pretty well up here."

First Facebook, then the small-time paparazzi, now this. Not to mention that we have a film crew with us. What a circus. I say nothing. And then, before I know it, I'm fully wrapped up in surfing the web, mouthbreathing at my screen. We go an hour without saying a word.

Wait a second, this is so messed up! I put down my phone and try to make conversation. Kevin and Brett both answer me in monosyllables, then look back down at their phones. I give in again to the gizmo and make a Face Time call to Becca. She is beaming and the sound of her voice instantly warms me. She props Fitz on her lap and whispers in his ear: "Tell Daddy what I taught you."

Fitz looks at the phone and says in his adorable little voice: "Crush it, Daddy."

At 12:30 p.m. I make an announcement. "All right, boys, time to put our phones away and go send the gnar!" We rappel down to where we left off the night before.

Pitch 6 is two hundred feet long and super complicated, the first truly heady pitch of the route. The scary pitches, like this, aren't always the most technically difficult, but fear can certainly make them feel harder. This one isn't easy to begin with, at 5.13c. Hard bouldery sequences are separated by good rests and tricky gear placements. I wait until the wall goes into the shade to start up. For seventy minutes I climb and rest, climb and rest. By rest, I mean contorting myself in ways that relieve the burning intensity in my forearms, alternately shifting my weight and holding on with one arm while shaking out the other, all the while trying to relax. And simultaneously strategizing about the difficult moves and long runouts still to come.

It's a mentally taxing type of climbing, the sort that I can endure only a few times each day. One small foot slip near the end is like blowing a game-winning free throw. I pull through, though, feeling more solid than ever. My nerves seem to have settled. I feel more like myself. Kevin follows it cleanly on his first try and the mood for the day is set.

Pitch 7 is the most dangerous of the route. It follows an existing aid pitch, with dodgy and infrequent protection, much of which must be placed from strenuous positions. If you get too pumped and don't set the gear perfectly, it could blow out under the force of a fall. Here, that could mean falling sixty or a hundred feet or more—it's a clean fall, though, so you'd probably get more mentally rattled than physically injured. Technically it's 5.14a, but, like the pitch before, it feels much harder. In the unwritten rules of climbing, it's poor form to change the character of pitches you didn't establish yourself, so we didn't add any bolts.

Until now we've been hanging in our harnesses to belay. But as the harder pitches often take us multiple attempts, we start to haul along a small belay portaledge to stand on. Kevin goes first and gives it a good effort, but slips near the end. Luckily the gear holds.

"Guess I needed to work out the jitters," he mumbles. He lowers, we pull the rope, and I give it a try while he rests. I totally bone crush it. "Wow, that felt so easy," I say sarcastically. "Are we still on the Dawn Wall?"

Kevin cruises it on top rope. The jitters are officially worked out.

An hour later we've also sent pitch 8, another 13d. "Holy crap, this is going unbelievably well," I say. I'm feeling cocky. "Shall we try another?" If we can climb pitch 9 tonight, a 5.13c, we will be way ahead of schedule. We send it as the sun sets and jumar one hundred feet back to our portaledge camp, arriving by 8:00 p.m.

The morning of day three is a repeat of the last. I prepare breakfast and we surf the Web. I make my daily announcement and we head to the start of pitch 10. It's the first 5.14b pitch, the one with the wet streak and the lift-the-car-off-the-baby move. It takes longer than expected to get ready. It's nearly 4:00 p.m. by the time I start climbing. I sprint through the wet part, dry my shoes at a dainty little stance, and continue. With my confidence peaking I rush to lift the car off the baby but my pinky misses its mark by half a finger width. I hesitate, my foot slips, and I take my first fall of the route. I lower back to the ledge.

"Had to happen eventually," I say with a shrug. To be honest, I was surprised that I hadn't fallen yet. It's a relief to get it out of the way.

Kevin gives it a warm-up burn. He climbs ten feet, hangs on the rope. Marks some holds with chalk, reworks the subtleties of the moves. He repeats the process for eighty minutes. By the time he's done working out the moves I'm well rested. We pull the rope and I lead the pitch feeling, once again, as if we are climbing on a whole new route. "Oh, yeah!" I shout as I clip into the anchor.

Brett is hanging just above me, and he reaches down and slaps me a high five. I have little doubt that Kevin will cruise the pitch belayed from above. When the protection is dodgy, as it often is on this route, it's mentally easier to climb on top rope. Since I seem to be on a roll—my training is clearly paying off—it makes sense for me to lead pitches like this until Kevin gets his groove on. Soon enough, on the traversing crux pitches, we'll both lead anyhow—it's easier that way with traverses.

Kevin flies through the bottom sixty feet, then comes to the section of dripping-wet slime. His breathing gets loud but he manages to pull through to a tenuous rest stance and calm down. He stands there rocking back and forth, shaking feeling into his toes and forcing his heart rate down. Ten minutes later he chalks up, dusts his hands on his pants with an audible whack, and explodes back into action. He cruises through sloping sideways holds into the crux. Under a small roof, Kevin presses upward with his hands while simultaneously walking-up his feet until he is curled nearly into a fetal position. He exhales hard.

"C'mon, man, you can do it!" I say.

I can tell he's tired; he hesitates, and then peels off only a few feet from the anchor. Frustrated, he rests for an hour as darkness falls. His third try is a repeat of his second. He pulls onto the portaledge and slumps into a sitting position.

"Three days in a row is a bit much for me," he says. "Maybe I should call it for the night." I make sure to look sympathetic even though my silence indicates that I want him to take another crack at it. He sees right through me and sighs. "All right, I'll try again."

While he rests he pulls out his phone. "Whoa, check this out." His eyes get wide. He's got a weather app loaded, and it has a blinking red bar at the top of the screen. *High wind advisory, arctic blasts to eighty miles per hour, beware of falling trees. High twenty-five degrees.* We won't be climbing tomorrow.

After another hour of rest, Kevin gives pitch 10 a last-ditch effort. He pulls it off at the very end. I am starting to understand Kevin's psyche. He essentially has to give up in order to be free enough to perform his best.

That night, as the cold front moves in, our fixed lines dance in the wind. Come morning, Brett and I cook breakfast with the portaledge zipped shut. When I reach out to pass Kevin his coffee, the wind instantly numbs my hand. By noon it's blasting, and despite two bodies holding down our ledge, it occasionally hovers like a magic carpet. In the late afternoon Kevin bundles up, climbs over to join us, tightens up the tie-down straps, and tosses me the whiskey. He piles in, and it's three dudes, clothes, cameras, food bags, and plastic water bottles piled chest high, all smooshed together. The steam from our laughter fills the space with fog. Pellets of condensation drip down on us. Soon Kevin cracks open the whiskey and takes a swig.

"Even though New Year's Eve isn't until tomorrow, I say we party tonight."

The tent fly vibrates against the wall like a machine gun, *whap-a-pap-pap.* Far below, pine needles swirl in furious little tornadoes and tree branches dance until they crack. The wind howls like ghosts, warning us of the danger, so we turn up the volume on Brett's iPhone speakers. Bob Marley. We sing away the evening, swilling whiskey and talking about life, women, and exploring faraway places.

I'm overcome with gratitude simply to be here, surrounded by friends. As the stars shine and the wind cranks up for another round, I look at Kevin and state the obvious. "This is an experience we will not soon forget."

His eyes meet mine and he smiles. As we continue talking and laughing I feel a great connection, as if, for this moment, in this little spot, all is right in the world. Brett smiles, too, nods his head, and takes another pull of whiskey.

I want to reach over and hug them both, but I don't because we're three smelly dudes crammed in a portaledge.

CHAPTER NINETEEN

An icy wind continues to blow the next day. I call the Yosemite weather hotline. Most of the roads in the valley are closed due to wind-downed trees. We wrap ourselves tight in our sleeping bags, and I emerge periodically to stretch and do portaledge push-ups and sit-ups. The hardest sections of the climb await us. Over and over in my mind I review the forthcoming pitches, like a film or TV actor watching a scene on video replay, looking for nuances of the performance to either be discarded, repeated, or refined, memorizing everything down to the tiniest detail.

The next two days remain cold but the wind abates. When the morning sun beats down on the wall, ice starts to fall. At first it's little cubes. Before long, however, baseballs start whizzing by. We had opted against my genius ice-deflecting shield invention, figuring that the absence of precipitation would mean that no ice would form. We were wrong. A few watermelons roar past. The only thing we can figure out is that there must be water seeping from the ground above us, and it's suddenly gotten so cold that the water freezes before the sun can burn it off.

"Man, the likelihood of one of those chunks hitting us head-on is so slim." My reaction, as usual, is denial and justification. "I am *sure* the portaledge fly would deflect it anyway. We've bailed in storms in the past and had to leave our ledges in place, and never found any signs of damage."

Kevin isn't usually one to show anger, but something about this brings it out of him. He tenses and slaps the wall. "I hate this shit!" I wonder if he is mad at me and my attitude, or just the scenario. His minor fit seems to relieve the pressure, however, and he settles down and accepts our fate. With a sigh he adds, "Not a whole lot we can do about it now, I guess."

Someone later told me that if we'd gotten smacked by one of those baseball-sized chunks, one that weighed nine ounces like a baseball, and if it had fallen roughly 2,000 feet from the top, it would have hit us at a speed of more than two hundred miles per hour, striking us with more than 4,000 pounds of impact force. I was glad I'd learned this after and not before.

By afternoon the ice has mostly stopped falling. In the two days before the storm, we'd been on a roll, dispatching the opening ten pitches: 12b, 13a, 13d, 12b, 12d, 13c, 14a, 13d, 13c, 14b. While that sequence was more stacked than on any existing El Cap free route, it was only a warm-up compared to the upcoming middle section of the Dawn Wall. We make our way to pitch 11. The ambient temperature is near freezing, so, for once, we climb in the direct sun. The rest afforded by the storm has done us good. The rock feels tacky as I begin to climb, almost as if I'm sticking my tongue to a piece of metal. The vicious gusts return, dropping the temperature into the low teens. Halfway up the pitch, despite the solar warmth, my fingers go numb. It's an unnerving feeling, and I can't help but think that the sharp holds are turning my skin into hamburger meat. After every move I glance at my fingertips, just to make sure. Luckily, at 5.13c the pitch is easier than many of the others, and I manage it clean, despite barely feeling my fingers.

Kevin takes a totally different strategy to the cold, dealing with it up front. He slowly climbs the bottom half of the pitch, forcing himself to hold on to the rock until his fingers go completely numb. Then he hangs on the rope and rewarms his hands in his jacket. The freeze-thaw cycle creates a horribly nauseating pain that alpine climbers call the "screaming barfies." Fortunately, the vasodilation usually lasts for several hours, making it useful for barehanded climbing in frigid temperatures. The pain passes in a few minutes, Kevin lowers to the bottom of the pitch and frees it without any problem.

We've now matched Kevin's high point in 2010. Time to haul our belay portaledge to the base of pitch 12. There we sit, side by side, gazing outward and saying little. The snowy peaks of the High Sierra unfold in the distance.

The route has been angling steadily rightward as it goes, placing us above a huge depression. It's as if we're sitting at the end of a crane atop the tallest building in the world. Kevin reaches into our mini haul bag full of supplies and pulls out an insulated flask. He tucks it beneath his chin and cackles like the Wicked Witch of the West.

"I brought us a little treat, it's hot coffee."

We pass the flask back and forth as the last rays of light flicker out and the wind calms. On our push in 2010, climbing to here had felt like a war, with frazzled nerves and hands that looked as if they had been caught in a blender. This time, at least thus far, has been wholly different.

Kevin again takes a cerebral approach to pitch 12. He starts with a practice lap. Like a musician tuning up before a symphony begins, Kevin rehearses each of the crux moves individually. It's 5.14b, and though not the hardest pitch of the route, it's still quite desperate. He stubs his fingertips into a flaring seam above his head, pushing upward into a small roof. With each hand placement, he wiggles his fingers back and forth until the skin pushes as far into the seam as possible. He digs the rubber on his shoes into grape-nut-sized footholds. Every few feet he hangs on the rope. He makes minor adjustments to his body position, fine-tuning the subtleties. Once everything feels right, he lowers down.

I take a burn, repeating the same process. I've climbed this pitch clean twice before, so I'm confident. But we both know that if Kevin can take the reins here and lead a pitch that had shut him down last time, it will be a huge breakthrough. We don't even discuss it. Kevin ties in. Then he starts up, climbing like a wound spring, blasting through his previous high point. At thirty feet he throws his foot up on a shoulder-high edge, sloping and two inches deep, and with a loud grunt pulls himself onto a rest stance. Intensity spills from him in strong, audible exhalations. Then he climbs around the corner and out of sight. I close my eyes, trying to visualize his position. I can read his emotional temperature through the rope. When it moves slowly I know he is climbing methodically. When it moves fast I know he is dropping the hammer and my palms begin to sweat. Forty gripping minutes later I hear a relieved "Yaaaooo," and I know he has done it. Kevin is on fire.

Following, I blow it twice. Rushed, sloppy attempts. Despite the constant reminders to myself that the Dawn Wall is an enormous mental challenge that calls for keeping my emotions in check, I'd gotten carried away. Having seen Kevin complete the pitch with relative ease, I'd become overconfident and paid the price. I force myself to rest for thirty minutes and then send the pitch cleanly from the belay.

Back at camp, I feel nauseated. Five days without walking seem to be messing with my metabolism. Eric jumars up the ropes and delivers a fresh batch of food and water. I cook for everyone, but barely touch the food myself.

I spend the night tossing and turning as 2014 becomes 2015 and fritter away the morning chewing my fingernails. There's so much riding on these moments, these coming days. Seven years.

The warm weather returns and we resume our schedule of climbing in the shade. At 3:00 p.m. on day six, we warm up by sending pitch 13, a relative respite at 5.13b. We've now reached my previous high point. Pitches 14 and 15 loom above. They compose the crux of the route: back-to-back 5.14d traverse pitches. They look as smooth as glass, and they climb that way. Everything else on the route is easy by comparison. Kevin is riding high from yesterday's success on pitch 12, while I'm having PTSD flashbacks to my failures here in 2010 and 2011. I'm excited, nervous, and eager to move forward but still wary of the weather holding and whether our bodies will hold up.

In a way, the Dawn Wall is a throwback. In the late eighties, many thought that the difficulties of rock climbing had nearly reached a ceiling. At some point the holds would simply become too small. But then people began climbing on the undersides of overhangs, where the holds are comparatively large and difficulty comes from a style reliant more on power and spectacular, gymnastic-style movements. For twenty years that style defined the cutting edge, and near-vertical, small-hold climbing, with its excruciatingly tedious technique, became a forgotten art.

I imagine that's one reason why the climbing community thought that El Capitan was climbed out. Parts of the Dawn Wall were simply too blank, too smooth. While the first twelve pitches weren't much harder than what had been done in the past on this kind of rock, pitches 14 and 15, set smack in the middle of this 3,000-foot monolith, brought it to the next level.

The next three pitches—the two cruxes, followed by the dyno pitch—had kept me up at night for years. Climbing them individually is very different from climbing them after nearly a week on the wall. Like trying to run a four-minute mile after finishing a marathon, from the couch it sounds possible. But doubt looms as a constant threat, like a virus ready to attack.

We spend a few hours swinging back and forth on the rope, feeling the holds and mapping the sequence with chalk marks. I stroke and whisper to the holds, asking them to be kind to me today. We each take a warm-up burn, and then wait until the right moment for our first try. For me, this is just before dusk, when the rock has had the maximum time to cool from the midday sun, but there is still enough light to see without a headlamp. Before climbing I sit cross-legged on our belay portaledge and meditate. I listen to the hum of my body and reduce my world to the bubble of the pitch. I block out the exposure. I nod at Kevin and he nods back, and then I step off the portaledge into a cold blast of air blowing from the valley floor straight up the wall. Right away I notice that I'm not trusting my feet. I try to compensate by pulling harder with my fingers. I climb twenty feet to a resting position, and try to recompose.

Pull yourself together, you can do this.

But doubt has already seeped in. I step up the tempo. I pull hard on the razor-sharp holds, too hard. My body position is off, my foot slips, and I feel a microscopic shift in my left middle finger. I let go and swing onto the rope. A drop of blood falls and is whisked away by the wind. I look at my hands. *Damn it.* There is a perfect V-shaped gash in my left middle fingertip. I have Kevin lower me back to the portaledge. I apply pressure to stop the bleeding, then wrap it in tape.

"I just felt a little off that time," I mumble, staring at my finger. "I feel strong though. Conditions are perfect."

Kevin is only half paying attention, thinking about his own attempt. I let him stay in the zone. Since most of our rehearsals of this pitch have been in the dark, Kevin decides to wait. When daylight fades to black, he clicks on his headlamp and sets off. As he climbs the easier part at the beginning, he makes small talk.

"I remember the first time you showed me this pitch. I thought you were crazy for thinking it would go free."

I understand his strategy. He is trying to relieve the pressure, act as if this is just another practice round. After twenty feet of climbing he rests for a few minutes on decent footholds. As he pulls into the first crux sequence his body begins to shake. I'm sure he's about to fall. But he lets out a herculean grunt and, somehow, manages to climb through to another micro-stance.

"Yeah, Kevin, that was crazy!" I shout.

"I showed that move who was boss," he replies.

I can't help but chuckle at his light but determined mood. He alternately shakes his hands for a minute, resets his focus, and pulls into the second crux. He climbs flawlessly, absolute perfection.

"Oh, hell yeah, that felt great," he shouts. He hangs from a finger-width edge and pumps a fist. I can't see his eyes, but I can sense his fire. He rests for another minute and I hold my breath. Just one more sequence of desperate climbing. Stealthily, fiercely, he growls and then crosses his right hand over his left. Places his left foot on a pea-sized bump and presses it hard. He reaches far with his left hand until he is spanned out like Christ on a crucifix. He inchworms his fingers onto a razor blade, hops his right foot in, directly under him. He crosses his right hand over again. For a moment, he hesitates. The universe falls away beneath him. Ever so carefully he reaches his left hand to a good hold. The moment he touches it, his other limbs cut loose but he hangs on and shuffles his feet onto the ledge that marks the end of the pitch.

My eyes bug out.

"Did that just really happen?" Kevin mutters through labored breath.

"Oh, yeah it did!" I yell.

Kevin makes his way back to the portaledge—on the traverse pitches, it works better for each of us to lead. When he arrives I grab his shoulders and shake him like a rag doll. "That was freaking incredible!"

"Thanks, man." He gives me a big hug and looks in my eyes. "Now it's your turn."

I sit for a few minutes, somewhat dumbstruck. I've never considered that

Kevin might actually outclimb me. I've always been impressed by his climbing skill, but this is a whole new level. Before this attempt, he hadn't cleanly climbed pitches 12, 13, or 14. Pitch 14 is the hardest stretch of climbing he's done in his life, and he did it by headlamp after a week on the wall. Since 2010, we had failed to set a new high point. And now Kevin just did it. I am both exceedingly proud and filled with envy.

On top of it, the odds are momentarily against me. On a climb where molecules of skin contact make all of the difference, I now have only three fully functioning fingers—including my thumb—on my left hand. Next to my missing index finger, my sliced-open middle finger is covered in tape.

As these thoughts swirl in my head, they're overtaken by a determination that I have rarely experienced in life. *I must find a way.* I look again at my torn fingertip.

I wrap my finger tightly in a fresh layer of tape, switch on my headlamp, and start climbing. I feel light and airy, aware of every detail. A few moves in, blood seeps through the tape. My headlamp casts shadows across the stone. I become disembodied. Time slows. Through Kevin's stare I can feel his unwavering focus, willing me to stay attached to the wall. I feel his strength flowing through the rope.

I climb through the first sequence perfectly, rest for a moment, and notice my breath rising in the darkness. I enter the second sequence. My feet dance across microscopic ripples. I place my fingers on the holds one at a time, letting the texture of my fingerprints settle into the granite. I get to the next resting position, pause, and take a few breaths, exhaling forcefully. Just six more feet. I pull into the final moves.

My hand blurs into focus under the beam of my headlamp. I watch my fingers curl, my knuckles extend up. A tiny roll of skin pushes itself behind a micro flake. Excitement wells in my chest, building.

I know I will not fall. I can't fall. I mirror Kevin's moves, extend into the crucifix position, cross my hand steadily but powerfully to the good hold, then drop my feet onto the ledge. I let out a scream that leaves me hoarse for two days.

CHAPTER TWENTY

Somehow we've just danced through one of the two hardest pitches on the Dawn Wall. We're on the roll of a lifetime. But our rapid pace has battered our fingertips. I think how huge this wall is, how crucial these little layers of skin, and we're not even halfway there. We decide to rest for a day.

Inside I'm freaking out. For the first time in seven years I feel that there is a high probability that we will actually send. But I try to keep my cool, keep the mood light, avoid added pressure.

January 2 feels surprisingly mundane. The three of us chat and surf the Web. Brett is still with us filming the action. Alex Honnold jumars up to say hello. He brings us shelled pistachios and chocolate, and jokes that the route looks scrappy and low angle. After an hour he gets bored and heads down.

The next morning isn't much different. At around eleven Corey Rich jugs up. "Wow, you guys seem so chill." Kevin relaxes alone in his portaledge, listening to music. Brett fiddles with his cameras. I rise from the seated position for the first time in eighteen hours, stretch my arms out wide, and yawn. "Don't know what I was expecting," says Corey, "but this wasn't it, being as how you are in the middle of sending the hardest rock climb in the world." I glance at our leisure tour setup and laugh.

"Yeah, man, mostly we just eat snacks and sunbathe."

A few minutes later I look down and see several people ascending the fixed ropes to our camp. Eric has recruited some friends to help him deliver another batch of supplies. Big Up added a shooter in El Cap meadow, and now a second cameraman, Corey, on the wall. There is a growing crowd down in the valley. Our bubble of intimacy has fully burst.

Later that afternoon, I take a warm-up burn on pitch 15. Corey and Brett hang directly overhead. Brett's in an unbelievably exposed position, out in space. Eric hangs from the anchor at the end of the pitch, managing a rope that allows Brett to track directly behind us as we climb—pure rigging wizardry. I finish warming up and return to the belay portaledge. I dust my hands with chalk. Finally it's time to climb, and as I step onto the wall the strangest thing happens: Suddenly I am alone. Everything else becomes white noise. The only sound I recognize is my own breathing. The 1,500 feet of exposure, the biting wind, the clicking of cameras, and the cheers riding on the breeze from El Cap meadow all blur into the background.

As I climb the next one hundred feet I feel I have left my body. The opening sequence flows like nothing, that sequence that for so long seemed impossible. I simply observe as pinhead-sized points of contact between shoe rubber and rock mate like tiny magnets, as the tips of my right fingers cross my body to the left and touch a nearly invisible hold. Time slows. The granite passes before my eyes. I float into the middle portion, pausing for no other reason than that it feels right, right now, this place. I chalk-up again, blow into my hands.

I've heard athletes from other sports talk about how the game slowed down for them at crucial moments, how they were able to visualize the whole playing space and what was about to unfold. Like an outside observer, I watch myself glide across the rock, left arm high, two-finger hold, hips in, scoot right foot beneath me. I barely notice the effort. Flow, that state of optimal experience in which one feels fully engaged, is one of the most magical experiences a person can have.

In many ways my entire Dawn Wall quest, and maybe most of my life, has been a search for this sensation. But I know that the pull of gravity will soon return. These thoughts flutter like butterflies in the fading rays of daylight, and I'm only half aware that the crux of the climb has passed before me.

Suddenly, magically, I'm standing on a six-inch ledge at the anchor. Kevin is shouting. Shutters are clicking. I lean against the golden granite, arms draped by my sides. My cheek presses against the cool stone. Birds fly beneath my feet. Slowly I return to reality. *No, no.* I don't want the moment to end. But it already has. Pain throbs in my shoulder. I suddenly feel self-conscious. Should I turn around and yell to the crowd below, or look into the cameras and pump my fist? I shout to Kevin, "Oh, hell yeah!" The words feel awkward and forced. I make my way back over to him and manage a smile. He looks dumbstruck.

"That was the most impressive piece of climbing I have ever seen in my life."

All I can do is lower my head. "Thanks. It felt good."

Just like that I've done the two hardest pitches of the climb. I can't believe it. For years I've had so many doubts over whether the Dawn Wall would ever come together. And now I'm left wondering if it's even that hard.

I figure Kevin will easily follow suit. The sun sets and he prepares to climb. The filmers re-rig for night climbing, and here, on our perch, it looks like a vertical sports field with miniature stadium-style lights. We sit and wait, struck by the strangeness of the artificial illumination. The brightness blocks out the stars and the moonlit trees far below, creating a circle of light bound by impenetrable darkness. It looks and feels surreal, as if I'm peering inside another person's imagination.

"This is truly an experience we will never forget." I tell Kevin. "You've got this."

As he steps off of the portaledge, the spiderweb of ropes and people and lights makes it hard to play this off as *just another practice round.* Kevin doesn't look like himself. I can sense right away that his belief has abandoned him. He fumbles through the first eighty feet, shoes skipping along the wall, gasping breaths penetrating the night. I know he is going to fall moments before he sails off and slumps onto the rope.

"Damn it!" he shouts. "That felt terrible."

"No big deal, Kevin. You'll get it next try." My attempts to alleviate the tension ring hollow.

On his second try he looks more energetic, and for a moment I think he will do it. But just as he's pulling to good holds at the end of the pitch, his foot slips. He makes a sound as if he has been punched in the face and falls

313

aggressively onto the rope. Dangling below, he looks at his hands. "Shit, I just poked a hole in my finger."

Oh, no, that's bad. These crux holds are tiny and razor sharp, yet so specific that our fingers contact the rock at the exact same spot each time. Every subsequent attempt will grind at the tear.

"No worries, man, you've climbed much of this route with at least one fingertip taped already. I am sure you will be okay."

He returns to the start of the pitch, tapes up, and tries again.

He falls even earlier. His defeated body hangs limp. Dead weight. I feel a flash of concern. Our momentum has been suddenly shattered. I force the thought from my mind and wonder if I should say something to cheer him up.

The next day, as we rest in our portaledges, Kevin gets a text message. John Branch, a reporter from the *New York Times*, wants to interview us. We talk with him on the phone. More people appear in the meadow. Kevin spends the day obsessing over his finger.

Come nightfall, he tapes it up and tries pitch 15 again. He falls, and then falls again. He makes multiple attempts. In the process, the split in his finger worsens, a terrible gash at precisely the spot where he has to grab a crucial hold. He lets out a frustrated roar. "I guess I have to just see if I can get this to heal." We return to the portaledges.

The mood stays heavy. Kevin is in precisely the same situation that caused me to fail in my 2011 push: battered skin and frazzled nerves, downtrodden. I can see the anxiety in his eyes. To be truthful, I have little faith that he will be able to recover. I keep my doubts to myself. *It's not over until it's over.* Secretly I am stressed out.

The following morning, our tenth day on the wall, I call Becca and she tells me that we are on the cover of the *New York Times*. The jaw-dropping photo shows us climbing on one of the crux traverse pitches from a dramatic angle. And for once, a mainstream article about climbing is tastefully done, not overdramatized. Branch tells it like it is, gets the facts right, and captures the spirit of the climb. I guess that's what a Pulitzer Prize–winning journalist does.

"It's getting pretty crazy," Becca tells me. "CBS News is at your parents' house right now. They want to come to our house next. Is that okay?"

"Do whatever you want, baby, I'm going to try to ignore it." While we're on the wall, our voicemail and e-mail in-boxes are filling up. I stare at my phone with detached fascination. *What is going on here?* Then my phone rings.

"Hi, Tommy, this is Melissa Block from NPR." *Melissa Block?! I listen to her pretty much every morning.* "Thanks for taking my call. So, tell me what you see when you look down." She wants to hear about the daunting exposure, which Kevin explains with his usual poise, but all I can think about is the growing crowd down in El Cap meadow.

Problem is, we aren't even halfway up. We spend the next several hours on our phones reading articles. Many of the mainstream stories are overflowing with blatant, absurd inaccuracies, while also portraying climbing as a game for roulette-wheel-spinning maniacs. Inside I feel as though a part of me has died.

I climb over and sit in the door of Kevin's portaledge. "Man, I think it's really important that we keep our heads in the game up here. This media stuff is getting out of hand."

"I agree," says Kevin. "Maybe we should just keep it outgoing. We can do our Instagram updates. Adidas has asked me to post little videos for them. But other than that we won't accept any interview requests."

We decide to make exceptions for the most legit sources: the *Times* and NPR.

"Sounds good."

Until now, Kevin and I have climbed at the same pace; when one of us succeeds, the other has been able to ride the send train. Pitch 15 was the first break in the pattern, and I grapple with a difficult decision. *Should I wait?* Momentum is a powerful wave, and I still have some hard pitches left, especially my nemesis, the dyno. It's up next. Since Kevin is resting his fingers today, he can belay me. Ultimately that's how I justify it. If I climb ahead while he recovers, I can put all my energy into helping him when he is ready.

I study the eight-foot gap that the dyno spans, and then look down and around. While training for the dynamic move in Colorado, I had torn the labrum in my shoulder. The pain had been manageable, but now, after a week on the wall, it's flaring up. The joint feels unstable and fragile.

For years I've thought that the dyno was the only option for pitch 16. But on the last day before heading home for our Christmas break, I had willed a potential alternative into existence. Out of desperation, for about the hundredth time I had searched for a way to climb around it. The solution had escaped my notice because it's so bizarre. Fifteen feet before the end of the previous pitch, which traverses from right to left, a small, obtuse corner drops down to a good ledge eighty feet below. That ledge extends leftward and then rises in another dihedral that finishes a few feet above the hold at the end of the dyno. It is a little like walking around the block to cross the street. The workaround is essentially a big loop, nearly two hundred feet of climbing resulting in only twelve feet of forward progress, and 5.14+ on its own, but in a type of climbing that suits me better than an eight-foot leap.

I know that the dyno will risk worsening the tear in my shoulder and put the whole climb in jeopardy. I try the workaround for two hours by headlamp, and fail. Putting it together is harder than I had thought. I tear another hole in one of my fingers. My foot slips and I gash open my ankle. Blood saturates my climbing shoe.

A distant panic begins to rise. I rest for an hour, and on my next attempt I fall just before the end. After another hour of rest I grit my teeth and try again.

I smear my feet downward in that weird, flared corner, then delicately traverse to the rising dihedral. The pitch contains all the crazy subtleties and impossibilities of 5.14+ climbing—terrible footing, awkward liebacking, subtle body positioning, huge effort load. I feel like a rank beginner, trembling, my feet skating, but somehow, some way, my body adheres to the wall. Maybe by nothing but thirty-some years of experience and sheer, absolute will.

While the pitches below had flowed together almost effortlessly, the Loop Pitch was an epic conflagration. *A muerte*, as the Spanish climbers say. "To the death." Brett says I made it look twice as hard as any other pitch on the climb. But I did it. I've often cracked that the best thing about beating your head against the wall is that it feels so good when you stop. While my determination may be my greatest asset, every strength can also be a weakness. My obsessiveness can blind me. I chuckle to myself, thinking that this makes a great mantra for life: If you find yourself failing over and over, sometimes it's best to just give up and find another way.

It's our eleventh day on the wall. Kevin stares at his fingertips. He decides to crowdsource finger taping and skin care techniques through Facebook. Doctors from around the globe chime in. He spends most of the day sorting through advice and playing with different ideas. By evening, he's found a technique he wants to try. He rips the tape into three-millimeter-wide strips, douses his fingertip in superglue, then half mummy wraps, half basket weaves the tape all the way down to his second knuckle. Then he superglues over all of the exposed edges. "Worth a try," he says.

He waits for the sun to drop. He climbs easily to the crux, then falls. He plays with his foot sequence and refines his body positions. He climbs the crux sequence on its own, but when he tries from the beginning he falls again. Kevin battles hard, trying to will his way through. Drops of blood float to earth from his fingertips. Eventually, he hangs from the end of his rope and kicks the wall. He needs to let his skin heal for two more days, and then try again without the bulky tape.

Inside our portaledge Kevin barely speaks.

My personal success weighs on both of our minds. I want it, but I want to do it with him.

"I just don't want to hold up the program," he says, again and again.

Everyone in the climbing world would understand if I decide to send the Dawn Wall myself, with Kevin or somebody else relegated to a supporting role. These days, the individual send is generally the norm anyway. But it isn't what I want.

While Kevin said the "right thing" about not holding me up, his tone, his body language, his determination—every other element—shows how badly he wants it, too. I love that he doesn't want to quit.

The next day, I'm eager to climb. I have only one more 5.14, pitch 17. The rest of the hard climbing is of a style that suits me, flaring corners, tiny holds. At the moment I'm feeling unstoppable, and I want to finish it off before the momentum shifts. I do pitch 17 first go in under thirty minutes, and then I send pitch 18, rated 5.13c, for good measure. We are back at base camp by 9:00 p.m.

Kevin's stress is palpable. I try to be supportive, but the pressure continues to build. Perhaps worse than not sending himself, Kevin doesn't want to be the reason that I fail to climb the Dawn Wall. The longer we stay up here—we haven't set foot on earth for twelve days—the more we'll deteriorate, physically and mentally. And the more likely bad weather will roll in. No one has ever heard of its being this dry in January. Our luck can't last forever.

"What about this, Kevin?" I suggest. "While you heal up I can try to lead my last three pitches to Wino Tower." (It's named for Warren Harding and his prodigious drinking on his 1970 aid siege of this same general aspect of El Capitan.) "Then I'll have them out of the way, and from there it's much easier. I could make it to the top in a day if a storm showed up in the forecast." After pitch 21, the remaining eleven pitches ease up to mostly 5.11 and 5.12, with nothing harder than 5.13–.

There's a long pause. "I love being up here, Kevin," I continue. "I can't imagine topping this out without you. I am willing to stick it out as long as it takes."

He realizes that I've already been waiting, and that I'll wait some more. "Thanks, man, that means a lot to me." We go to sleep with a slight sense of relief. At least I do.

"Jesus, we're in the *Times* again," Kevin says over coffee, looking at his phone. It becomes a pattern, and during our climb they run profiles on us, an interactive route map, a piece on what we do on rest days, explanations about climbing and its nuances, and even a reader question-and-answer about climbing and El Cap, with answers from "celebrity climbers" like Alex Honnold and my ex-wife, Beth.

One day they run a photo of me standing in the portaledge in only my Dr. Seuss–striped long underwear bottoms, a single sling girth-hitched around my waist, muscles glistening in the sun. Becca sends me a text:

Grrrrrrr! Some 450 comments appear on my Instagram page, mostly from women, lots of lighthearted sexual innuendo. I have a huge laugh thinking back to my third-grade picture, with my buck teeth, bottlecap glasses, and huge ears. In one day, my Instagram following goes from five thousand to fifty thousand.

Today's big news story, in the *Times* and everywhere else, is about Kevin's struggle with pitch 15, and the emerging subplot of whether I'll ditch him and blast for the top. *Kevin the Underdog holds up Tommy the Supermodel.* No pressure.

I look below. Four news trucks are parked in El Cap meadow, satellite dishes pointed skyward. Cords run from the trucks to reporters with microphones. Probably a hundred people gather around Tom Evans's telescope. Few of the people are climbers, so the news stations seem to be interviewing anyone they can find.

Alex Honnold gets approached by a female reporter from the Bay Area's ABC affiliate. She asks if he is familiar with El Capitan. "Yeah, I'm pretty familiar with El Cap," he says. (Alex knows it as well as anyone.) Somehow the interview goes from the reporter asking Alex about our climb, to his plan for getting my infant son to the top of El Capitan to greet me. The hike around the backside is long and boring, so Alex plans to go up the East Ledges—exposed scrambling and ascending fixed ropes—with Fitz strapped to his back. "I honestly don't think it'll be any problem."

The aghast reporter asks how they'd get down.

"We'll all rappel down the ropes."

"How do you get a baby to rappel the ropes?" she shoots back, protective or borderline incensed.

"Put him in the backpack," Alex says, completely unfazed. "It's not like I've ever done this, I don't really know, but that's just the obvious solution that comes to mind."

The seven-minute news clip continues almost like a deadpan comedy routine as Alex tries to convince the reporter that it is—of course—no big deal.

"He's only a twenty-five-pound baby," Alex concludes. "I'm sure it'd be fine."

Perhaps best of all, in the station's haste they did no fact-checking. In the original video clip (later edited), they botched Alex's last name. He swears it wasn't him playing a prank, but flashing across the screen was the name: Alex Honnlove. He's not only the world's greatest free soloist, but he now has a porn-star last name.

It's 10:00 p.m., day thirteen. I switch off my headlamp and stare at the stars. The sky is perfectly clear, the wind calm. The last hard pitch, pitch 21, 5.13+, rises above me. One hundred and fifty feet to the top of Wino Tower. I've just climbed pitches 19 and 20, both 5.13 as well, on my first try. If I can do this, I know that the rest is in the bag.

Seven years.

Kevin and I sit on our belay portaledge. I've lost nearly ten pounds by this point in the climb—a combination of exertion and nervous energy sucking up calories. Inside I'm buzzing, but I have to keep it contained. Almost as important as this pitch, in my mind, is that I don't put any more pressure on Kevin. I keep my voice low, my face relaxed and calm. I switch my headlamp back on, slide my feet into my climbing shoes, and tighten the laces so hard that they screech. I stand up, check my knot, and dust my fingers with chalk.

As I begin to climb, my whole body trembles. The intensity is almost too much for me to handle. I try to force it out of my head. *Focus, breathe.* I climb slowly, careful to execute every move perfectly. I let the air whistle through my lips with each exhalation. My body stops trembling. I channel my concentration to the circle of my headlamp. When I get to a small ledge halfway up the pitch, I stop. For ten minutes I hesitate. Thoughts come rushing in. *Do I really want this to end?* I have known the Dawn Wall longer than I have known my wife and my child. What happens with my life without this driving force? Will I still have motivation? Will I still be a good father? What if I fall into depression? And what about Kevin? What will it be like for him to know that I am only a day away from finishing?

I know I can't stop. All the blood and tears, the countless days spent abusing my body on this beautiful wall. The months away from my wife and son. The humbling support of my entire family. Now, this moment. I look up. My headlamp illuminates a few rusty pieces of metal sticking out of a hairline fracture in the granite. I am not sure that they would hold a fall. But at this point I don't care.

I gently bring my foot up and smear it onto a bump no larger than a peppercorn. I grab a tiny flake and feel it flex away from the wall. A drop of sweat falls from my cheek and disappears into the blackness. The end is so near. My body shakes. My breath rattles. My forearms fill with lactic acid and my fingers begin to fail. Twenty, ten, five more feet. The stubble on my lower lip stabs me in the nose. I pop up my foot and gasp, then shoot my hand into a small opening in the crack and pull onto the first real ledge in twelve days. Kevin is 150 feet away and around the corner. I try to quiet my crying. I can't let him know what I am going through. I sit on the ledge for twenty minutes, staring into the stars, my chest heaving in and out.

Before I head down, I pull myself together. I know I must temporarily push this moment from my mind. My job now is to be there for Kevin. I want him to have this experience, too. I wipe my face with my shirt, thread the rope through my rappel device, and descend to him.

"Nice job, dude," Kevin says at the anchor, his eyes hanging low. He offers up a fist bump. "Thanks, man." We barely speak as we rappel back to camp.

CHAPTER TWENTY-ONE

That night I keep the portaledge fly unzipped so I can gaze at the stars. My mind swirls with the galaxies. I repeat to myself again and again, *I did it, I actually did it.* I replay the final few moves, the outrushing of emotion and the melancholy-tinged exaltation.

I desperately want to hold on to this experience. My body and mind came together in a crescendo of meaning that was years—more than years, decades, my whole life—in the making.

I once heard a description of how waves are formed. They start with far-off storms that result in tiny ripples carried great distances by the wind. Over thousands of miles, these undulations combine, organize, build in size. A pattern emerges and creates a swell. When the swell approaches land, the bottom of the ocean pushes the energy skyward and a wave forms, standing upright for one glorious moment. Generally, the bigger and fiercer the storm at its genesis, the bigger the wave. If Kyrgyzstan was my storm, maybe the Dawn Wall was my wave.

I spend so much of my life chasing experiences like this. But as the night draws on, the joy of the moment gives way to a growing emptiness, like the moonlight washing away the most distant stars.

I just don't want it to end.

I don't sleep a wink, and run through a year's worth of thoughts and emotions. I wonder how different this moment might feel if it were just Kevin and me, without the media glare and high-production cameras, doing the kind of climbing that my dad taught me and that real climbers the world over all know. Would we be closer friends? Or would he even be here? Would I be experiencing the same conflicted emotions? Even in physics, matter behaves differently when being observed.

By the time the sun rises, I decide that I spent the night being an over-analytical sap. I return to the simple fact that I did it, and that what's next is a singular task: Help Kevin do the same.

"How are you doing, homie?" I ask, poking my head into the cold morning air. Kevin squeaks out a meager, "Okay."

He doesn't look okay. I glance down to the valley below. Again he says, "I just don't want to hold up the program."

"Don't worry about it," I respond, "I'm having the time of my life up here, and the weather forecast is great. I am willing to stick it out as long as it takes." I pause to cough. "How are the fingers doing?"

"They still feel pretty thin," he mutters. "But they seem to be healing."

I can tell he's on the verge of unraveling. He won't make eye contact with me, he mumbles his replies. I try to imagine being in his position right now, and I don't know if I could deal. He's been stuck on this pitch for seven days. I try to take the pressure off by acting all Alex Honnold about the situation, *This is no big deal.* But we both know we can't live like veal in these hanging bags forever, and that our luck with the weather will ultimately expire. Also, I'm starting to feel funky. Each time I rise from the sitting position I get a severe head rush. My shoulder continues to flare up, and I've developed a hacking cough. Except for his hands, Kevin looks better. He's now taken two consecutive rest days and plans to climb this afternoon.

He passes the morning on his phone, following every word of news coverage, which, at this point, has become a worldwide discussion of the skin on his fingertips, and, especially now that I've climbed to Wino, whether I will ditch him and blast for the summit.

God must have grown tired of my complaining about the damned phones. That morning, while I'm leaning over to grab some food out of the haul bag, I feel a shift in the chest pocket of my jacket. I look down as a silvery reflection falls out of sight.

"Oh, crap! I just dropped my phone."

Kevin turns to me. "Seriously," his eyes bugged out. "No . . . you're joking."

The moment of shock passes and is replaced by a realization. I hesitate, and then raise my arms.

"Oh, yeah! I just dropped my phone!"

Kevin just stares at me.

"You know what, dude, I'm psyched. This is going to allow me to fully embrace the rest of this experience."

Sure enough, with my Wonder Killer gone, within hours I start noticing things I hadn't before. The oak trees across the valley still hold their red autumn leaves. The angle of the sun stretches familiar shadows farther, longer than I'd ever seen from here. Each day, around noon, the chunks of ice that form on the shore of the Merced break away and float downstream.

I start organizing all of our supplies. I unpack the haul bags and take inventory of everything we have. I make plans for every possible scenario of how many days the rest of the climb might take.

I may have gotten a little overzealous. After all, I've still got eleven pitches to go, even though they're comparatively easy. Kevin is less than halfway up, with three 5.14 and five 5.13 pitches remaining. But I joke and am relaxed when I talk to the crew. The sky seems to be a deeper shade of blue. A fountain of appreciation flows from me. I ramble on about friendship and family. I verbally replay the highlights of the climb. "Remember that night when we both sent pitch fourteen, that was so cool."

I notice that Corey and Brett are keeping their phones tucked away more now, too. The sound of laughter overtakes the sound of tapping thumbs. I go over and unzip Kevin's portaledge, where I find him (as always) staring at his fingertips.

It's early afternoon when a light cloud layer moves in and a biting breeze kicks up. Kevin sticks his hand out the door and flutters his fingers in the wind. "It feels kind of cold. This could be good."

At three I jumar to the start of the pitch and set up the belay ledge. An hour later the sun leaves the wall and Kevin joins me. Brett dangles above with his camera, and the wind sends him in thirty-foot arcs. Higher up, his rope skips across the wall. His nerves show in his body language but he remains silent, intent on not distracting Kevin.

Kevin takes a warm-up burn with the tape still on his fingers. He climbs through the beginning of the pitch looking as smooth as I have ever seen him. When he gets to the micro-rest before the crux, the wind gusts hard. Brett flies sideways through the air and lets out a little shriek. But Kevin is in the zone and doesn't even notice. It all comes down to belief. He needs to believe that the conditions will be such that he will outperform his nine attempts over the last six days. He needs to believe that his skin won't peel. He needs to believe in himself. I am in a down jacket, shivering. Smart and strategic as always, Kevin decides to drop off before the sharp crux holds.

Before his next try he peels the tape off his fingers. He starts across, climbing quickly and without hesitation. He is light on his feet, smooth with his movements. He gets to a resting position and shakes out. I can see his confidence. I can feel it in the air. My own heart pounds in my chest. Kevin lets out a deep growl and starts into the hard moves. When he gets to the razor-sharp holds that have been shredding him, he pauses for a moment, and then carefully places each finger one at a time. He shuffles his feet across. He bumps his right hand, steps onto a good hold, and pauses again. He is through the hardest moves. I've been holding my breath the entire time. Kevin climbs around the corner. I can't see him anymore but the rope continues to flow away from me. Then he lets out a huge scream. Cheers erupt from El Cap meadow. I look down to see more than a hundred people watching.

Back on the portaledge, we exchange high fives. Kevin is smiling. But it's nothing like the emotional flood I was expecting. He shows me his index finger. There are five cuts, small but severe, drops of blood seeping through the skin into little red balls.

"Good thing I did it that try," he says, almost catatonic.

"Yeah it is," I say between coughs, and then I grab him. "You just freaking sent pitch fifteen! We should throw a party or something."

He responds in a slow, almost astounded-sounding drawl. "Yeah, I thought pitch fourteen was hard when I sent it, but fifteen, that was a special kind of hard."

He rides the wave and sends the dyno, pitch 16, that night, too.

The next day, our fifteenth on the wall, Kevin also sends pitches 17 and 18. It's as if the dam just broke. I haul gear, manage ropes, and belay, anything to support our progress. I relish the role of big wall caddie. We're headed for the top.

Kevin decides to rest a day before the final push. Once he makes it to Wino Tower, we could do the remaining eleven pitches in a single push if we had to, but the weather holds steady. I spend the morning observing the traffic jam in El Cap meadow. At one point I see my Sprinter van, weaving through the maze of cars and satellite trucks. Becca and Fitz are here. The sight of them instantly makes me homesick. I borrow Corey's phone—you gotta make exceptions now and then—and call them. She informs me that it is total chaos down there. She's been sneaking around the back of the meadow to avoid reporters. When Becca tells me that she and Fitz have been spending time with Beth, her now-husband, Randy, and their child, for a split second I feel this pause, a strangeness, but then as quickly as it comes it passes. We've all grown from the past and started anew. Maybe it's the fleeting nature of life, or our mutual love for wild places, or the beauty we see in our children. Probably all three.

The scene is once again surreal that night. Clouds have blown in, creating a feeling of urgency even though the weather forecast remains perfect. As Kevin climbs the last three pitches to Wino Tower, the valley floor disappears from view. A rapidly moving wall of clouds whistles a few feet from his back. It looks as if he's climbing inside a narrow slot. He falls a couple of times on each of the pitches and considers throwing in the towel on pitch 21 for the night. Kevin had been walking that line between success and failure for so much of the route that I'd almost gotten used to having my heart in my throat while watching him. But then, as always, he pulls it off.

When he tops out on Wino—the end of the hardest climbing—he is smiling, but seems detached. I give him a big hug. I try to count how many times Kevin has succeeded when the odds seemed stacked against him. I consider the distance Kevin has traveled, from boulderer with zero big wall experience to this. It's much farther than my own. I'm damned proud of him. He's only thirty years old.

I rise from my cocoon at 5:00 a.m. I feel like hell. It's been more than four days since I last climbed. That's the most rest I've taken in more than a year, though it hasn't been exactly relaxing. My sickness has moved into my throat. Swallowing is excruciating. My body is one giant painful knot. I guzzle water, then coffee and Advil, and start coming to life. Our base camp is starting to smell. A bucket of excrement hangs just inches below my bed. For the last seventeen days, our urine has been floating in the wind, often blowing back up the wall and speckling our camp. A fine layer of dry, foul, orange-tinted protein dust now coats everything. I am ready to be off the wall.

The only people I want to see on top are Becca, Fitz, and my parents. But I learn that my dad isn't going to be there. My mom, in her round-about way, says that this whole thing is emotionally too much for him to handle. Dad has always been very proud of me. He is such a tough guy, yet so tender inside. He doesn't want to be caught weeping on live television. After seeing the Honnlove interview, the PR department at my main sponsor, Patagonia, sends a message advising me that it would probably be best if Alex didn't cinch Fitz into a backpack and ascend fixed lines. "It might come off like the Michael Jackson incident." Although Alex offers to hike the eight miles around, in the end Becca decides to leave Fitz with my parents.

For the first time on the climb we take down one of the portaledges and stuff it into a haul bag. We'll make one more camp. There's no rush.

We lead up largely unrehearsed terrain, but it's easy enough. A hold breaks and Kevin pulls a Matrix maneuver, dodging the flying hunk of stone. The rest of the day goes as planned and we set up our portaledge atop pitch 28 at around 9:00 p.m. The smell of pine trees wafts down from the summit, just a few hundred feet above. I crave flat ground. We have now been on the wall for eighteen days.

We've heard that there will likely be around fifty people waiting for us on the summit. I want to see my family, but am uncomfortable about sharing the coming moments with strangers. I wish I could just tell them to give us a day.

Once again, for the last time, I lie awake in the portaledge staring at the sky, thinking a million things. I feel lucky that my dad showed me the way of climbing and the mountains, and that my mom was strong and brave enough to support all our crazy notions. I feel lucky to have found Kevin as a partner to see this through. I even feel lucky for how Kyrgyzstan made me tough. Without that, I don't know if I would have recovered from my run-in with the table saw. I even feel lucky that Beth left me, which started this elevated dream. Then again, maybe it started in 1978, when I weighed four pounds and came out seven weeks early, fighting for life.

As the sun crests the horizon I sit upright, leaning my back against the wall. This part of El Cap, the top of the Dawn Wall, is the very first place to get sun in all of Yosemite Valley. Below is darkness, frost, and cold. We sip coffee and listen to music. We are so small. I feel part of something so much greater than myself. The sun's radiation, combined with the caffeine, energizes me in a way that makes my body hum with energy.

When I try to speak only a rough wheeze comes out. The sickness has now attacked my vocal cords. Kevin looks at me and laughs. I wish I could freeze this moment in time, put it in a pill, and save it for later. El Cap now glows like an ember and life in the valley begins to stir.

Becca is walking to the top with Alex, Kevin's family, and some of our friends. In addition to my parents and my sister, my extended family has come, too: two nephews and four uncles. They decided to turn the event into a family reunion and are gathering in the back of El Cap meadow, as far from the cameras as possible.

As the morning draws on I see two small figures, one big and one little, playing on the banks of the Merced, away from the crowd. Ripples of water break the otherwise glassy surface and extend outward. I think it's my dad and Fitz. Fitz's favorite Yosemite pastime is casting stones in the water. And these days my dad enjoys nothing more than spending time with Fitz.

Tears start to form when I remember what it was once like between us. Dad used to look at me with the same eyes that he now reserves for Fitz. People still tell me all the time what a badass my dad is. At sixty-five, he still lifts weights five days a week and spends the majority of every day outside, fishing, hiking, and, even though arthritis makes it so he can barely lift his arms above his head, climbing. He loves bolting new sport climbs, and manages to find little roadside gems that others have somehow overlooked. Each time he does a new route he calls it "the best climb of my life." And each day he fishes, he swears that he caught "at least a hundred fish, a few big ones, too."

When he and my mom are together, he likes to stand directly behind her, wrap his arms tightly around her shoulders, and squeeze. The same way Fitz hugs a teddy bear. Then he kisses her softly on the back of her head. In recent years, he has taken on some of the nurturing attributes I used to see only in my mom. He tells her the sweetest things, and cooks her dinner several nights a week. I never remember him cooking anything but microwave burritos when I was a kid. I wonder if it's his way of demonstrating something that I feel as well: We would be nothing without her. They seem more in love now than ever. I guess I'm still trying to be more like my parents.

Dad still wears tank tops and short shorts, at least when he is feeling fit. His muscles are still well formed, even if they sit a little looser on his bones. His eyes hold a hint of sadness, at least when he looks at me. I know he misses climbing together.

But while mountains, climbing, and physical fitness used to take priority—they remain lifelong pursuits, and our way of life—I think his priorities shifted a few years ago, when his own father was leaving this world. His death reminded them, and me, of the fleeting nature of life. At the time, I promised myself that I would spend more time with Mom and Dad. I haven't. The Dawn Wall and kids and life have gotten in the way. I need to change that.

I'm especially pleased to see my mom so happy. She's a remarkable grandmother to Fitz. I realize now that I never really worried about her, how she'd manage. It couldn't have been easy to see her husband and her son embarking on risky outings. She never complained. She never asked us to reconsider. She knew that we had to live our lives with richness and meaning, and she sacrificed her own comfort for us. She also knew when to speak up and intervene.

As Kevin and I linger in our sleeping bags, relishing these last hours of solitude, a party is forming atop El Cap, along with reporters and news cameras. Many people started hiking at 2:00 a.m., to be sure they made it up in time to greet us. A large group of Kevin's friends arrived at nine with beer and champagne. They've already started drinking. They're all wearing matching green T-shirts, and Kevin has one on, too. They have declared the Dawn Wall climb a tribute to his friend Brad, who died the previous summer while climbing in the High Sierra. He and his girlfriend, Jainee, had gotten engaged that very day. The shirts bear a drawing that Brad sketched before he fell. I wonder why Kevin had never mentioned any of this to me. I only know because of an on-camera interview he did in the portaledge with Brett a few days earlier.

I'd sensed that something was troubling him, and I suppose I could have asked, probed more deeply. But I suspected that even then he might not have told me. Maybe our chemistry was always off. I let it go, glad that the climb had served some deeper purpose for Kevin.

In a few hours Kevin and I will join the party, but I only want to see Becca. She avoids the cameras, sitting by herself on a rock slab a few hundred feet from the top, staring out into the mountains. I can't wait to see her, to hold her, to thank her. I think of Fitz and how I love to watch him as he sleeps, to see his small chest rising. How I love his little giggle, and the way his eyes shine as he explores this infinite world.

Our gear clicks and clinks as we rack up on the portaledge. A warm winter breeze blows off the face from the east. Distant chatter filters down from the summit. Kevin and I barely speak. I'm up first. I tie in. I take my time; there's no rush. Never again will I have this exact view, in this exact place, with all that it holds. This moment. I take a breath and lace up my climbing shoes. Kevin smiles and gives me a fist bump.

I settle my fingers into El Cap's exquisite granite. Before I go, I take another look down to the valley, to the walls on the other side, and out across to the High Sierra, unfolding and uncaring with the ages. I try to hold on just a little longer.

EPILOGUE

A couple of months before that final climb of the Dawn Wall, Becca, Fitz, and I were playing in a nearby area called the Church Bowl. A warm morning breeze fluttered down from the thousand-foot slabs up-valley. Yellow and brown leaves blanketed the ground. Becca and I sat together and watched Fitz, on his eighteen-month-old legs, stagger over to a short, table-shaped boulder. Perfectly flat on top, about as tall as he was, it sat in a soft, grassy area that would cushion any fall.

He looked over at us as if to say, "Watch me."

Becca said, "It's a mantel move," using climbing lingo for pressing over the top of something flat.

"Man-tel," Fitz imitated. He drummed his little hands on the boulder, then he started to climb—it's such a natural activity for kids. His feet skittered and he stepped back down, and then tried again.

"Man-tel," he said again, with a hint of frustration.

Becca rose and walked over to him, encouraging, "You can do it, buddy."

"Man-tel," Fitz said, more neutrally this time, looking like he was tasting the word.

For a couple of long minutes he struggled, frequently glancing at Becca as if to say *help me*. He whimpered.

"Remember, Fitz," she said, "you've got to try hard and focus." He climbed a little farther, dropped back down, looked around, and cried a little harder.

Becca spoke in a higher, sweeter voice, "Try hard, Fitz."

He took exaggerated, forceful breaths, a habit he surely picked up from

333

watching me. He committed more on his next attempt, getting halfway over the mantel. He looked like he was about to fall back down.

"Help," he said.

My heart was breaking.

I glanced at Becca. Becca did not help him.

Instead she encouraged him in her sweetest voice. "Stick with it, you can do it. You got it, push hard."

Fitz bore down, grunted through his tears, and kept trying. He found his footing and pulled his body halfway over. His little feet kicked in the air. He set his knee on the top, crawled forward, stood up, and clapped.

"Good perseverance," Becca said, walking over. "Nice mantel, buddy." Fitz glowed. She gave him a high five. Fitz smiled and swatted at her hand. "Boom," he said.

I thought of my dad, of course, and how his encouragement, much like Becca's, rang throughout my childhood. How he and my mom showed me the importance of developing a mind-set to persevere, which is the greatest gift they ever gave me.

My life today is much different than it was two short years ago—the aftermath of the Dawn Wall surprised and overwhelmed me. Everyone has a story to tell, though, and we all experience triumph and hardship. Through our stories, we can deliver inspiration and knowledge. So for now I'm trying to do justice to the opportunities before me. While I used to focus on what I could gain through experience, I am now thinking more about what I can give.

I always thought my deepest fulfillment came from the mountains, and that's why climbing has been my art. But as I wrote this book I was surprised to find that the act of creating, even behind the keyboard or when speaking to an audience, feels deeply rewarding. Maybe all along the appeal had lain in the satisfaction of giving fully of myself. Maybe climbing wasn't always the answer, but the venue.

In March of 2016, Becca and I welcomed Ingrid Wilde, our daughter, into our family. My children simultaneously enlighten me to life's infinite possibilities, while causing me to continually reevaluate the meaning of risk. I used to think that adventure and risking one's life were intrinsically linked. I now realize that adventure might be more about embracing the unknown. That's not to say that I no longer feel the call of the mountains, but simply that life's big goals have always felt a bit like thunderstorms, appearing with little warning and leaving me no option but to become engulfed. I still find myself dreaming of Arctic big walls and more time on El Cap, but those dreams are laced with a deep responsibility to balance adventure with forethought and care. The most important challenges and risks in my future will come in helping my kids (and perhaps other kids) grow into people who will engage the world with the same sense of boldness and confidence that my parents instilled in me.

Last summer I got a call from my old friend Adam Stack, the guy who climbed with me on the Dihedral Wall back in 2004. He had a harebrained idea to try to climb a big wall on the north face of Mount Hooker, in Wyoming's Wind River Range, car to car in twenty-four hours. The face rises nearly 2,000 vertical feet, and is fifteen miles from the nearest road. It gets climbed a few times every year, and the standard approach is to horse pack in, make camp, get acquainted with the area, then spend a few days climbing the wall. Typically it's a week-long outing. When Adam asked me to go, Ingrid was four months old and not sleeping through the night, and I had spent the last year deep in the writing cave and barely climbing.

"I don't think I can justify the time away from home right now," I told Adam. I was also somewhat concerned about how out of shape I was.

"I bet if we run I can get you back to the family in forty-eight hours," Adam argued. "You're not getting light on me, are you?"

Thirty miles of running with packs full of climbing gear would be fairly hardcore, even if I was in shape. But throw in a big wall? I didn't know if we could do it. It sounded absurd.

"Sounds like a pretty bad idea to me," I said.

"Yeah, definitely a stupid idea. I'm so psyched." Adam said.

We set out from the car at 2 a.m. The night was black and damp, the air biting. We jogged through pine forests, headlamps scanning the hoof prints. The steam of our breaths pulsed before us. For the first several miles I felt lethargic, and I struggled to keep up with Adam, who had been furiously training. By 4 a.m., however, my body started to remember the flow. At mile twelve we stopped to fill our water bottles in a crystal-clear alpine lake, as lavender and red twinkled on the horizon. We jogged down a steep dusty hill as daybreak illuminated a cirque of pyramid-shaped snowcapped peaks.

I looked at Adam. He was flush but as happy as I had ever seen him.

We scrambled toward the base of the wall through a maze of house-size boulders, climbing over some and leaping between others. My body hummed with endorphins. I could taste the exertion and it flooded me with a heavy dose of nostalgia for all those days spent in places like this. At the base of the wall we roped up. Our plan was to simul-climb in four- to six-hundred-foot blocks.

I started up, wandering between face holds and intermittent cracks. The rock was solid and the gear good. After 150 feet Adam let out a "Whoop" and we started climbing together. We judged each other's progress by the tension in the rope. When Adam slowed I would put in more gear and keep the rope between us tight. When I slowed Adam would watch me close. Through trust and faith in each other's judgment, we moved as if we were one. I thought about how different this was from the last big wall I had climbed. No camera team, no cell phone service, no expectations beyond our own. I thought about how the Dawn Wall had fulfilled a desire to explore limits, but had somehow left me longing for something deeper.

We kept climbing, and I thought of Chris Sharma, Alex Honnold, and Corey Rich. I thought of my close friendships that had been forged through climbing. I thought of my mom and dad, and Becca, Fitz, and Ingrid. How lucky I am to have been shaped by the mountains into a man who can love so deeply.

As I climbed higher, the pitches seemed to fly by with startling ease. Sometimes life works like that. Sometimes gravity releases its grip and you glide toward the clouds. There must be a pattern to this, but I have yet to understand it. Maybe that's okay, or maybe I'm wrong.

Five hours later we crested the top of the wall. We lay our sweaty backs on sun-warmed slabs and shared an energy bar. Looking out at the surrounding landscape, I was struck more by what I couldn't see. No roads, no people.

"Only six more hours of jogging and we get to sleep," I said.

"This wasn't such a dumb idea, was it." Adam smiled.

"We'll see if we still feel that way when we get back." I slapped Adam's arm and pushed to my feet to begin the descent.

By the time we finished, every muscle and bone in my body screamed. But I was flooded with the sort of contentment that only deep fatigue can bring. It was a hell of an adventure. And I never once thought I might die.

Embrace the unknown. Push through the difficult moments, work with them.

Just like Fitz on that mantel problem, when it gets hard is when we grow.

Forty-eight hours after I'd left, I walked back into the house, and Fitz ran across the room, latched on to my weary legs, and squeezed them tight.

"Come look at my epic train tracks, Daddy!" He looked up at me with his huge green eyes.

I picked him up and gave him a big squeeze. Becca came out of the bedroom holding Ingrid, telling her, "Daddy's here!" She walked over and gave me a kiss. It was good to be home.

ACKNOWLEDGMENTS

As with so many of the big moments in my life, the idea to write this book originated in a moment of delusional optimism. I had just finished my seven-year journey on the Dawn Wall and had this feeling that dedication can accomplish almost anything. Why not? It can't be any harder than what we just did, right? Sure, I expected it was going to be hard, but I was excited for an adventure. What I failed to consider is that I was not truly a writer. At least not of books. Therefore, I had to rely on the expert assistance of many people. What appears on these pages is a product of an intense collaboration between many great friends.

I approached this book the only way I know how: like climbing a mountain. I realized that this journey would be riddled with loose rock and threat of avalanche. The one path to succeed on such an endeavor is to team up with someone whom you trust with your life. Perhaps the greatest single piece of advice I have ever received came from a good friend, Jim Collins. He told me, "You have to get the right people on the bus." If there were one person on my bus who deserves more credit for this book than anyone else it is Kelly Cordes. He was not only the co-writer, but also my confidant, therapist, and best friend. He was always able to see things I couldn't and helped to turn my loose ramblings into something more cohesive. His attention to detail, his tireless work ethic, and his willingness to pour his soul into this book were absolutely invaluable, and I am forever grateful that he was willing to join me on this journey.

Acknowledgments

This book never would have left the ground were it not for Jim Collins and Jon Krakauer. In the summer of 2014, Jim invited me to a book club discussion for one of Jon's books, *Where Men Win Glory*. Jon also attended. Toward the end, the conversation drifted to the general practice of writing. I will never forget when Jim said that in the final stages of a book he usually loses up to twenty pounds and gets boils on his lips. Similarly, Jon said that he liked the research part of books but disliked the actual writing. He said it was like ditch digging—you just have to get in there and dig a few feet each day. Interestingly, these comments appealed to my affinity for deriving gratification from pain and got me through the darkest and most arduous days behind the keyboard. Furthermore, Jim had been encouraging me to write for years, thereby building the confidence that I otherwise lacked. Both Jim and Jon generously provided critical help in negotiating the publishing world from start to finish.

I must underscore the role that the team at Viking played, most notably my editor, Paul Slovak. Not only did he pore over several drafts, providing crucial insights, he also continually pushed me to make it better, especially in the final stages, when he introduced me to the highly experienced writer Gary Brozek. Gary helped to bring out emotional elements that had been eluding Kelly and me.

I would like to also thank my literary agent, David Larabell at CAA, who believed in my story and did an extraordinary job of presenting it to others. I am particularly indebted to my lawyer, Becky Hall, whom I now refer to as my guardian angel, and to Michael Kennedy, who became my "Yoda." These two served as valued critical readers and encouragers. The rest of my critical readers included Lance and Carrie Brock, Jill Cordes, and Adam Stack, whose collective insight helped guide my words. Thanks to Katie Ives, Christian Beckwith, Matt Samet, and Andrew Bisharat for their editing work on articles that ultimately metamorphosed into a few of the stories in this book.

Thank you to Joanna Croston and the Banff Centre for supporting Kelly and me with the Paul D. Fleck Fellowship Grant. They provided a quiet cabin in the Leighton Artists' Colony for two critical weeks preceding delivery of the original manuscript.

Acknowledgments

Besides Paul and his assistant, Haley Swanson, many other people at Viking contributed to the publication of this book. Sean Devlin was invaluable in copyediting the manuscript. The production editor, Eric Wechter, helped put together the many complex pieces of the puzzle, including the photo insert, and Brianna Harden designed a fabulous book jacket. The publicity team of Lindsay Prevette, Kristin Matzen, and Christopher Smith worked tirelessly to get the book media exposure and to keep me on schedule. I also want to thank Viking president Brian Tart and Viking editor-in-chief Andrea Schulz for believing in this project from the moment they first heard about it. To everyone else at Viking who contributed to the effort, I'm very grateful.

The visuals for this book have all been provided by friends. Thank you Corey Rich, Tim Kemple, Jimmy Chin, Topher Donahue, Becca Caldwell, Jim Thornburg, and Brett Lowell.

The greatest blessings in my life are a direct result of having Mom, Dad, and my sister, Sandy, as examples to follow. I thank them for showing me how to be curious, to love life, and to work hard. Any strength that I possess is a direct result of their love.

Finally, words cannot describe the appreciation I have for my wife, Becca Caldwell. I know you thought you were going to get me back after the Dawn Wall, but you didn't. Thank you for sticking by my side and putting up with my tendency to become consumed by projects like this. You are my best friend, most valued critic, and biggest inspiration. This book could not have been written without you. If I have one regret, it's that the writing process has kept me away from you, our son, Fitz, and our recently born daughter, Ingrid, far too much. Nothing shines brighter than the love I have found with my family.